AUSSIE AUSSIE AUSSIE

BEN POBJIE

Published by Affirm Press in 2017
28 Thistlethwaite Street, South Melbourne, VIC 3205.
www.affirmpress.com.au
10 9 8 7 6 5 4 3 2 1

National Library of Australia Cataloguing-in-Publication entry available for this title.

Title: Aussie Aussie Aussie / Ben Pobjie, author.
ISBN: 9781925475685 (paperback)

Cover design by Design by Committee
Typeset in 11.5/17 Bembo by J&M Typesetting
Proudly printed in Australia by Griffin Press

The paper this book is printed on is certified against the Forest Stewardship Council® Standards. Griffin Press holds FSC chain of custody certification SGS-COC-005088. FSC promotes environmentally responsible, socially beneficial and economically viable management of the world's forests.

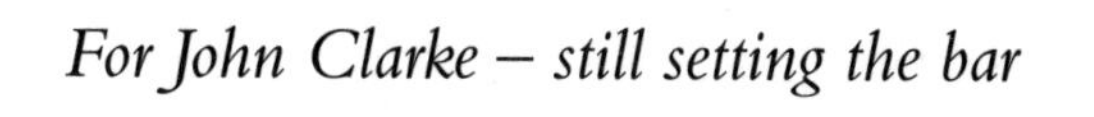

For John Clarke – still setting the bar

CONTENTS

INTRODUCTION

'AUSSIE! AUSSIE! AUSSIE!' The legendary cry that we happy products of the great southern land emit in order to inform the world that not only are we Australian, and not only are we present, but we are, above all, loud. When we gather in large groups to bellow these three simple words that are actually one simple word, we are affirming our identity, and expressing our pride in the country we call home.

But perhaps, when we express that pride, we fail to think deeply about exactly why we feel it. What, after all, is so great about Australia? Is it the glittering beaches? The rugged outback? The inefficient reproductive systems of the fauna? Do we really express pride in our nation based only on the natural wonders offered by the landmass?

Surely not. The real beauty of this country lies not in trees, seas, or cassowaries, but in the greatest resource that any country can have: its people. For is not the story of Australia the story of the Australian people? Onc hopes so, or else the story of Australia is just the story of a wide and distressingly dry slab of rock and some cuddly animals with eccentric child-minding protocols.

The Australian people define Australia, create it, represent it and make flesh the aspirations our young, ambitious nation has always had and never really managed to do much with. Without people, Australia would not be Australia. Every inhabitant adds something to Australia, makes it more Australian than it would otherwise be. But obviously, there are some Australians who have left a greater footprint on the pants seat of the world. As egalitarian as we pride ourselves on being, we would be naïve to deny the inescapable fact that most of us are incredibly unimportant, while a few of us are very special. It is those special few who have done most of the heavy lifting in making the country what it is today, whatever that might be: this extraordinary minority is responsible for putting Australia on the map – without them maps would have a big blue empty space down the bottom and ships would constantly be startled by the massive continent they bumped into without warning.

Great Australians come in all shapes and sizes (although mostly roughly human-shaped), and from all backgrounds. Some great Australians come from the city, some from the country, some from Perth. They come from every state and often from different countries, driven to become Australian by the indefinable urge that tells so many of the world's people, 'I simply must go to a better country'.

Importantly, as this book is about to show you, great Australians mark their greatness in a variety of fields and capacities. Over the course of its history, Australians have become titans of business, legends of sport, giants of science, colossi of philanthropy, and pygmies of politics. Australians have led the world in myriad ways, and whether generating wealth, inspiring youth, opening up the vistas of human potential, saving lives, or ending them, we have done it all in a peculiarly Australian way, with a swagger and style that marks a person out as an inhabitant of the scientifically determined greatest country on earth.

The following pages will introduce you to a selection of some of the greatest Australians of all. In the arts, sport, science, politics, warfare, business and humanitarianism, they did things that would be impossible for most of us, inept and slothful as we are. But the lessons these mighty figures of history have to teach us are massive and enduring. Should we wish to learn how to better serve our nation, how to leave a legacy worthy of the term, there is no difficulty: all we need do is look to the Australians contained within these covers, and drink in the cool, refreshing inspiration they devoted their lives to pouring out for us. To these earthly gods of the Antipodes, we salute you, the most Australian way we know: with the joyous cry, 'Aussie! Aussie! Aussie!'

INVENTING AUSTRALIA

THE FIRST INHABITANTS of Australia were of course the Aboriginal people, who generations of Australians remember from that one history class when the teacher mentioned them. But the original inhabitants would not have thought of themselves as 'Australian'; the 250 individual nations that occupied the continent had yet to gain the wonderful sense of national unity that white men brought to Australia, along with other marvellous innovations such as guns and smallpox. For many thousands of years, these people lived in total ignorance of what they were missing out on, not even knowing how deprived they were until their European benefactors came along to teach and/or kill them.

Of course, those white men didn't yet think of Australia as 'Australia' either. Prior to European settlement, the continent was known in the Old World by a number of names: 'New Holland', 'New South Wales', 'Old Zealand', 'North Antarctica', 'The Big Brownie', 'Snakeville', and 'Tatooine' were all common monikers for the great southern land. When the First Fleet sailed into Sydney Cove in 1788, its passengers filled with hope for a quick and painless end to their suffering, it was not Australia to which they thought they had journeyed. It didn't much matter what they called it, though: the Fleeters considered themselves British, and the fact that they were on the other side of the world would not stop them feeling that way, or wearing completely inappropriate clothing for the climate. In fact it took some time for the British and their descendants in Australia to stop thinking of England as 'home' – some say the tendency only really died out when Robert Menzies passed away in 1978 at the age of 6000. Australia – under any name – was viewed as an outpost of the British Empire far beyond the point at which this perception was literally true or even remotely reasonable.

And yet somehow, the diverse peoples of the Indigenous nations and the deluded white criminals of the motherland ended up forming a single nation, this amazing land we call Australia, which combines all the best of its brutally cruel origins with the finest in modern complacency and self-deception.

But when did Australia truly begin? Who were the 'first Australians' – the people who invented the idea of being Australian, and began the long, slow trek towards discovering exactly what being Australian means? From the very beginning of the clash of cultures that set this land on a collision course with nationhood, there were a few remarkable individuals who, however they began their lives, ended them fully deserving the prestigious and only slightly insulting designation of 'Great Australian'. These then are their stories.

BENNELONG
First Contact High

GOVERNOR ARTHUR PHILLIP was under pressure. Dispatched to Port Jackson and given the task of founding a new colony on the alien southern continent, he was finding it a lot tougher than anyone had anticipated, mainly because nobody had ever bothered trying to figure out how tough it would be. A combination of factors, from the climate to the unproductive soil to the fact the British government had not allowed anyone with any practical skills to come to New South Wales, was threatening the success of Phillip's burgeoning settlement. The government, for their part, weren't that fussed: just by getting a thousand-odd surplus criminals as far away from their country as possible, they had already hit their main KPI. So the Governor was largely on his own, in a hostile land, trying to figure out the best way to build a successful colony out of malnourished convicts, drunken soldiers, and racism[1].

One of the most problematic of Phillip's responsibilities stemmed from an instruction given by King George III of England, to the effect that the governor of the new colony should 'endeavour, by every possible means, to open an intercourse[2] with the natives,

1 And of course four goats, without which they really would have been stuffed.

2 Grow up.

and to conciliate their affections, enjoining all subjects to live in amity and kindness with them'. This was in the days when people still took instructions from George III relatively seriously – before he began ordering people to move Buckingham Palace to Antarctica and knighting giraffes and so forth – so young Arthur felt he should at least make an effort to do as he was told.

This was awkward, though, as the local Indigenous population wasn't particularly keen to have any kind of intercourse opened up with the people who had turned up uninvited and started clogging up the land with their huge ugly animals and weird dying crops and ill-mannered men with incredibly lax attitudes to gun safety. It wasn't that the Eora[3] people who were living in the Port Jackson area at the time weren't a friendly bunch: it's just that they realised early on that the benefits of multiculturalism were basically restricted to bullets and smallpox, and no matter how many dinner party invitations the governor sent them, continuing to breathe was a more attractive option.

Phillip was most vexed by the Aboriginal people's standoffish nature in the face of what he had tried to make as relaxed and comfortable an incipient genocide as possible. He searched desperately for a way to achieve his goal of learning more about the culture and customs of the locals. Anthropologists have over the years devised myriad methods of making contact with and discovering the secrets of Indigenous peoples, but Phillip was no anthropologist. He was an officer of the British Empire, and the only way he knew to get things done was the British Way. And so, in the interests of living in amity and kindness with the natives, he told his men to go kidnap a couple of them.

To our modern eyes, abduction seems a brutal act of violence

3 Eora means 'people', making the phrase 'Eora people' rather silly, but that's history for you.

by an invading commander against an invaded people. But it's important to understand the historical context, i.e. back then the British were dicks to everyone. Whatever the rights and wrongs[4], the fact is that Phillip's henchmen did their job conscientiously, found two Aboriginal men at Manly Cove[5], tied them up and brought them back to Sydney. And so, in November 1789, Bennelong and Colebee were introduced to settler society. Colebee escaped from Sydney town a few weeks later, but Bennelong was to stay longer, and have a profound impact on the earliest conceptions of what Australia meant.

Woollarawarre Bennelong had been born around 1764-ish, in the country of the Wangal clan of the Eora, on the south shore of the Parramatta River. Although Bennelong is the name by which he is now best known, he had five different names, as was common among his people. Besides Bennelong, he was also named Bunde-Bunda – meaning 'hawk' – Woollarawarre, Wogletrowey, and Boinba. These were recorded by the British under several different spellings, because white men can simply never make up their minds. The First Fleet officer Watkin Tench, the vaguely irritating source of much of our knowledge about everyday life in the early colony, called him 'Baneelon', but Tench was notoriously terrible at spelling, and also called the Aboriginal people 'Indians', so he's as unreliable as they come.

Bennelong was about 25 when brought to Governor Phillip, and in the words of the dubious Tench, 'of good stature, and stoutly made, with a bold intrepid countenance, which bespoke defiance and revenge'. Tench, whose notoriety as a bad speller was matched only by his deficiency in emotional intelligence, probably never considered the possibility that the defiance and revenge might have

---

4 Mostly wrongs … if we're honest.

5 The obvious place to find men, really.

been a result of having just been kidnapped by a bunch of pasty-faced bell-ends in stupid trousers.

Despite the unfortunate circumstances of his introduction to white society, his vengeful countenance, and the fact that Watkin Tench called him fat, Bennelong got along well among the colonists. Phillip insisted he be treated well, apart from the whole captivity thing – and in the 18th century if you came into contact with the British Empire and the worst thing that happened to you was wrongful imprisonment, you were getting off lightly.

It seems that once in the custody of the colonists, Bennelong resolved to make the best of the situation. Tench wrote that 'he became at once fond of our viands', an assertion that has caused many a historian to ask the question, 'What are viands?' This may forever remain a mystery. What is clearer is that Bennelong took his captors for everything he could in terms of food and drink. He ploughed through the colony's food supplies, and drank everything offered to him. He was, in every way, Australia's original party animal, and the British were in awe at the man's vast capacity to enjoy life. Tench said that 'love and war seemed his favourite pursuits', which probably came as a major shock to men from England, who had always tried to restrict themselves to war.

Of course, by 'love and war', what was meant was 'fucking and fighting', and perhaps Bennelong can be best summed up as a kind of 18th-century Oliver Reed. The marks of his proclivities were all over him: he had scars all over his head, the remnants of spear wounds on his arm and leg, and half a thumb on one hand.

Besides wowing the settlers with his astounding appetites and re-enactments of the film *Roadhouse*, Bennelong also became close with Governor Phillip, who he considered one of the nicest men to ever invade his home and forcibly remove him from his family. He referred to the Governor as 'Beanga', meaning 'father', and to himself as 'Doorow' ('son'). For his part Phillip, who had no sons of his own and had always longed to be the proud dad of a strapping young black man who he could drink whisky with and keep under armed guard, was extremely attached to his loving abductee. The two often exchanged gifts: Phillip would give Bennelong extra rations, clothes, knives or fishhooks, and Bennelong would give Phillip Aboriginal weapons and artefacts. In this way the Governor learnt more and more about the fascinating culture of the Indigenous people who sincerely wished he would piss off.

In six months of living at the Sydney Cove settlement, Bennelong also learnt English, adapting easily to Western civilisation and impressing everyone with his intelligence, good humour, and awesome spear wounds. But in May 1790, he proved the truth of the old aphorism, 'Even a man you've given loads of knives and fishhooks to might not want to live his entire life in prison'. Feigning illness one night, he convinced his guard to let him go into the backyard, whereupon he jumped a fence and disappeared into the night.

The Governor was doubtless distraught at his friend's escape, being forced now to spend all his time among a bunch of boring white dudes. But the Phillip-Bennelong bromance was not over yet: in September Phillip saw his protégé once again at Manly, where he was part of a large group of Indigenous people who gathered to meet the Governor. It wasn't the happiest of reunions, the mood spoiled somewhat when one of Bennelong's countrymen threw a spear through Phillip's shoulder. Some saw this as a pretty harsh act, considering that Phillip had always been at pains to demand that the colonists treat the local populace well, and punished severely anyone who disobeyed. On the other hand, if you ever find yourself in a position where you have to order your underlings to treat the natives well, you may not be entirely in occupation of the moral high ground.

In any case, Phillip seemed to take the massive hole in his shoulder as a sign of youthful high spirits, and didn't order volleys of gunfire or napalm bombing or any of the things that almost every other head of a colonial government in history would have done in the same situation. It certainly didn't sour his relationship with Bennelong: the younger man began to pop round to Sydney Cove to see how his old Beanga was going and whether the spear-hole was healing up okay. Bennelong and his friends became regular visitors to the settlement, and in 1791 Phillip recognised the role he played in the colony's life by building a brick hut on the eastern point of Sydney Cove, a spot which became known as Bennelong Point. Years later this hut was replaced by the Sydney Opera House, which is widely believed to have been a step backwards.

The year after Phillip's hut-based reconciliation program, the governor sailed back to England and took Bennelong with him, promising him that in England he would experience emotional repression and general dampness beyond his wildest dreams.

In England, Bennelong was presented to George III. Not in a gold watch kind of way, it just means he met him. Exactly what they did during this meeting is unknown, but probably Bennelong showed George his scars, and George asked how he got them, and Bennelong said, 'Fighting dudes with spears and stuff,' and George said, 'Cool,' and Bennelong asked George what he did for a living, and George said, 'I declare war on France and sometimes America,' and Bennelong said, 'That must keep you busy,' and George said it was okay but he was thinking of making a change and going insane for a bit, and Bennelong high-fived him and then the conversation sort of flagged a bit. Of course, there are some historians who claim that Bennelong never met King George at all, but that's not much of a story, is it? 'The Amazing Tale of the Man Who Never Met the King'? Sometimes historians can be real killjoys.

There is, however, definite evidence that while in London, Bennelong and his companion Yemmerrawanne visited St Paul's Cathedral and the Tower of London, and at some point hired a boat. It seems likely that they also went to Big Ben and posed for a picture next to the sign for Cockfosters station.

Arthur Phillip stayed on in England, but Bennelong returned to New South Wales on the *Reliance* in early 1795, unwell and dispirited due to homesickness and the British climate – always a problem for anyone raised in a country where the sun is visible.

On his return to Sydney, Bennelong maintained friendly relations with the white settlers, acting as an adviser to the new governor, John Hunter. However, it was the pull of his own people that was strongest, and he returned to a lofty position among the Eora. It can't have been easy re-entering Aboriginal society, reacquainting himself with his kinsmen, and trying to reassure everyone that the years he'd spent hanging out with the guys who kept trying to exterminate them were no big deal. Bennelong overcame these hurdles to become leader of a clan of 100 people on the north side of the Parramatta River, near Kissing Point – named after its resemblance to an enormous point. Despite his distinguished position among his own people, white men of the time reported him as having been rejected by other Aboriginal people, and descended into alcoholism and squalor. At the time of his death, he was described by the *Sydney Gazette* as 'a thorough savage', in an obituary that is now seen as the founding document of the Murdoch media empire's editorial policy on Indigenous issues.

Bennelong, among his many achievements, was also responsible for the first known text written in English by an Aboriginal person, being a letter to Mr and Mrs Phillips, who had cared for him in

England. In it he thanks them for their kindness, relates how he has been speared in the back but is 'better now'[6], and asks them to send him stockings, shoes and a handkerchief: the colony was apparently struggling so badly that these were impossible to find in the shops. It's not necessarily the most eloquent letter you'll ever read, but I can't stress this enough: not a single British person of this period ever sent a letter written in the Eora language, which makes Bennelong pretty much the most educated man in Australia.

Bennelong died at Kissing Point in January 1813, aged around 50. Today he is commemorated in the name of Bennelong Point, and in the electorate of Bennelong, once held by John Howard: a man who, much like Bennelong himself, was born over two hundred and fifty years ago.

Bennelong's importance in Australian history is enormous and often underappreciated. As one of the first Aboriginal people to join white society and form a relationship with colonial forces, he was a pioneer in cross-cultural dialogue, as well as one of history's most forgiving kidnap victims[7]. He might also represent something of a missed opportunity: the affection between Bennelong and Phillip shows that it might just have been possible for the British invaders to establish genuinely friendly relationships with the Indigenous population of their new home, but it's not particularly surprising that instead they went down the dispossession and massacre route (it had been so successful for them in the past). Nevertheless Bennelong was one of the most important figures in the first days of the colony. He did more than anyone to teach the colonists about the people of New South Wales, and showed all in Sydney Cove the pride and strength of the Aboriginal people. In the long trek to nationhood, Bennelong's story symbolised the tension that would always be at

---

6 Men really were men back then, you know?

7 Him and Belle from *Beauty and the Beast*.

the heart of that journey, and while he demonstrated the potential for understanding between cultures, he also showed how difficult it can be for peoples from different worlds to come together in harmony; especially when one of those peoples is a bunch of greedy rapacious bastards.

As the Sydney colony grew, the theme of greedy rapacious bastardry would develop strongly.

FUN FOR YOU AT HOME: Make friends with a person of a different race. Find out about their culture and make a list of all the differences between their background and yours. Show them how open-minded you are by dressing up in their national costume for a day. Make sure you tell them you're not a racist first.

JOHN MACARTHUR
A Man of the Sheeple

LIFE IN SYDNEY in the late 18th and early 19th century was tough. To survive, you needed a thick skin[8], a cunning mind, and a streak of healthy masochism. John Macarthur had all of these, but he had something else besides, something that would prove of enormous importance both to him and to the fledgling nation just beginning to poke its beak through the colonial eggshell. What John Macarthur had was sheep. In the days before mobile phones and stretch hummers, when humanity's priorities were wildly out of whack, sheep were a man's ticket to paradise. Or if not paradise, at least Parramatta, which was the closest you could get back then.

John Macarthur, like many of the most arrogant Australians, was born in England. His father, Alexander Macarthur, had fled to the West Indies in 1745 after the Jacobite uprising, when an army of furious Scots revolted against King George II to protest his refusal to reveal what a 'Jacobite' was. Returning to England, Alexander became a linen draper[9] and 'seller of slops', making his fortune in the mid-18th century drape and slops boom, when the citizenry's growing eagerness to drape things and intensifying appetite for

8 It was an even bigger advantage if it was white.

9 In the vernacular of the time, a person who drapes linen.

slops made many men rich beyond their mildest dreams. In 1767, Alexander fathered John, an act which would have far-reaching repercussions but which at the time impressed almost nobody.

John grew into a fine strapping lad, and in 1782, his father, believing that 15 was quite old enough to be sent overseas to be killed, got John a commission as an ensign[10] in Fish's Corps, a regiment formed to fight in the American War of Independence. The regiment never made it to America, as the Americans had the appalling bad taste to win the war early, and so the teenage Macarthur headed to a farm in Devon, where he spent five years staring blankly at cows and thinking about becoming a lawyer: the legal profession being one of the most popular for young Englishmen with no qualifications. Deciding that there were some occupations too degrading even for the son of a slops-seller, Macarthur instead returned to the army in 1788, excited about the recent settlement of Australia and the opportunities it might offer to kill and be killed in uncomfortable clothing on oppressively warm shores.

Recognising that in New South Wales he might need someone around to help him by doing all the work and having the occasional baby, he married Elizabeth, a farmer's daughter with a powerful urge to get out of Devon. The move paid off for her, as shortly after the birth of their first child, the Macarthurs upped sticks and boarded the *Neptune* for Sydney, where John would take up his post as a lieutenant in the New South Wales Corps.

The Macarthurs did not have a happy time on board the *Neptune*, with the combination of cramped and squalid conditions, rampant disease, and the beating, starvation, and murder of convicts causing some little discomfort to the travellers. John responded to the provocations in a manner which was to serve him well all his life: by challenging the captain to a duel. This was the first major

10 Nobody knows what this means.

indication that Macarthur would give of his lifelong dedication to being an aggravating dickhead. Eventually the Macarthurs got themselves transferred to the *Scarborough*, a more comfortable ship, although it was still in the Second Fleet, so everything's relative. I mean, having your big toe cut off is 'more comfortable' than being shot through the eye, know what I mean?

The point is, eventually the Macarthurs got to Sydney, and John immediately began providing for his family's future by starting fights and corruptly amassing wealth. In 1793, he received 100 acres of land at Rose Hill from acting governor Major Francis Grose, who had been living up to the duties of his office by giving all his friends presents. Grose gave Macarthur another 100 acres in 1794. Grose then made Macarthur paymaster of the New South Wales Corps, and superintendent of public works, realising that he needed a right-hand man as avaricious and amoral as himself. In 1796 Macarthur resigned from his job misappropriating government funds, in order to devote himself more fully to private grifting.

By this time, Macarthur's business and farming interests were growing fast. In 1794, he had begun experiments to cross Irish wool rams with Bengal ewes from India, hoping to create an unholy monstrous super-sheep. He was delighted to find that the offspring produced 'a mingled fleece of hair and wool', which was the kind of thing that really got the blood pumping in 1794. 'Have you heard?' the townsfolk would ask breathlessly. 'Mister Macarthur has, it is said, produced a mingled fleece of hair and wool!' 'Can it be true?' another townsfolk would ask. 'Can this long-cherished dream of Man have finally attained fulfilment?' 'Apparently so!' cried the first townsfolk. 'Society will never be the same!' And so on and so forth until they all died of smallpox.

If the experiments with Indian and Irish sheep had produced pleasing results, Macarthur found that even better results could be achieved by the clever expedient of buying a bunch of sheep from another country. Macarthur purchased several Spanish merino sheep from the Dutch Cape Colony, which is what South Africa was called before anyone knew where it was. With these sheep, he started a flock that produced some of the finest wool in the world. Cultivating his sheep at Elizabeth Farm, the Rose Hill property he had named after his wife because it looked remarkably like her from a distance, he soon became the colony's biggest sheep rearer – in number of sheep reared, that is, not in total personal mass.

In 1801, Macarthur sailed to England with some samples of his wool[11]. His hope was to establish in the imperial consciousness an idea of the superiority of Australian wool. In this he was successful: London society was abuzz with talk of Magic Macarthur and his Wonder Wool, and when he presented to the British government his incendiary work *Statement of the Improvement and Progress of the Breed of Fine Woolled Sheep in New South Wales*, wool fever absolutely exploded. Now not only one of the Empire's most renowned fabric-owners but also one of its most provocative authors, Macarthur easily won permission from the government to go home and take a tight, tyrannical grip of the New South Wales wool industry. To help him do this, the government gave him another 5000 acres, because what the hell, it wasn't their land, they could give bits of it away all day without feeling a thing. It was going to be 10,000 acres, but Sir Joseph Banks, the eminent botanist who had been hanging around boring everyone stiff with his stories about flowers, had the grant halved because he didn't like Macarthur's face. A boring man, but an excellent judge of character, was Sir Joseph.

The pioneering sheepman had increased his influence to the extent that he was now easily the most powerful man in the colony, free to basically do as he pleased to advance his business interests,

11 Well, not *his* wool, the wool from the sheep.

assist his personal friends, or just generally go around shooting at people. Back in the 1790s he had destroyed the career of Governor John Hunter, who had attempted to break the New South Wales Corps' control of the courts, lands, public stores, and convict labour. Macarthur, incensed at this completely unprovoked attempt to enforce the law, moved to safeguard his commercial interests and those of his Corps pals by spreading word that Hunter was corrupt and trafficked in rum. Macarthur got the idea for this scheme from himself, who was corrupt and trafficking in rum. Hunter denied the charges, but who were the authorities going to believe: some jumped-up little so-called governor, or a man capable of convincing Indian and Irish sheep to have sex with each other?

Hunter was recalled, but Macarthur found to his chagrin that when you get rid of one governor, another one just comes along to replace him. Hunter was replaced by Philip Gidley King, who tried to continue the Sisyphean task of introducing the rule of law to New South Wales. King's attempt to stop the illegal trade in alcohol ran into the same problems as Hunter's: viz, nobody ever did what he told them to do. It's a lonely life, being a governor who's not allowed to govern anything, and King quickly grew sick of it, especially after he overturned a one-year prison sentence for Lieutenant James Marshall, who had been convicted of assaulting Macarthur. The Woolfather took this as a personal insult and tried to get the rest of colony society to ostracise the governor. Macarthur's then-superior, Colonel Paterson, refused to join in these shenanigans, which caused Macarthur to attempt to blackmail him. This caused Paterson to challenge Macarthur to a duel. This caused Macarthur to shoot Paterson in the shoulder. This caused King to have Macarthur arrested, then released, then sent to Norfolk Island[12]. This caused Macarthur to refuse to go to Norfolk Island, once again proving his

12 Also known as 'a fate worse than death'.

keen intelligence. This caused King to send Macarthur to England for trial. This caused England to tell King that they didn't want to try Macarthur and send him back, by which time Macarthur had quit the army and couldn't be sent to Norfolk Island, making the whole exercise a total waste of time for everyone but Macarthur himself, who had had a lovely holiday, cemented his position as an international wool tycoon, and had the satisfaction of shooting a guy.

King eventually left his post, a broken and grouchy man. He was succeeded by William Bligh, the protégé of Sir Joseph Banks who, by getting Bligh the job, was wreaking a terrible revenge on Macarthur for daring to have a higher and stiffer collar than his own. Bligh was previously best-known for flogging so many of his own men that they threw him overboard and made him row all the way to Indonesia.

Bligh was a stickler for rules and correct procedure, but the main difference between him and his predecessors as governor was that he was every bit as stubborn and insufferable as John Macarthur. A mighty clash of wills was about to unfold.

Bligh had been assigned to New South Wales for the express purpose of cracking down on the lawless behaviour of the New South Wales Corps, or 'Rum Corps' as they had become known due to their control of the rum trade, which gave them control of the whole colony and was in flagrant breach of the law against public officials engaging in private enterprise. Macarthur had many friends in the Rum Corps and was profiting mightily from their activities himself, and Bligh's arrival to stamp out corruption and graft in public service really put his nose out of joint: corruption and graft were basically his two favourite things.

Macarthur's usual way of dealing with a problem like Bligh was simple: challenge him to a duel. But Bligh was such a stiff-necked square that he wouldn't even fight duels, leading to his popular nickname, 'Guvnor Spoilsport'. Unable to shoot the governor, Macarthur watched in horror as Bligh put a stop to his supply of cheap rum to the Corps, halted his importation of stills, and cancelled a lease on government land that Macarthur held. It was as if Bligh was running a personal vendetta against Macarthur, which he was, a bit, but to be fair Macarthur was absolutely asking for it. It was one of those catch-22 situations where on one side you have a man committing crimes, and on the other side you have a man trying to stop crimes.

The Bligh-Macarthur feud came to a head thanks to the dramatic yet boring saga of the *Parramatta*, a ship co-owned by Macarthur that had been named after the football team. A convict had stowed away on the *Parramatta* and thus escaped to Tahiti, which was in direct contravention of Bligh's commitment to preventing anyone at all from enjoying life. Bligh demanded that the ship's owners forfeit the £900 Transport Board[13] bond; Macarthur, who was not much of a one for demands in general, refused to comply. And so, Bligh had the *Parramatta* seized when it returned to Sydney, and in December 1807 ordered Macarthur to appear before the courts to answer for his crimes and general air of douchebaggery. Macarthur refused to appear before the courts – he was on a bit of a refusal roll and was finding the refusing lifestyle suited him perfectly.

Bligh responded by having Macarthur arrested, an act which sent shockwaves through a fledgling colony that had literally been founded on the principle that only poor people ever needed to pay for their crimes. Macarthur's trial was set down for January 25, 1808, before a panel of judges consisting of Judge-Advocate Richard Atkins and six members of the New South Wales Corps. Atkins happened to be an enemy of Macarthur's – after all he was

13 A long plank on which ship-owners had to balance large sums of money before being allowed to set sail.

only human – and so Macarthur objected to his presiding over the case. The six officers, by strange coincidence, all agreed, and the court was dissolved.

The next day Major George Johnston, head of the Corps, released Macarthur from prison. Macarthur immediately drafted a petition requesting that Johnston arrest the governor. 'Well, you're the boss,' said Johnston, recognising the now-established Australian principle that whoever has the most sheep is in charge. The Corps subsequently marched to Government House, pulled Bligh out from under his bed, where he had been busy flogging dust mites, and put the governor under house arrest.

Macarthur had won, and though Bligh made concerted efforts to reclaim his office, including the supreme act of desperation – sailing to Tasmania – he would not return to power in Sydney. Satisfied that he had shown everyone the folly of challenging the shepherdocracy, Macarthur returned to his farm to continue enriching himself and buying ever more restrictive collars.

The controversy over his clashes with officialdom, his frequent duels, and his lifelong commitment to shameless criminality can sometimes obscure the enormous contribution Macarthur made to Australian agriculture and to the early development of the colony's economy. Well into the 20th century it was said that Australia 'rode on the sheep's back', and if this was so, it was John Macarthur who strapped on the saddle and hit the sheep with a stick until it ran in the right direction. The man bred a lot of sheep and sold a lot of wool, and was one of the major contributors to New South Wales's evolution from a penal colony to a genuine player in the world economy.

It's worth mentioning how much Macarthur owed to his wife Elizabeth, after whom he named his farm. It was Elizabeth who managed the farm and the Macarthur business empire while her husband was away, which was quite often, what with the trips to England, and the duels, and the courts-martial, and the going to jail, and the defaming governors, and the illegal liquor-supplying, and so forth. Elizabeth was the first soldier's wife to arrive in New South Wales, and was perhaps the most influential woman in the colony of the day.

Not only did she supervise all wool production and sheep breeding during John's absences, she also managed to maintain the family's good standing in society despite her husband's struggles with being an ill-tempered graceless pig. Elizabeth was reputed to be a far more gracious and charming person than her husband, and really could've done better than him – what she got up to between 1801 and 1805, or 1809 and 1817, when John was away, who can say, but whatever it was I don't blame her.

John Macarthur did more than just infest the Australian countryside with sheep. He was also the owner of more than 100 horses, which is far too many horses for a man to own by any reasonable standard, and founded Camden Park Stud, which he named after himself despite Elizabeth's denials. Macarthur also established Australia's first commercial vineyard, which was in line with his twin vocations of agricultural pioneer and alcoholism facilitator. Whether wool, rum, wine or corruption, Macarthur led the way in laying down an example for future generations to follow.

Later in life, Macarthur was elected to the New South Wales Legislative Council, but was sadly suspended in 1832 after being declared insane, a fate that continues to befall state politicians in New South Wales to this day. Placed under restraint at his home at Camden, John Macarthur died there in 1834, aged 67-ish. It was a sad end, but few men have packed more into their years than John Macarthur. A lad of humble birth, he travelled across the world to make his fortune, created a major industry in a distant land, brought down governments, distributed alcohol, and every now and then shot a guy. We can only hope we make our own lives as full of achievement and incident.

Macarthur's legacy lives on in the name of the federal electorate of Macarthur and in the heritage listing of his estates at Camden and Elizabeth Farm. The now-defunct two-dollar note bore his visage, and in 1934 a postage stamp was issued to mark the centenary of his death. But most of all, Macarthur lives on in the Australian entrepreneurial spirit, the tradition of hardy men venturing onto the land to exploit natural resources and inseminate ungulates. In his determination to let nothing stand in the way of his ambitions, Macarthur was the prototype of the classic anti-authoritarian Australian, the self-made man who refuses to let stifling bureaucracy or petty laws prevent the wealthy from doing whatever they want. A thousand rich criminals have followed in his footsteps, and they – like all of us – owe a great debt to John Macarthur.

FUN FOR YOU AT HOME: Search your local area for sheep. When you find one, shear it. Take the wool home and try to make a jumper out of it. Not as easy as you thought, is it? Now do you respect your ancestors? You better.

JOHN BATMAN
The Dark White Rises

EVERY NATION'S STORY is, to some extent, one of missed opportunities. America continues to kick itself that it didn't annex Canada when it had the chance. Sweden's failure to reclaim Bremen in the Swedish-Bremen wars following the Peace of Westphalia haunts it to this day[14]. And Prussia has always deeply regretted the fact that it no longer exists. But has any opportunity been so badly missed, or so powerfully rued, as the chance that Australia had, and spurned, in the first half of the 19th century, to name one of its major cities 'Batmania'? The decision to go with the more prosaic and less heroic 'Melbourne' is one we've had to live with for the best part of two centuries. But should we curse our forebears for passing up the future tourist dollars that would today be flooding in to a DC Comics-themed city, or thank them for turning down an association with John Batman: a man who, though impressively named for any fan of costumed vigilantism, also possessed qualities that might be described by the blunter brand of historian as those of an utter prick.

John Glover, the artist known as the 'father of Australian landscape painting' due to the reluctance of other artists to claim paternity, was a neighbour of Batman's in Van Diemen's Land, or as

14 History!

it is now known, 'The Democratic Republic of Taswegia'. Glover described Batman as 'a rogue, thief, cheat and liar, a murderer of blacks and the vilest man I have ever known'. But we can't assess a man's entire character purely on the testimony of one person, which is a pity because this chapter would take a lot less time to write if we could.

John Batman was born in 1801 at Rosehill, quite near to where John Macarthur was at the time firing guns and encouraging sheep to bang. His parents had come to Sydney from England in 1797, having no more idea of how amazing their surname was than John would. John grew up in the burgeoning farming community of Rosehill, but since the district already had a violent sociopath, he knew he would have to relocate to really fulfil his potential. In 1821, therefore, he moved to Van Diemen's Land, the windswept island to the south of Australia named in honour of Anthony van Diemen, the governor-general of the Dutch East Indies, because why the hell not.

Several years later, Batman achieved a measure of fame when he hunted down and captured the famous bushranger Matthew Brady[15]. Brady had been wounded in a gunfight, but escaped, and was found by Batman limping in the bush. The bushranger, sick and in pain, surrendered to Batman. This achievement greatly enhanced the reputation of John Batman, whose amazing feat in accidentally stumbling upon a severely wounded man and dragging him to the police impressed the role-model-starved people of Van Diemen's Land.

Just like the other Batman, young John had proven himself capable of apprehending and bringing to justice dangerous criminals, and just like the other Batman, he also steadfastly ignored the confluence of social and economic factors that force

15 One of approximately 73 men known as 'the Gentleman Bushranger' in the 1800s.

the underclass into a life of crime. For the rest of his life he would maintain his love of addressing symptoms rather than underlying causes, paving the way not only for myriad superheroes, but every elected government in Australian history.

Batman had settled into the life of a grazier in Van Diemen's Land, and as a grazier he naturally had a duty to hunt Aboriginal people. Nowadays, few if any graziers feel the need to track and capture people of different races, but in Batman's day it was simply expected that if a man wanted to farm livestock, he had to be prepared to hunt human beings, lest he be exposed to adverse comment at the Graziers' Ball. Batman was, in fact, a bounty hunter, the nastiest kind of bounty hunter you could get: the kind who shoots or captures black people for money. Not that his nastiness was unique in Van Diemen's Land: after all, for bounty hunting to be a profitable occupation there have to be bounties, and the colonial government's attitude towards the Indigenous population was vicious even by Imperial standards[16]. The 'Black War', in which Batman was a significant participant, saw the whites wipe out the majority of Tasmania's Aboriginal people. It's estimated that there were about 1000 Aboriginal people on the island in 1826; by 1832 there were about 100 left.

To say that colonial procedures in Van Diemen's Land do not represent the high point of Europe's contribution to world history is an understatement roughly on par with saying that the Jonestown Massacre should not be considered a blueprint for local churches' community outreach. The Black War began because the governor, George Arthur, a man who suspiciously refused to give anyone his surname, was deeply concerned by the Aboriginal people's increasing attacks on white settlements, attacks that just wouldn't let up no matter how much the settlers murdered, kidnapped,

16 And again, we're talking *Star Wars* here.

raped, and drove to starvation the original inhabitants. Realising something had to be done, and that that something definitely had to be as maniacally violent as possible, Arthur declared martial law, effectively making it legal to kill Aboriginal people. From 1830, rewards were given for capturing Aboriginal people and bounties paid for killing them, thus providing men like Batman their lucrative sideline.

So Batman, although a murderous piece of shit by modern standards, or indeed by almost any other standards, was by the standards of Van Diemen's Land just one of many murderous pieces of shit. And in one of those irritating incidences that are always cropping up in the lives of historical bastards and making everything look messy, there were even some times when he behaved in a less murderous and shitty way than might have been expected. For example, in 1829 Batman led a group that fired on an Aboriginal party of 70 people[17], killing 15: but afterward he raised a little boy who survived the attack as his own. That boy, Rolepana, and another, Lurnerminer, who had previously been captured by Batman, were fiercely protected by the bounty hunter, who refused the governor's demands to hand the boys over to the government. Batman believed that Aboriginal people could be 'useful members of society'. Admittedly, he thought they would become useful members of society by being removed from their families as children and raised by white settlers, but you can't expect too enlightened a view from the man – I mean he was a murderer.

---

17 Although he only fired on them because they attacked his men. But then they only attacked his men because they had come to imprison them. So, it was one of those common historical incidents where there is fault on both sides, but also only on one side. Even when history is simple, it is complicated.

In 1833, Batman was diagnosed with syphilis, which was the sort of thing that happened a lot in those days, with people starved for entertainment and always willing to try new things. How the disease affected his state of mind or future actions cannot be known for certain, but one thing's for sure: after he got syphilis he left Van Diemen's Land, so it's possible there are beneficial side-effects that doctors are overlooking. Could a lot of the demographic and logistical problems of modern Australia be solved by infecting planning authorities with syphilis? That's not for me to say: I simply report the facts.

By 1835, Batman was not only syphilitic, but also in possession of more than 7000 acres of fairly rubbish farmland. He decided that he would seek more fertile climes on the mainland, or as patriotic Van Diemeners called it, 'the northern sandbar'. He applied for land grants around Western Port, but the New South Wales government knocked him back, having not yet been informed that Western Port is not in New South Wales. He tried the Victorian government, but they wrote back to say they didn't exist yet and it might be a while before they could process his application. Batman therefore decided to head across the Bass Strait himself and explore Port Phillip in hopes of finding some useful turf.

So it was that in 1835, Batman sailed for the mainland in *Rebecca*, which to everyone's relief turned out to be the name of a boat. Exploring the land around Port Phillip, he stumbled on a strip of land between Geelong and the Yarra River that interested him strangely. It was lush and green, with plenty of space for wine bars and art galleries, and Batman found that when he stood on the land he became inexplicably obsessed with finding a quality cup of coffee. Satisfied with what he had discovered, Batman made what would become one of Australian history's most famous declarations, saying, 'This will be the place for a village'. Or rather, he wrote it down in his diary, which he then locked and placed the key on a chain around his neck so nobody would ever know, sadly underestimating the ingenuity of future historians.

Of course, as it turned out, it wasn't the place for a village: it was the place for a big bloody city with skyscrapers and trains and everything. No wonder John Batman became known after his death as John 'Failure of Imagination' Batman. But there wouldn't be a city there without Batman's sad, lonely fantasies of a village, so it was a fairly important development.

But you can't just decide that a place is a place for a village and get building: there are procedures to follow. The land on which Batman hoped to build his village was already occupied by the Wurundjeri people of the Kulin Nation, and in a startling break from tradition, he and his fellow settlers decided that this mattered to a certain extent. He therefore entered into negotiations with the Wurundjeri on the banks of Merri Creek in what is now Northcote[18]. He was helped, in these negotiations, by the legal advice of former Van Diemen's Land attorney-general Joseph Gellibrand, the support of his own Aboriginal companions from Van Diemen's Land and Sydney, and his heartfelt belief that 'ethics' was a county in England. The fact that he was negotiating at all could be said to be a huge leap forward in Batman's moral development compared to his younger days; but he still entered the talks with the standard Empire approach to dealing with natives: screw 'em quick, and screw 'em hard[19].

After several meetings with the Aboriginal inhabitants, during which he presented them with gifts of blankets, handkerchiefs and food while restraining his innate urge to shoot them – and the Wurundjeri gave him gifts of baskets and spears and restrained their

---

18 No. 3 in the latest edition of *Melbourne's Most Pretentious Suburbs*.

19 And not, let's be clear, in the good way.

innate urge to tell him to fuck off – the signing of Batman's Treaty, as it came to be known[20], took place on 6 June 1835.

Batman's Treaty specified that in return for about 600,000 acres of land that would soon become the Melbourne metropolitan area, the white settlers would pay the original inhabitants: 40 blankets, 30 tomahawks, 100 knives, 50 pairs of scissors, 30 looking glasses, 200 handkerchiefs[21], 100 pounds of flour and six shirts[22]. On top of this, Batman pledged to pay an annual 'rent or Tribute' for the continued use of the land, of 200 blankets, 100 knives, 100 tomahawks, 50 suits of clothes[23], 50 looking glasses, 50 pairs of scissors and five tons of flour. This is a fairly generous rent: it's certainly more than I pay for my place[24], but on the other hand my place is less than 600,000 acres, and I also do not commit genocide against my landlord.

The Wurundjeri people were happy with the treaty, the only potential sticking point being that they probably had no idea they had just signed a treaty. In fact, some historians believe they didn't sign it, alleging that Batman had simply gotten his Aboriginal companions from Sydney to make the marks on the paper that he claimed were the elders' signatures. Even if the signatures were genuine, it's unlikely that the elders knew what was going on: they didn't speak English, and neither Batman nor his Sydney associates spoke the language of the Wurundjeri, so the probability of clear communication was low. It's more likely they believed it was a

20 Not to be confused with the treaty of the same name that brought peace between the warring tribes of The Penguin and The Riddler.

21 These would come in particularly handy once the Wurundjeri realised what had been done to them.

22 Most of the Aboriginal people didn't wear shirts, but Batman's brother-in-law owned a dry cleaner and had asked him to drum up some business.

23 He anticipated demand would grow, clearly.

24 In fact I don't pay any tomahawks at all for my house.

tanderrum – a ceremony undertaken by Kulin peoples to allow temporary access to their land. Had they known Batman was assuming ownership for himself of the entire Melbourne area, they may not have been so accommodating. Which, from Batman's point of view, was probably kind of the point. Whatever the problems of the treaty, it was the only attempt made by any European to negotiate directly with Australia's original inhabitants for the occupation of their lands. The fact we have to give Batman credit for this does tell you something about how the British Empire came up with its famous slogan: 'Britain: Setting The World's Lowest Bars Since 1066'.

In the end, any doubts over the treaty's fairness were swiftly rendered moot, as Richard Bourke, the governor of New South Wales, declared Batman's Treaty null and void on 26 August 1835, on the grounds that the land in question belonged to the Crown, and the Aboriginal people with whom Batman had negotiated had no claim to it. In other words, the British government proclaimed that Batman's attempt to scam the Indigenous population out of their land didn't count, because scamming people out of their land was too generous to be legal. Instead the government stuck to the time-honoured legal principle of *terra nullius*, which is Latin for 'everything on earth belongs to England'. Bourke's proclamation also declared that anyone on 'vacant land of the Crown' without official authorisation to be trespassing, thus neatly rendering any Aboriginal person who hadn't asked permission to live in their own home a criminal.

In the interests of balance, I will pause here to note that the British Empire also did some good things probably.

John Batman, the racist mass murdering mercenary, was devastated to find himself officially declared too nice to black people, and even more outraged that while he popped back to

Launceston to spread the word of the wonderful new village of Batmania, he'd been gazumped by John Pascoe Fawkner, who led his own party to the site of Melbourne and set up his own village, responding to news of Batman's Treaty with a hearty laugh and a rude gesture.

Batman and Fawkner ultimately agreed to share the settlement, which just goes to show that men of good will can come to mutually agreeable terms and live together in peace and harmony as long as they're both white and recognised by an imperial government as human beings.

That settlement continued to be called Batmania, until mid-1837, when it was officially renamed Melbourne, after William Lamb, 2nd Viscount Melbourne, best-known today as the United Kingdom's least memorable prime minister. And this was the moment that many reputable historians[25] believe our nascent nation really missed a trick. The arguments are complex on all sides. On the one hand, nobody knew that 'Batmania' would one day be such a beautifully evocative name. On the other hand, they surely had to suspect it would at least be more impressive than 'Melbourne'. Even in the 1830s, the name of Batman had to have slightly superheroish connotations, didn't it? And even if it didn't, 'Batmania' includes the word 'mania', and who would turn down the opportunity to have that in their name? Nowadays thousands of cities would kill to be named Beatlemania, or Wrestlemania, if only trademark considerations prevented it – the merchandising opportunities should've been obvious even to the people of the 1830s, who science has proven were stupider than normal people. And even then, wasn't it obvious that Lord Melbourne was a bland and forgettable man who would never be worthy of commemoration?

25 Probably. If they were honest.

Obviously, as a more enlightened age made it clear that John Batman himself wasn't exactly a paragon of virtue – in the sense that Stalin wasn't exactly a Meals on Wheels volunteer – one can see that naming a city after Batman might be slightly problematic. But all of the horrible things Batman did were on behalf of the government that was being led by the Viscount Melbourne, so it's a bit of a wash on that front anyway.

And, I mean, no matter what the facts of history might be, can you seriously tell me that living in a city named Batmania wouldn't be a blast? If need be we could just pretend it was named after the fictional character. It's not like Melbourne isn't used to dishonesty: we're still calling ourselves the sporting capital of the world[26].

Still, the opportunity was missed and a fortune in T-shirt sales forgone. John Batman settled at the suspiciously named Batman's Hill at the western end of Collins Street[27], and a few years later, disfigured and crippled, died of syphilis, having been cared for in his final days by the local Aboriginal people, in what was either a classic case of irony or a classic case of the thing that people call irony but isn't. He was only 38 when he died, and had done a lot for his age by any standards – especially when you consider that in between the graziering, the bounty hunting, the race warring, the city founding, and the syphilis catching, he had also fathered eight children[28]. In a twist that he would've found massively annoying if he'd been in any state to do so, he was years later exhumed and reburied in the Melbourne cemetery named after Fawkner.

---

26 Incidentally the actual sporting capital of the world is Fargo, North Dakota. Look it up.

27 This is either the 'Paris end' of Collins Street, or the other one.

28 At time of writing, I myself am 38, and I've only fathered three children, and founded no cities whatsoever.

Batman would not be remembered in the name of the city he had sort of started, but his name would certainly not be forgotten. Numerous streets and parks in Melbourne and elsewhere bear the name of Batman, as does a federal electorate and a railway station. There is also the comic book character, whose creators claim is named after the popular flying mammal, but bears a lot of striking similarities to his 19th-century Australian forebear, including:

- Working as a vigilante
- Having lots of money
- Distinctive headwear
- Syphilis.

What sort of legacy did Batman leave? He was undoubtedly a pioneer, and it cannot be denied that he had a huge impact on the development of colonial Australia. But neither can the fact that his life, particularly in Van Diemen's Land, featured numerous atrocities. A complex man who enriched himself by hunting Aboriginal people, but also wished to improve their lives, lobbied for what he considered fairer treatment, and attempted a fairer deal with them than any of his fellow colonists; perhaps the best summation of John Batman is that he contained the problematic contradictions inherent in the growing nation that he was such a notable part of. But if it's difficult to pin down the essential truth of the man, one thing is certain: his name was Batman, and nobody can ever take that away from him.

FUN FOR YOU AT HOME: Create the John Batman experience in your own backyard! Get a group of your friends together and set out to hunt the most dangerous game: man! Feel ashamed of yourself? So you should be.

CAROLINE CHISHOLM
Emigrate Expectations

IF MEN OF COLONIAL AUSTRALIA like John Batman and John Macarthur provoke furious debate as to whether they should be labelled heroes or villains, there can be no such disagreement about Caroline Chisholm. She was a woman of such overt and indisputable kindness, selflessness, and charitable intention that you probably would've hated her if you knew her. Indeed, Chisholm was so remarkable a woman that it is no exaggeration to say that I used to live on a street named after her.

Caroline Chisholm was not the first woman to make a mark on history: many experts have suggested that women, if they really put their mind to it, can do things. Obviously, this allegation has been contested, and in some quarters the debate continues to rage. But careful analysis of the facts seems to strongly support the thesis that things have, at times, been done by women, including Joan of Arc, Golda Meir and Barbara Windsor to name just a few. But can any great woman be a more great woman than that woman so great that she dedicated her life to helping other women be as great as they could be? Assuming I read my last sentence correctly, there cannot.

Who was Caroline Chisholm? An easy question to answer, but a difficult answer to comprehend. In one sense, she was an

Australian hero, but in another sense, she was actually an English hero. Though she scorned public position and the pursuit of status, she became one of the most famous women in both England and Australia. She was once given a bust of herself by Pope Pius IX, yet never gave her own bust away to anyone, not even the Pope. The woman was a walking conundrum[29], but if she can be summed up in a few words, they are these: a bloody nice lady.

Caroline Chisholm was born Caroline Jones, a suspicious discrepancy that leads one to ask: what else was she trying to hide? Her father was William Jones, a Northampton pig dealer with 16 children who was married four times, his first three wives presumably dying of exhaustion. Caroline was his last child, William recognising that he'd finally got it right when she was born in 1808. As a young girl, Caroline saw her father bring a maimed solider home, and instruct his children on the debt they owed to this man who had fought for them. Caroline learnt an important lesson that day: treating the disadvantaged as props in your homespun morality plays can work wonders.

At the age of 22, Caroline sadly made herself a willing accomplice to the patriarchy by marrying Captain Archibald Chisholm of the East India Company, a rising star in the field of violent mercantile colonialism.

In 1833, Caroline joined Archibald with his regiment in India. Here she was immediately struck by the bad influence that the soldiers were having on the young girls in the barracks. As children are wont to do, the girls were mimicking the behaviour of the soldiers, staying out late, smoking, drinking, and conducting rapacious invasions of peaceful foreign nations. To address the poor behaviour, Caroline founded the Female School of Industry for the Daughters of European Soldiers, an institution that overcame

29 Yet often sat or stood still – see how contradictory she was?

the handicap of having a stupidly long name to teach the girls of the barracks reading, writing, cooking, nursing, and also religion because it was the 1830s and you just couldn't get around it.

After five years of pursing her lips at soldiers and forcing girls to conform to her own rigid ideas of propriety, Caroline left India due to Archibald taking sick leave. Believing, adorably, that the Australian climate would be beneficial for the Captain's health, the Chisholms arrived in Sydney in October 1838, making their home in Windsor for some reason[30]. Not long into their Australian sojourn, the couple began to notice something about life for immigrants in the colony, that something being that it sucked. People would arrive in Sydney, wide-eyed and full of enthusiasm for the exciting new life they were under the impression was about to begin because someone had told them a vicious lie. Their illusions were shattered in the most abrupt and devastating way when they discovered that life in the colonies was, like Queen Victoria herself, nasty, brutish and short.

Caroline was most distressed to see the predicament faced by many young women who had emigrated with no money, no source of employment, and no friends or family in the new land. Some might say that the fact that these women embarked on a journey around the world in such personal circumstances proved that they were naive idiots, but many of them quickly proved such assessments wrongheaded: intelligent and resourceful, they showed real initiative, took responsibility for their own welfare, and got themselves jobs on the streets. And by 'on the streets', I mean exactly what you think I mean.

Caroline, a good Catholic and every bit as judgmental as that implies, was horrified that so many women were forced into such degrading and immoral work just to feed themselves. No doubt she

30 Your guess is as good as mine. I've been to Windsor.

was not the only one, but unlike most of us, who see the corruption and filth of the world around us and recognise almost immediately how futile it is to waste energy trying to effect change, she went and did something about it.

In 1840, Archibald was called back into active service with his army of bloodthirsty corporate gangsters, but Caroline and her three sons[31] stayed in Windsor, from where she made frequent trips to greet the immigrants disembarking at Sydney Harbour. Caroline found many immigrant girls jobs, and even provided accommodation to some in her own home.

But Caroline knew that her house in Windsor was not sufficient to contain every desperate immigrant who discovered that the promise of the new world was illusory and the reality of the British Empire a squalid deception. In order to give these women a home, she realised, she would need to establish some kind of home for women, or 'women's home': a home in which women could live, in other words. With this in mind, she approached Governor George Gipps and asked for his assistance in combining these twin concepts of women and homes.

Governor Gipps was surprised when he met Caroline, saying that he had expected 'an old lady in white cap and spectacles' only to be confronted by 'a handsome, stately young woman'[32] who despite being quite blatantly female, spoke to him as if she was an actual human being. Though she had already gained a head start by arousing the governor's masculine lust, Caroline knew she would have to broach the subject of the women's home delicately, as anti-Catholic sentiment in the colony was high and the governor would be likely to quash any project suspected of being a front for the dissemination of papal propaganda. She

31 By the way, while all that other stuff was happening, she'd had three sons.

32 Genuine historical quotes: accept no imitations.

therefore used the utmost tact in her approach, sneaking up quietly behind Gipps and whispering softly into his ear, 'How about a women's home then?'

'What?' replied the governor, startled yet intrigued.

'How about we do a little women's home, here in Sydney?' Caroline pressed. 'Just a little one, a home for women to be at home in.'

'Is this a Catholic thing?' the governor asked suspiciously.

'God, NO!' bellowed Caroline.

'But you are a Catholic, aren't you, Caroline?' said Gipps, who had recognised her from her picture on the five-dollar note[33].

'I may be a Catholic, sir,' declared Caroline, drawing herself up to what may or may not have been her full height, 'but before I am a Catholic I am a woman. I am a human. I am a citizen, dammit,' here onlookers gasped at the boldness of her language, 'and I seek only to provide a public service to the needy, with no mention whatsoever of the indivisibility of the Trinity.'

'Well,' said George Gipps, 'frankly I am convinced. Here you go,' and with that he handed Caroline part of Sydney's old immigration barracks and she was away.

The immigration barracks was in fact nothing but a decrepit shed full of rats, which Caroline eliminated by lying in wait at night with poisoned bread, much like Val Kilmer in the film *The Ghost and the Darkness,* except that he was hunting lions instead of rats, with a gun instead of bread. The result, however, was much the same: a bunch of dead animals, and Caroline Chisholm standing triumphant amid the carnage, knowing her greatest dream was now several hundred rats closer to fulfilment.

In that once-filthy shed, refurbished and spruced up à la Calam's

33 They replaced her with the Queen: can you fucking believe that?

shack in the film *Calamity Jane*[34], Caroline created the Female Immigrants' Home, an institution that offered shelter and aid to women who arrived in Sydney without available means of support[35]. Attached to the home was Sydney's only free employment registry, meaning that Caroline was not just keeping these women afloat during hard times, but actively assisting them in forging their own path in the colony. Such an establishment was unprecedented: in an era when the prevailing philosophy of life was dog eat dog, Caroline Chisholm not only refused to eat dog, she gave the dog a thorough brushing and took it shopping for a new collar.

Caroline did not discriminate: she helped those from all backgrounds and beliefs, even though she must surely have known a lot of them were going to Hell. Her only concern was for the welfare of those whom callous society had deemed surplus to requirements. She wished to transform New South Wales from a remorseless meat grinder turning eager young immigrants into human sausage, to a welcoming meat-grinder, turning them into socially useful and spiritually fulfilled kranskys.

Having established the Sydney Immigrants' Home, Caroline set to work to solve one of the greatest problems of migration to Australia: workers were needed in the rural districts, but those who arrived in Sydney were understandably reluctant to journey to the outback, because they had an extremely accurate idea of what it was like. Caroline determined that she would bring migrants to the interior and persuade them that a life on the land was not the terrifying nightmare that facts suggested it would be. She spent most of 1842 riding back and forth between city and country on her white horse, Captain – named after her husband, whose rank she had amusingly mistaken for his first name – bringing

34 History is really nothing but a succession of similarities to movies.

35 Financial support, I mean. I'm sure they had … you know, garments.

groups of young migrants to the New South Wales frontiers and showing them that things weren't so bad if you gritted your teeth and invented flyspray. Caroline quickly established a chain of new immigrant homes throughout the regions, facilitating the flow of migrants from the docks of Sydney to the sunburnt expanses of the bush in a way that all the men who had previously been in positions of authority in New South Wales had utterly failed to do.

Chisholm's organisation continued to expand, and she quickly became known as the guardian angel of all who came to Australia seeking a decent life. Her work attracted opposition, but Caroline's attitude to opposition had always been, and would always remain, 'they can all go fuck themselves'[36]. Her plan for settling migrant families on the land with long leases was repeatedly knocked back by officialdom, the government being dominated by those who feared the loss of their land-owning supremacy – it is difficult for we of the 21st century to imagine it, but back then government was greatly dominated by self-interested arseholes. It was a very different time – but Caroline never stopped fighting for the rights of families on small farms against the wealthy oligarchs of 'squattocracy', so named because they treated the rest of the population like their toilet.

Together, the Chisholms toured New South Wales and collected statements from more than 600 inhabitants testifying to the reality of life in the colony. With these they hoped to encourage more prospective emigrants to make the journey, and provide them with the information they needed to prepare: a radical departure from previous practice, which had been to lie as much as possible about what Australia was like in order to trick people into coming here, and if necessary, to drug them and transport them in barrels.

36 There's no record of her actually *saying* this, but she didn't need to say it when she lived it.

Her interests grew to embrace the conditions found on the journeys from Europe to New South Wales themselves: migrants suffered cramped and dirty quarters, and young women were vulnerable to sexual assault. Caroline became the first woman in New South Wales to bring a case to court, against the captain and surgeon of the ship the *Carthaginian*, after a passenger named Margaret Ann Bolton complained about the mistreatment of women on board, and was punished with a night on deck in stocks. Caroline got in quite a state, and her righteous fury as usual proved successful: she won the case and struck fear into the hearts of all other ship's captains who were hopeful of continuing to be human garbage undetected.

In 1846 the Chisholms returned to England, where her crusade continued: she lobbied for, and won, free passage to Australia for the wives and children of former convicts, and for children that emigrants had left behind. She published some of the statements she had collected in New South Wales in a pamphlet titled *Comfort for the Poor! Meat Three Times a Day!* This became one of the most popular meat-themed pamphlets of the mid-19th century[37] and convinced the public of the great joys of colonial life, where meat flowed like water and you could hardly swing a cat without hitting a hamburger. The flesh-filled colons of the hardy colonials[38] became a powerful selling point.

In England Caroline also founded the Family Colonization Loan Society, to provide financial assistance to families wishing to start anew in Australia. She hoped to replace the savagery and violence of unattached colonials with the savagery and violence of families. The society won praise from no less a personage than Charles Dickens, who advertised the society in his magazine *Household Words*, and

37 And up against some stiff competition, as you can imagine.

38 Colon-ials, ha!

honoured Caroline herself in his novel *Bleak House*, by basing the character of insufferable bitch Mrs Jellyby on her[39]. Caroline Chisholm thereby attained a unique place in Australian history, as Australia's only English philanthropist to both found a home for immigrants and be fictionalised as a deeply unpleasant hypocrite by a legendary novelist.

By 1854, the Family Colonization Loan Society had helped more than 3000 people migrate to Australia, something that today is not only hard to imagine, but probably illegal. That year, Caroline returned to Australia and toured the Victorian Goldfields, where she proposed shelter sheds be built along the route for the comfort of prospectors and their families. The government supported this scheme because by this time nobody could really summon the energy to *not* support anything Caroline Chisholm proposed.

Yet by this time, Caroline was flagging a little herself. As the old saying goes, 'sooner or later everyone gets kidney disease', and she demonstrated the truth of this proverb by getting kidney disease. It did not stop her from working, but it did slow her down, and she moved back to Sydney for medical attention.

Caroline made her final return to England in 1866. She passed away in London at the age of 68, on 25 March 1877. Archibald died later that year, having never at any stage of his life had much point to him apart from his wife, and this being truer than ever now that she was dead. The Chisholms were survived by five of the eight children that Caroline had occasionally remembered she had, but which we don't really need to pay any attention to at all.

In 1859 the *Empire* newspaper of Henry Parkes said of Caroline Chisholm:

> *If Captain James Cook discovered Australia – if John Macarthur planted the first seeds of its extraordinary prosperity*

39 Dickens had his own ideas of what 'honouring' meant.

> *– if Ludwig Leichhardt penetrated and explored its before unknown interior – Caroline Chisholm has done more – she alone has colonised in the true sense of the term.*

These words rang true in 1859, and they ring even more true now that we know full well that Captain Cook didn't discover Australia, John Macarthur was a psychotic gangster who left most of the hard work to his wife, and Ludwig Leichhardt was such a great explorer that he got lost and never came back. If Caroline Chisholm towered over these men even then, she towers even more toweringly over them in these days of recognition that they weren't all that great to begin with.

Caroline Chisholm's tombstone in Northampton bears the words, 'The emigrant's friend'. True, but hardly sufficient. In this amazing woman was united a phenomenal work ethic, an agile and imaginative mind, irresistible determination, a burning passion for social justice, belief in the innate dignity of all people no matter how humble their station, and a conviction that the world could, through concerted effort by good people, be made a better place. She fought for women's rights at a time when few were concerned with such things, and made the powers that be take notice through sheer force of will. She stood up for the poorest and most downtrodden in her society, and changed the way that governments and social institutions treated them. She did all this with minimal official assistance and while also carrying the intolerable burden of children, the waking nightmare that so many of us know so well.

The best way to sum her up is perhaps to say that she proved the theory that one person can indeed make a difference in this world, despite that theory being basically bollocks. Let Caroline Chisholm's legacy to the world be this: don't try to follow her example too enthusiastically; you'll only be disappointed.

FUN FOR YOU AT HOME: Get to know an immigrant in your community. Ask them about their experience. Where did they come from? How is Australia different to their country of origin? Have they committed any crimes? Inform the police as soon as possible.

MARY MACKILLOP
Sainted Love

IT'S NOT EASY to become a saint in the Catholic Church. For a start you have to be dead, which is never a fun part of a job application process. Secondly, before you were dead you had to have been possessed of 'heroic virtue', a phrase meaning, 'so good it just makes you sick'. Finally, you have to be proven to have performed at least two miracles, or to put it another way, some slightly strange old men have to decide that you performed at least two miracles.

Given all those hoops one has to jump through to get that coveted 'Saint' in front of your name, anyone who gets there is clearly an impressive person. Not even Caroline Chisholm is a saint yet, and she was so good that if she were alive today someone on Twitter would call her problematic. So it can safely be said that St Mary of the Cross MacKillop is one of Australia's highest achievers: indeed she may be the highest achiever of all, given that almost every other notable Australian ceased their achievements upon death. In future St Mary might be joined in the Australian Saints Club by other great Aussies: perhaps Chisholm, or the great humanitarian Father Bob Maguire, or Hugh Jackman. But at the time of writing, MacKillop is all we have, saint-wise, and that's a pretty big feather in one's habit.

Mary Helen MacKillop was born on 15 January 1842, in Newtown, New South Wales – not to be confused with Newtown, New South Wales. The area MacKillop was born in is now Fitzroy in Melbourne, but as at that time neither Victoria nor yarn-bombing had been invented, they decided it would be best to confuse everyone by calling it Newtown while they waited for the hipsters to arrive. Mary was the daughter of Alexander and Flora MacKillop, Scottish immigrants who had travelled around the world in search of similar weather. Alexander had trained for the priesthood, but quit just before being ordained after hearing a rumour that sex was fantastic – a rumour that fortunately never reached his daughter's ears. Mary, the eldest of eight children[40], was christened Maria Ellen, but continued to be known as Mary Helen because nobody in the MacKillop family understood how names work.

Alexander MacKillop was not a success as a farmer, possibly because he'd been expecting to be a priest until he was 29 and never learnt how to plant seeds[41], or possibly because Fitzroy was a terrible place to have a farm due to all the second-hand bookshops getting in the way. Due to his failings, the MacKillop family frequently needed to rely on income earnt by the children to survive, which can't exactly have been a boost to Alex's self-esteem. At 14, Mary got a job in a stationery store. 'Better than a store that keeps moving around,' joked her dad. 'Get a job, you deadbeat,' Mary retorted, in no mood.

At 18 Mary, still striving to meet the needs of her poverty-stricken and parentally deficient family, found employment as a governess at her aunt and uncle's estate in Penola, South Australia. This means Mary started out as a governess before becoming a nun,

---

40 Catholics, eh. What can you do?

41 Except in Jesus's parable about the seeds, which is extremely sketchy on agricultural detail.

in a rare example of the reverse Von Trapp. Here Mary displayed an early flair for philanthropy, allowing other children of farm workers on the estate to attend lessons with her aunt and uncle's brood.

In 1864, after moving to Victoria, she opened her own school, the Bay View House Seminary for Young Ladies. After founding the school, Mary was joined by the rest of the MacKillops, who were taking their mastery of the art of sponging to a whole new level.

In 1866, Mary received a plea from Father Julian Woods, an English priest and friend of hers from Penola, who asked her to come back to the SA town to open a Catholic school. Mary, always a sucker for a handsome man in a dress, duly returned with her sisters Annie and Lexie: anything to cut down on their parents' food bill. Woods and MacKillop founded their school in a stable, having badly misinterpreted a passage of the New Testament. They got the MacKillop girls' brother to renovate the stable, because the Catholic church, then as now, was terribly short of funds.

On 21 November 1866, the feast day of the Presentation of Mary[42], several other women joined the MacKillops in Penola, and Mary adopted the name 'Sister Mary of the Cross', which everyone thought seemed a bit pretentious but didn't like to say anything[43]. Mary and Lexie MacKillop began wearing habits, and the group, calling itself the Sisters of St Joseph of the Sacred Heart[44], moved to new digs in Grote Street, in Adelaide's growing Nun District.

At Grote Street the sisters founded a new school, something that was beginning to be something of an obsession with Mary: her

---

42 Commemorating the time the Virgin Mary presented her plan for a restructure of the sales and marketing departments to the board.

43 I feel like it shouldn't be this easy to just become a nun. Isn't there a test you have to do or something?

44 Not to be confused with the Sisters of St Joseph of the Profane Kidney, a far louder and less demure order.

friends worried that school-founding was getting to be her whole life. 'Don't you think you should cut down on all these schools you're founding, Mary?' they'd ask. 'I'm sorry,' Mary replied, 'but I can't stop. I guess it's ... getting to be a habit with me!' And then everyone would share a hearty laugh and forget what they were talking about.

The new school was the first religious institute to be founded by an Australian, and would've made Mary pretty cocky if that weren't such a bad look for a nun. MacKillop came up with the 'Rule of Life' to act as a guiding principle for her new order: it focused on poverty (i.e. how great it was to be poor), no ownership of personal belongings (which came in handy given the poverty bit), dependence on divine providence (i.e. relaxing and letting God get on with stuff), and willingness to go where needed (which technically was nowhere, since everyone was supposed to depend on divine providence, so depending on nuns going places would violate that completely, but nobody was claiming the Rule of Life was internally consistent, just that it was nice). The Rule of Life proved wildly popular, and women began to flock to Adelaide to get a chance to own nothing and work interminably for the benefit of others. Ten new sisters joined the order by the end of 1867, and MacKillop started to realise she really had something here: it was a lot like Beatlemania.

The Sisters of St Joseph of the Sacred Heart, or Josephites, also became known colloquially as the 'Brown Joeys', due to their plain brown habits and tendency to carry each other around in pouches to save wear and tear on boots. The Joeys were dedicated to the education of the poor, in a time when the prevailing view of the ruling classes was that educating the poor was as useful as reading aloud to firewood. In October 1867 yet another school was opened in Yankalilla[45], South Australia, and by the end of 1869 21 schools

45 Named after the first lewd act to be prosecuted in the area.

were being run by Josephite nuns around the state, which seems a ridiculously rapid expansion and goes to show that when nuns put their mind to something, they are utterly terrifying.

In December 1869, driven by her insatiable lust for philanthropy, MacKillop went to Brisbane to establish the Queensland branch of the Joeys, basing it at Kangaroo Point[46]. By 1871 there were 130 Josephites working in more than 40 institutions in South Australia and Queensland. Australia had not seen such a powerful force for the welfare of the poor and marginalised since the New South Wales Corps offered a 2-for-1 deal on rum.

Obviously, you can't be a hard-working, selfless woman committing your life to the care and education of the less fortunate without making many powerful enemies, because the world is a gigantic pile of burning garbage. Local South Australian clergymen clashed with Mary's friend Father Woods, now director-general of Catholic education, over education policy, and began a campaign to discredit MacKillop's order – one priest declared that he would ruin Woods through the Sisterhood, just one of countless historical examples that have given Catholic priests their famous reputation for kindness and humility*.

Rumours began to circulate of financial mismanagement – which is a bit tasteless given the whole poverty thing – and that Sister Mary herself had a drinking problem. In fact, she drank alcohol on doctor's orders, to gain relief from her dysmenorrhea, a painful condition that had presumably been visited upon her by God to indicate his dislike of poor children.

One of MacKillop's most formidable adversaries was Father Charles Horan OFM[47], a nasty and vindictive man who, even by the standards of the priesthood, was about average really. Horan had

---

46 I know: a bit on the nose.

47 Standing for Obnoxious Fucking Maggot.

been a colleague of Father Keating of Kapunda, north of Adelaide. In 1870 MacKillop heard that Keating had been sexually abusing children. One has to remember that this was a different time, when positions of trust and authority could be given to cruel and predatory men who were allowed to take advantage of their position to violate children. We can all be thankful we live in different times now*.

The Josephites informed Father Woods of the allegations against Keating, and Woods relayed the story to the vicar-general, Father John Smyth, who sent Keating back to Ireland under the church's traditional 'if it's happening somewhere else, it's not happening any more' rule. Keating's dismissal so enraged Horan that when he became acting vicar-general after Smyth's death, he looked to poison the mind of Laurence Bonaventura Sheil, Bishop of Adelaide, against MacKillop and her Joeys.

In September 1871 Horan convinced Sheil that the Josephites' constitution should be changed in such a way as to render the sisters homeless. MacKillop refused to obey this order, on the grounds that it was transparently dumb, and as a result, Sheil excommunicated her for insubordination. This meant she was forbidden contact with the Catholic church, but nevertheless many people considered it a punishment. It was an upsetting time for MacKillop and the Josephites. Most of the order's schools were closed, but there were some Josephites who chose to stay under the jurisdiction of the Adelaide diocese, and were dubbed 'Black Joeys' for their split with the founder of the order, and their disturbing scavenging activities during bushfires. The Black Joeys maintain a presence to this day, under the title of the Federation Sisters of St Joseph, and must have some guts to go around boasting about how their group was founded by throwing a saint under the bus.

Mary's excommunication didn't last long: on his deathbed, Bishop Sheil pondered the advisability of coming face-to-face with

God with his file still marked 'Incredible Douche', and ordered Horan to lift the excommunication.

Back in the fold and as hot for good deeds as ever, Mary set her sights on even loftier peaks. In 1873, she travelled to Rome to seek the approval of Pope Pius IX – commonly considered one of the all-time best Piuses[48] – for the Sisters of St Joseph, which would make them an official, papally sanctioned religious congregation and not just a bunch of weird ladies in brown poking their noses into everyone's business[49]. The Pope's approval was forthcoming, but not before the Vatican altered the Rule of Life in regard to the vow of poverty. This angered Father Woods, who hated to see women owning things, and a rift developed between he and Mary.

Returning to Australia in 1875, Mary continued to face opposition from priests and bishops over her order, which flouted convention by living in the community rather than in convents, and being under the control of a superior general chosen from within the congregation rather than the diocesan bishop, which in the world of 1870s Catholicism basically made them hippies. The Josephites further enraged the conservative/dickish religious hierarchy of the day with their approach to education: they refused to accept government funding, which angered those who didn't like looking a gift horse in the mouth; they refused to teach instrumental music, which angered those who thought that was kind of a weird thing to refuse to do but to be fair were themselves a bit weird in thinking that instrumental music was so freaking important; and they refused to teach girls from wealthy families, which angered those who adhered to Jesus's

48 But then, most fans will tell you that the odd-numbered Piuses are always the best.

49 That role in Australian life having since been taken over by the CWA.

famous admonition, 'Be nice to rich people, they're the best people in the world'.

Their idiosyncratic eagerness to piss off the authorities saw the Josephites expelled by intolerant bishops from Bathurst in 1876 and Queensland in 1880. But the order continued to expand throughout South Australia and New South Wales. MacKillop established the Josephites in Victoria and New Zealand, despite being replaced as Superior General by Sister Bernard Walsh in 1883, a controversial move among many who considered it deeply suspicious that a nun was called 'Bernard'. In 1899, Mary became superior general once more after Bernard's death, yet again proving her peerless ability to grind her opponents down.

In May 1901, Mary suffered a stroke at Rotorua, New Zealand, and most people who'd been there didn't blame her. She was an invalid from then until her death on 8 August 1909. The Archbishop of Sydney, Cardinal Patrick Francis Moran, said, 'I consider this day to have assisted at the deathbed of a saint', and it would be charitable to assume that he meant spiritual assistance rather than assisting her to die. Mother Mary MacKillop was buried at Gore Hill cemetery, where pilgrims immediately began removing earth from around the grave, because Christians are a bit strange and they thought it would give them superpowers or something. The ongoing soil theft resulted in Mary being exhumed in 1914 and moved to a vault before the altar of the Virgin[50] Mary in the memorial chapel in Mount Street, North Sydney. Here nobody could move earth from around her, which was far more respectful, but caused a massive rise in whatever it was the Christians were hoping the earth would stop.

In a way, what Mary MacKillop did after her death was the most important part of her story, although in another way, this is not even

50 Alleged.

remotely true. However, it was her post-mortem shenanigans that got her sainted. The process to have her declared a saint began in 1925, initiated by the then-Mother Superior of the Brown Joeys, Mother Laurence. Archbishop Michael Kelly of Sydney established a tribunal to continue the process, and as quickly as possible, nothing happened. Decades went by while church elders faffed around examining Mary's writings, discussing her life's work, and generally debating the provocative proposition: 'Mary MacKillop: quite nice?'

In 1973 the initial phase of investigations was completed, demonstrating the ultimate source of the Catholic belief in an afterlife: if they didn't live after death they'd never see anything get done. Further investigations resulted in MacKillop's 'heroic virtue' being declared in 1992. So only 83 years from death to official recognition that she was great: bravo, speedy apparatus of church officialdom.

But obviously heroic virtue is not enough to become a saint: the real crux of sainthood is the performing of miracles, i.e. curing terminal diseases after people have prayed to you. Before Mary could become Saint Mary, she had to prove to the church's satisfaction that she was a qualified ghost doctor, and this can be a tricky thing to prove, what with being invisible and incorporeal, and proof of such a thing being by any measure utterly impossible. Plus, to be a saint you have to do it *twice*. But Mary MacKillop was no quitter: she was determined to provide undead first aid, and she would not rest until she had. Which is a bit sad really: you'd think she deserved a bit of rest after dying.

The same year she was declared heroically virtuous, the church announced that it had been persuaded that in 1961, Veronica Hopson was cured of leukaemia by praying for Mary MacKillop's intercession. Intercession is a useful process whereby if you want something, but find that when you pray directly to God the line is busy, you can instead pray to some dead person who you know is very nice, and they'll go let God know what you want. God is, after all, a busy man, and cannot be expected to answer every call personally – but His operators are standing by and He promises your prayer is important to Him. And if the person you pray to is actually able to tap God on the shoulder and say, 'Hey, mind zapping that leukaemia away, chief?' and God then does just that, then you know the person is actually a saint, because it's not like he's reading Post-It notes from every upstart little ghost who tries to get a tumour shrunk.

As a result of MacKillop's efforts in paranormal triage in the Hopson case, Pope John Paul II[51] beatified her on 19 January 1995 – beatification being one of the many processes devised by the Catholic church to make everything as pointlessly convoluted as possible. It recognises a formerly alive person's entry into Heaven and ability to, as noted above, get through to God's personal number. Being beatified, Mary was now entitled to call herself 'Blessed Mary MacKillop', which may or may not have seemed like a big whoop for a dead woman who'd had to wait 86 years for it.

It was on 19 December 2009 – just over a hundred years since Mary first moved into Jesus's gated community – that the Congregation for the Causes of Saints issued a papal decree recognising a second miracle. Kathleen Evans had recovered from inoperable lung and brain cancer in the 1990s after praying to Mary, and the Vatican had decided that these two events were causally linked because, you know, why the hell not.

Now that two miracles had been ascribed to MacKillop, there was simply no way to deny that she was a ghost doctor of the highest calibre. Her canonisation was announced on 19 February

51 A rare case of a sequel that lived up to the original.

2010, and officially took place on 17 October that year. Finally, Mary MacKillop was a saint, and nobody could take that away from her, no matter how many paedophile-shielders she upset. Eight thousand Australians were in Vatican City to witness the canonisation[52], a 900 per cent increase in the Vatican's population and an equivalent decrease in the Vatican's standard of grooming. Whether, after becoming a saint, MacKillop has continued to tug God's sleeve and make him fix sick people, or simply sat back, KPI achieved, resting on her laurels, is unknown.

It's hard to overstate the impact Mary MacKillop had on the world, and on Australia in particular.[53] Simply the fact that she was the first Australian saint is huge: our country has had multiple gold medallists, award-winning artists, Nobel Prize winners and serial killers, but only one saint; she stands alone on that particular pedestal. But more than that: in a time when life in Australia was cruel and difficult for most, she brought compassion and generosity to the unforgiving frontier. She defied convention and the authority of the church itself to bring Jesus's message of charity and love to the poorest of her country. There were many who sought to bring her down, but she never gave way to bitterness or rancour: she simply carried on doing what she believed to be right, driven by devotion to her God and love for her fellow humans. Like Caroline Chisholm before her, she reached out across the land to lend a hand to those most in need. The poor, the sick and the infirm were her business, and she never stopped ministering to them. In so doing, she showed

52 A term for making someone a saint, dating back to the Middle Ages, when an announcement of sainthood was marked by firing the saint out of a cannon.

53 Well, not that hard. I mean you could say, 'Mary MacKillop discovered fire' or 'Mary MacKillop raised Africa from the sea', and you'd have overstated it pretty easily. But you know what I mean.

that Australia was not just a country of convicts, fortune-hunters, and being kicked to death by kangaroos: it was a land of faith, hope, and love. Was not this her real miracle? No – curing brain cancer is much more impressive. But still.

FUN FOR YOU AT HOME: Find a friend or relative suffering from a terminal disease, and pray to a saint to cure them. Did they get better? You probably didn't pray hard enough. For shame.

SEEKING IDENTITY

AS AUSTRALIA APPROACHED the end of the 19th century, it was a restless country. For a hundred years, the inhabitants of the continent had worked to build a society and establish the idea of Australia in the mass consciousness, in between exploiting the land's natural resources and trying to wipe out its Indigenous population. Memorable figures, ranging from the monumentally selfless to the nauseatingly violent, had made their contributions, and the development of agricultural industries by the likes of John Macarthur, Samuel Marsden and William Farrer had been followed by seismic events like the Gold Rush and the boom in armed robbery that followed it. Australia had a society, it had an economy, and it had a place in the world. What it didn't have, though, was an *identity.*

What Australia was had become clear: it was a great big brown land in the middle of the sea where it was always far too hot and everything wanted to kill you. But who were Australians? What defined the Australian identity, and what did it mean for a person to say, 'I am Australian'?

Part of the problem, of course, was that many people didn't really say, 'I am Australian' at all. Most Australians still thought of themselves as British, which was fair enough because legally they were: Australia was no more an independent nation than the Isle of Wight. It wasn't even a united colony: New South Wales, Victoria,

Queensland, Tasmania, South Australia and Western Australia were separate entities with their own colonial governments, bound together by nothing but geography and the fact that they were the cringing lapdogs of a kleptocratic empire.

And yet a culture was developing that was more than just Britain in the South Pacific, or dying of thirst. There was something growing in the great southern land that would come to make the word 'Australian' mean something. The Australian people, whichever corner of the continent they happened to live in or had stolen from an Aboriginal person, were gradually moving towards a moment of definition: of announcing to the world – but more importantly announcing to *themselves* – who they are.

The first step was cricket. In 1877, the first test match was played between England and Australia. Australia won by 45 runs thanks to the dashing batting of Charlie Bannerman and the canny slow-mediums of Tom Garrett. It was a marvellous moment for the young nation, tempered slightly by the fact that it wasn't a nation yet. The embarrassment of being a country with a successful cricket team but no central government spurred Australians on to attaining a more concrete sense of self. And as time went on, not only would Australians define themselves as something more than just good cricketers, at several points in history, they would thoroughly define themselves as considerably less.

It was in 1901 that Australia became a united and independent nation, but in the years just prior to that landmark, and those following it, great men and women would do more than just declare independence: they would declare their identity. Having built Australia, they took it on themselves to take the next step in nationhood. These are their stories.

HENRY PARKES
The Santa Claus in Federation's Chimney

YOU MAY HAVE NOTICED, as you progress through this damn thing called life, that Australia has a number of states – six, to be exact. Yet these states do not all exist independently of each other, but are rather combined into one spectacular whole. A country, for want of a better word, that we call Australia. The states do have a certain amount of autonomy, but it tends to be that kind of autonomy that could best be described as 'not autonomous'. Basically, if the states ever want to do something that the federal government doesn't want them to, they don't get to: which is an excellent and efficient way of running things, and avoids Australia becoming like, say, Europe, which has a bunch of different countries all speaking their own languages and declaring their own national meats and causing utter chaos across the continent. Our continent has one country in it, and that is all we need. And for this happy state of affairs, we have one man to thank[54].

The Henry Parkes story is an old and straightforward one. On 27 May 1815, a boy was born in Canley, Warwickshire, England. In 1839, that boy migrates to Australia. There, he enters politics

54 Actually we have many men to thank, and possibly even some women. But I'm going for a certain effect here, so bear with me.

and changes the entire course of a nation's history, and then dies. A country town is named after him. A radio telescope is built in that country town. The radio telescope is used to broadcast the moon landing around the world. A movie is made about that broadcast, starring Sam Neill. A simple story, but one with far-reaching consequences. Is the moral of this story that without Henry Parkes, man would never have landed on the moon? Probably. At the very least Sam Neill's career would be less rich and varied. And yet there is so much more to Henry Parkes's life than space travel. The bare bones of facts are scarcely sufficient to encompass the impact that he had on all of our lives.

Henry Parkes was the son of a tenant farmer, who in his youth missed out on a comprehensive formal education, instead becoming apprenticed to a bone and ivory turner, a profession that in all likelihood is made up[55]. As a young man, he became involved in political movements that sought to improve conditions for the working class, beginning a lifelong interest in hampering economic growth and general troublemaking. According to the *Australasian Dictionary of Biography*, 'Though he has recently denied that he ever formally associated himself with the Chartist agitation, it is undoubted that he was warmly interested, as a working youth, in the advanced Liberal movements of the time'. Can we believe Parkes's denial that he was formally associated with the Chartist agitation? That's the question that vexes historians – and if indeed he was lying, can anyone with a formal association with the Chartist agitation be considered a great Australian? Also, what is the Chartist agitation[56]? These questions may never be resolved.

---

55 Why do you need to turn bone and ivory? Was it facing the wrong way?

56 I'm joking. I know what the Chartist agitation is. But I'm not going to tell you.

One question that *can* be resolved is, 'Did Henry Parkes arrive in Sydney on 25 July 1839?' The answer to this question is, unequivocally, 'Yes'. Parkes and his wife had come to Australia as a result of a series of unfortunate events, which history tells us is the only reason anyone ever comes to Australia.

Back in England, Parkes's business had failed, possibly because he was spending too much time informally associating himself with Chartism and not enough time on inventory control. He was also distracted by poetry, the scourge of the working man from time immemorial. His poetry was political in nature, railing against injustice and crying for a fair go for the common decent filthy unpleasant working man. One poem he wrote as a teenager was on the wrongs of Poland, though what Poland had ever done to him I have no idea.

Anyway, the business had failed, and the Parkes had had two children, both of whom had died in infancy, which was a pretty run-of-the-mill occurrence in those days of negligible antenatal care and low-quality nappies, but even so was bound to get you down. The couple decided to make a fresh start in Australia, a move that paid dividends almost immediately: two days before reaching Sydney, their third child was born, and she didn't even die[57]. All in all, Parkes would father 17 children during his life, which doctors agree is too many.

Ensconced in Sydney with his darling wife Clarinda and his even more darling daughter Clarinda[58], Parkes became a labourer

57 Well, she did, but not till 1915, and by that time it was fair enough.

58 You might think Clarinda was named after her mother, but she was actually named after the second baby who died, who was named after her mother. Would it be unsettling to know you were named after your dead sister? Discuss.

on the estate of Sir John Jamison[59]. But Parkes's restless soul soon felt again the irresistible pull of weird old-timey jobs that wouldn't exist for very long. So, off to the city he went, working in an iron-mongery[60], a brass foundry[61], and the Customs Department, where he worked as a tide-waiter, serving drinks and finger food to incoming waves[62]. Through these jobs, Parkes was able to save up to buy tools and by 1845 had set himself up as an ivory turner – hoping the ignorant colonials would not realise this wasn't a real thing.

Finding Australians far more willing to pay for his turned ivory than the persnickety English twerps who had driven him out of business, Parkes met with early success, expanding his business with branches in Maitland – 'the Parramatta of the Hunter Valley' – and Geelong – 'the Maitland of Werribee'. These branches adhered closely to the traditions of the Parkes family by failing miserably, and by 1850 young Parkes was fighting to keep his head above water, pretty much as he had been in England, but worse this time because of the humidity.

During this difficult time, Parkes supplemented his income by writing, contributing articles and poems to newspapers which in those days would publish pretty much anything that turned up in their mailboxes. In 1842, in the classic act of a desperate man, he published a book of poetry. Writing regularly on political and social matters, he soon expanded into practical activism, campaigning publicly for universal suffrage: this caused authorities to flag him as a dangerous radical and a threat to the hereditary privilege and

---

59 Described by Governor Macquarie as 'an intriguing and discontented person'. So imagine how his labourers felt.

60 A place where one mongs iron.

61 A place where one founds brass.

62 One of the Department's most curious Customs.

unaccountable power that had made the British Empire the wildly successful and homicidally racist enterprise it was.

With the market for ivory turning in decline, thanks to the mid-century craze for DIY ivory-direction, Parkes had plenty of spare time to devote to his new passion for shooting his mouth off in public. In 1850 he joined the Australian League, a body formed to push for universal suffrage and the formation of a 'Great Federal Republic' of Australia – an ambition which is due to be fulfilled any day now.

The Australian League was short-lived, as was Parkes's fervour for republicanism, and five of his children. But he remained active in the liberal movement[63], campaigning for self-governance for the colonies, and against the transportation of convicts to Australia, which he knew to be unspeakably cruel because he lived there. It was also in 1850 that he founded the *Empire* newspaper, staying true to the adage, 'Never let the fact that you are currently operating a failing business stop you from starting another one'.

But his political career was booming. Entering the New South Wales Legislative Council, he became involved in debate over a new constitution for the colony, butting heads with former mountain-avoider William Wentworth over the latter's proposal for a constitution based on the principles of letting the rich guys keep doing whatever the hell they wanted to everyone else all the time.

In 1856, under the new, somewhat more democratic constitution, Parkes stood for and won the seat of Sydney City. Later in 1856, he resigned his seat, having been reminded by a friend that he still owned a newspaper and he might want to check on it. He may also still have owned his ivory turning shop at this stage, but he'd certainly forgotten all about it. He was in fact a

63 Not to be confused with today's Liberal Party, which is not a movement in any but the most strictly digestive sense.

very forgetful man: contemporary portraits indicate he frequently couldn't even remember to shave.

Checking on the *Empire*, he found it failing miserably, and reassured, he went back into Parliament in 1858, before resigning again due to insolvency caused by the collapse of the *Empire*. During these years, his popularity and esteem amongst prominent men of the colony only grew: the people had enormous respect for anyone willing to dedicate so much of his life to standing for, and shortly afterwards quitting, elected office. Sir Charles Gavan Duffy, the Victorian Premier, predicted that even 'ten generations hence', the name of Henry Parkes would 'best personify the national spirit of New South Wales'. Of course, as it turned out Duffy was wrong – it was Richie Benaud who did that – but he was prescient in his belief that Parkes would prove to be of historical significance.

Parkes returned to Parliament in 1859 in scenes reminiscent of those in *Cheers* when Norm would enter the bar. In 1861 he left again, to go to England as a 'commissioner of emigration': essentially his job was to tell English people they'd be happier in Australia. This was a difficult job as most English people knew full well that this was a lie. While he was away, his wife and six children were living in poverty, but at least in England he couldn't get Clarinda pregnant, which must have come as a blessed respite for her.

In January 1864 Parkes returned to Parliament for want of anything better to do that day, gaining the seat of Kiama, home of the famous 'Blowhole', and home of two of them after Parkes arrived. In 1866, he became Colonial Secretary in the ministry of Sir James Martin, a man who had himself fathered fifteen children despite looking like a stuffed capsicum in a wig. As Colonial Secretary, Parkes introduced the Public Schools Act 1866, which required that anyone working as a teacher be properly trained in teaching: daring stuff in a society built on poorly educated children.

Parkes's combination of progressive education policy and personal poverty had won him many admirers, but the political tides began to turn when in 1868 in Sydney, the visiting Duke of Edinburgh was shot by Henry James O'Farrell, an alcoholic recently released from a lunatic asylum whose erratic behaviour could have only one explanation: the Fenian Brotherhood. O'Farrell, who was not a Fenian, nevertheless claimed to be one, which unleashed a wave of anti-Fenian sentiment across the colony. He also claimed to be, and actually was, Irish, which unleashed a wave of anti-Irish sentiment across the colony. The anti-mental illness sentiment was already in place, of course, although the anti-alcoholism sentiment still hasn't arrived.

Parkes latched onto the rising tide of xenophobia, claiming the existence of a vast Fenian conspiracy in New South Wales, which was pretty unlikely, as there really weren't enough people in New South Wales for a vast conspiracy of any kind. The public, not knowing what a Fenian was but thinking it sounded fairly scary[64], embraced Parkes's theory enthusiastically, right up to the point when absolutely nothing happened and everyone realised Parkes was full of shit. Back in those days, proof that you were full of shit could occasionally be a political liability, and Parkes's position was weakened.

This didn't worry Parkes too much, because it was time for his next resignation anyway. It came in 1870, and again it was a result of financial difficulties, surely related to his inability to keep it in his pants around the house. Immediately after resigning he was re-elected, following which the Sydney Morning Herald published an anti-Parkes article, and he resigned again. He had really developed a nice rhythm by now.

Elected again in December 1871, Parkes then became leader of the Opposition, and in May 1872, ascended to the lofty position

64 It is, of course, simply a person from Fen.

of Premier, from where he now possessed unprecedented power to pursue whatever paranoid xenophobic fantasies he chose. In 1875, Parkes's ministry was defeated, and in 1877 he became bored with being leader of the opposition and decided to resign just to keep his hand in. A month or so later he became Premier again, and five months after that he became not-Premier again. Life moved pretty fast in colonial New South Wales, although not literally.

In 1878, Parkes and his rival Sir John Robertson, who had been engaged in a running battle for both the premiership and the title of the colony's most luxuriant beard, managed to find some common ground, and formed a government together. Parkes was Premier for the third time, and managed unexpectedly to do some things, including a trip to England during which he befriended Alfred, Lord Tennyson, with whom he had many long and heartfelt conversations about how great it was to have a beard and what a waste of time poetry was. Returning to Australia, he realised that he'd been Premier for more than four years and lost an election out of sheer embarrassment. Re-elected to another seat, he immediately went to England again for 14 months, before coming back and resigning again, for old times' sake.

At the age of 70, and with a still-growing battalion of children, many of whom were now old enough to embark on spasmodic political careers and disappointing business lives of their own, Parkes announced his retirement from politics. In 1885 he celebrated this decision by returning to parliament.

In 1887, Parkes became Premier for the fourth time, and his career had officially gone beyond a joke. This premiership finally allowed Parkes the opportunity to fulfil his lifelong dream of discriminating against the Chinese. Warning against the dangers of Asian immigration, Parkes expressed the fear that Chinese people were so awesome that if allowed into the country, they'd destroy the pathetic whites with their sheer brilliance, and struck a chord with a nervous populace who had also noticed how undeniably great the Chinese were, and how much they themselves sucked. Parkes managed to pass a law raising the tax on entering the colony to £100 a head, and satisfied with a good job well done, he stopped being Premier for two months, and then started again, for the fifth time.

Parkes's fifth premiership came shortly after he had married Eleanor Dixon, a year after the death of Clarinda, who had frankly performed superhumanly to last that long after the constant waves of babies that Henry kept putting in her. This second marriage caused a scandal in colonial society and upset Parkes's family, not surprising given that Henry and Eleanor had already had three children together before Clarinda had passed away. Henry was in his seventies at this time and honestly just the thought of it is horribly exhausting, a man that age carrying on like an untethered fire hose.

It was during his fifth and final premiership that Parkes would commit to the project that would come to define his life's work, rendering almost eighty years of work and accomplishment irrelevant and pointless in the eyes of history. Makes you think, doesn't it? Why do we bother? Why did Henry Parkes bother? Eleanor must have had a headache.

In October 1889, a report on Australia's defence suggested that the colonies merge their defence forces and implement a uniform rail gauge. This report sparked a memory in Parkes of that time, seven or eight children ago, when he had been pushing for the federation of the states himself. 'That sounds like a larf,' he said to himself, and combed his beard in preparation for the battle to come.

The first step came that very month, with the Tenterfield Oration, a speech delivered by Parkes at the Tenterfield School of Arts. In this, he called for 'a great national government for all

Australia', which was perhaps aiming too high: even today, 'great' is a bit much to ask. But the main thrust of Parkes's message hit home: the need for a convention to create a constitution for a new, united nation. The Tenterfield Oration, with its famously poignant passage, 'Ride again buckaroo/Think I see kangaroo up ahead', is seen as the de facto start of the federation movement, a movement that continues to affect us all today in ways that we can't even begin to understand.

From here things moved quickly, especially considering Henry's gammy leg[65]. February 1890 saw the Federation Conference, a meeting in which, amid much clamour and excitement, nothing happened, which led naturally to the 1891 National Australasian Convention.

At this convention were 45 delegates from the seven colonies of Australia and New Zealand, which would soon enough become just the six colonies of Australia after everyone realised that New Zealand hadn't been invited and nobody liked them. These 45, including such superstars of Australian history as former cricket umpire Edmund Barton and religious maniac Alfred Deakin, thrashed out important matters and debated weighty affairs and mulled over deep thoughts like nobody's business, and after much discussion the decision was reached to continue doing nothing just for the moment. This didn't mean progress hadn't been made: the first draft of a bill to create a Commonwealth of Australia was written, and the decision was made to call it the 'Commonwealth of Australia', after the bank.

As Premier, Parkes put the Federation Bill to the New South Wales Parliament in 1891, only to see it defeated. Fed up with the parliament's recalcitrance, and with the fact he hadn't resigned from

---

65 He actually did break his leg in 1890. His kids had sucked all the calcium out of his body.

anything for a while, he resigned. He stayed in parliament as an independent member for a while, but eventually he was defeated and finally, definitively, retired from entering and leaving and re-entering politics.

Despite his long career, the elderly Parkes was penniless. Forced to sell many of his most treasured possessions to provide for his family, the size of which would always remain his greatest mistake, he had nothing to show for his decades of service apart from the respect and admiration of the whole country, which was utterly worthless. While fighting his final election campaign, his second wife Eleanor died, and irritated at the disruption to his routine, he married his housekeeper three months later. Julia Lynch was 23, and Henry was 80, so just think about *that*. Does Mick Jagger really seem so bad now?

Sadly, despite what I have no doubt were his best and most energetic efforts, Henry Parkes failed to impregnate his third wife, and he died just six months later, in financial poverty yet rich in both historical legacy and widespread genetic material. On his instruction, a state funeral was declined, but his burial at his old home in the Blue Mountains was well-attended as befits such a giant of Australian public life. Unfortunately, dying in 1896 meant he never got to see his dream of Federation come to fruition, or his dream of anti-Asian discrimination grow and prosper.

But although he died with the colonies still divided, he had set the wheels in motion: more constitutional conventions followed that of 1891, including the Corowa Conference, the Bathurst Convention, the Adelaide Convention, and the Fairport Convention[66]. At each of these conventions, a little more incremental progress was made towards making Henry Parkes's vision a reality. Bills were drafted, statements were made, proposals

66 Bit of fun for you classic folk-rock fans out there.

were accepted, backs were scratched and strings were pulled, and the future soon hove into view over the horizon. The governments of the colonies, initially somewhat wary to commit to a process whereby they would be unable to fight wars against each other, eventually warmed to the idea of pooling their resources and fighting wars against other people together, and all was in readiness.

The final Constitution was mainly the work of Andrew Inglis Clark, the 'Australian Jefferson' (except that Clark was *opposed* to slavery) who emerged from obscurity in Tasmania to become an integral part of the foundation of Australia, and then went back into obscurity. But though Clark may have done the bulk of the writing, it was the spirit of Parkes that flowed through him as he worked: that great bearded ghost who jovially haunted all the endeavours of the federationists. When, on 1 January 1901, a hungover Australia celebrated its official transformation into one united nation, Henry Parkes must have been spinning in his grave: spinning with joy, as happy corpses do.

Few figures cast as great a shadow over Australian history as Henry Parkes. The *Times* called him 'the most commanding figure in Australian politics', and while admittedly this was before anyone knew about Barnaby Joyce, it was still a decent compliment. Alfred Deakin said, 'his personality was massive' and described him as 'a large-brained self-educated Titan', which makes him sound a bit like a terrifying telepathic alien, but then Deakin was always a bit weird. Besides the fact of federation itself, Parkes's legacy lives on in the name of Parkes the town, Parkes the observatory, Parkes the suburb of Canberra, Parkes the no-longer-existing electorate, Parkes the different and currently-existing electorate, HMAS Parkes the ship that fought in World War Two and was then sold to Hong Kong scrap merchants[67], and of course the Sir Henry Parkes Memorial

67 Make your own metaphor for this.

School of Arts in Tenterfield, where Parkes made his most famous speech and wrote 'I Still Call Australia Home'.

Sir Henry Parkes was truly the father of a nation, and not just in the sense that he was literally the father of several thousand children: he also gave birth to Australia as we know it today. Few nations go through a birth as painless and trauma-free as ours, and for that we owe much to the soothing epidural of Parkes's democratic passion and oratorical mastery. If ever a man deserved a gigantic solid gold statue of himself in all capital cities, and for all children to put on false beards and re-enact his greatest moments on his birthday every year, and maybe also a quiet prayer said to him before breakfast each day, it's Henry Parkes. Praise be to the Over-Father.

FUN FOR YOU AT HOME: Found your own nation. Declare independence, draw up a constitution, and recruit a standing army. Is it harder than it sounds? Easier? Have you been invaded yet? Is your economy growing? Keep a diary of your growing madness.

CY O'CONNOR
The Piper at the Gates of Dawn

SINCE THE DAWN OF TIME, mankind has gazed upon the world around it, and yearned for one thing above all else: a drink. Over the years, one of the most popular drinks of all has been water. This humble fluid, created when a previously fairly conservative couple of hydrogen atoms decided to spice things up in their relationship by inviting an oxygen atom in to get freaky, has shown genuine staying power when it comes to maintaining its place in humans' affections. Water doesn't have the glamorous image of some other beverages – it lacks the working-class appeal of beer, or the comforting maternal vibe of milk – but it has always had one major advantage in the public relations battle, which is that it is necessary for life to exist: something that can definitely not be said for Red Bull.

In fact, scientists tell us that up to 70 per cent of the human body is made up of water, a figure which can rise as high as 90 per cent depending on how misinformed the person you're talking to is. So water has always been fairly important when it comes to the survival of the human species, because if 70 per cent of the human body is water, that means that if that percentage drops below 70, your body ceases to be human and becomes god knows what. A horse? A Komodo dragon? It's in an attempt to avoid such a fate that men and women have always been drawn to water.

The trouble is, of course, that men and women have also always had the annoying habit of wandering off into places that have *no* water. Why they do this, nobody has ever quite figured out: it's some perverse need to rebel embedded in our DNA, as if evolution itself wants to kill us. Whatever the cause, the fact is that the history of humanity is the history of a bunch of damn idiots running off into the desert despite the fact that the desert is obviously a terrible place where nothing should live.

People being people, the discovery that there was no water in the desert did not lead to everyone leaving the desert, but to continuous and exhausting attempts to bring water to it. It's as illogical as spending money on running shoes instead of just not running, but what can you do? We're the worst.

The futility of the exercise notwithstanding, many great minds have been bent to the problem of hydrating the desert, and one of the greatest was that contained within the shapely skull of Charles Yelverton O'Connor, the man who changed the course of history by creating a thriving modern society out of a desolate sandy hellhole. He may not have been born in this country, but it was down under that O'Connor discovered the scope of possibilities that life could offer – if this is a land of opportunity, CY O'Connor helped make it so.

One would not have expected a boy born in Ireland to make a name for himself in desert renovation – that country containing precisely zero deserts and traditionally producing more alcoholic poets than irrigation pioneers. But growing up in County Meath, O'Connor developed an interest in water at an early age, spending much of his spare time building pipelines between his model railway and the bath, and amazing his classmates by fully irrigating his third-grade teacher using only a plastic funnel and the small intestine of a fruit bat.

But young O'Connor found his genius unable to fully bloom in Ireland, where every potato was a testament to the fertile soil and plentiful rainfall. There was so much water already in Ireland that O'Connor, a man with an ineffable talent for bringing water to unwatered places, felt useless and unappreciated[68], like a man selling coal to Newcastle, or poorly-designed transport systems to Sydney. He needed to find a homeland that truly needed him. With this goal in mind, at the age of 21 he moved to New Zealand, which was his first major mistake.

At the age of 23, O'Connor became assistant engineer for Canterbury province, which I know doesn't sound like much, but what were *you* doing when you were 23?[69] In this position, he constructed the Otira Gorge section of the road over Arthur's Pass, improving access to the West Coast goldfields[70]. He did such a good job that pundits predicted that soon he might be allowed to build an entire road, should New Zealand ever need one.

O'Connor parlayed his job as Canterbury's assistant engineer into one as inspecting engineer for the mid-South Island, and then Under-Secretary of Public Works. But inspecting and under-secretarying was not what CY wanted out of life: he had always felt he was destined for bigger things. Wandering the wilderness, gazing gloomily into the fragrant hot mud pools, he wondered: would his dream of moistening deserts ever come to fruition?

Restless and irritable, O'Connor tried to pass the time by fathering eight children, but even the brutal misery of fatherhood

---

68 This, of course, is how most of us feel all the time, but for someone like O'Connor it was hard to take.

69 I was at TAFE, doing Professional Writing. Paid off, right?

70 So next time you're at a trivia night and the old question, 'Who constructed the Otira Gorge section of the road over Arthur's Pass?' comes up, for once you'll be prepared.

failed to scratch his itch. It wasn't that his career was going badly: on the contrary, he was becoming well-known for his views on the construction and operation of colonial railways. But although he was setting the public aflame with his railway opinions, he knew he was a big fish in a small pond, and this was unacceptable: he was born for big ponds; vast ponds filled with luxurious lily pads and fragrant algae, where a pipeline-builder could spawn freely.

When, in 1890, at the age of 47, he was appointed New Zealand's Marine Engineer, Charles saw himself at a crossroads. Here he was, he bethought himself, twenty-six years of his life wasted building and inspecting and public worksing at the end of the earth, and what had it got him? Far too many children and a job as a marine engineer, which wasn't even a real thing – trains don't go underwater.

It was time for a change. It was time to finally embrace his fate and head for a place where sand and dust and hot, choking air was waiting to challenge him to a fight to the death: Western Australia. There he would find a challenge worthy of his mettle: Western Australia was dry even by the standards of Australia as a whole; and Australia as a whole was famous for being one of the few continents that actively tried to choke to death every living thing that entered it.

O'Connor arrived in WA at the invitation of Premier John Forrest, a large, bearlike man who contemporary photos indicate was played by British character actor Mark Addy. Forrest cabled O'Connor to ask whether he'd like to be Western Australia's engineer-in-chief. O'Connor cabled back to ask what, exactly, he'd be in charge of. Forrest cabled back, 'Everything'[71]. O'Connor, exasperated at this unhelpful response, hopped on a boat to Perth so he could ask again in person.

---

71 A true fact about the lack of seriousness in state officials in colonial Australia.

When he got to WA, O'Connor learnt that he was to not only serve as engineer-in-chief, but also general manager of government railways. This was a result of the fact that Western Australia was fairly sparsely populated at the time, and everyone who settled there had to take two jobs: Forrest himself sold ice-cream on weekends.

The first order of business CY had to address in his new home was the issue of Fremantle Harbour, which had long frustrated the business community of Western Australia by not existing. But up till then, WA had found no men or women of sufficient ingenuity and courage to build Fremantle Harbour. It was the 'white whale' of West Australian infrastructure, and John Forrest had found in O'Connor his Captain Ahab: the man brave, determined, and insane enough to essay this monumental task.

Upon O'Connor's announcement that he would build Fremantle Harbour, strong men went pale. There were shouts of 'He's mad' and 'He'll kill us all' and women were seen to faint from the shock. But O'Connor cared for neither public opinion nor British marine engineer John Coode's view that building a port in the mouth of the Swan River would be impractical due to the silting caused by lateral sand drift which would necessitate constant dredging. O'Connor scoffed at Coode's wasteful defeatism. 'British marine engineer John Coode,' he declared decisively, 'can bite me.' And with that same earthy pragmatism, he got to work.

Upon investigation, O'Connor discovered that the river's mouth contained a limestone bar. 'What idiot left this here?' he asked peevishly, and got rid of it. 'Also,' he continued, 'what's with all these sand shoals everywhere?' O'Connor hated nothing more than an untidy river. He would've built Fremantle Harbour purely out of obsessive neatness even if there'd been no infrastructural need.

The harbour was begun in 1892, and opened for business in 1897, which seems like a long time, but it's worth remembering one crucial fact: harbours are really big. In all likelihood, if you tried to make one at home, it'd take you just as long if not longer, and O'Connor didn't even have the internet. On 12 September 1897, the mail carrier RMS *Himalaya* berthed at Fremantle Harbour, and the locals threw their hats in the air in celebration[72].

More than 100 years later, Fremantle Harbour is still in use for heavy shipping, and British marine engineer John Coode is still a loser. If you see him, tell him that from me.

It was also in 1897 that CY O'Connor travelled to London, to be made a Companion of the Most Distinguished Order of St Michael and St George, an Order founded to commemorate the British amical protectorate over the Ionian Islands[73], but which had in subsequent years suffered a certain amount of mission creep, so that pretty much anyone could get one, even people who'd never even *been* to the Ionian Islands. In becoming a CMG, O'Connor proudly took his place alongside such luminaries as Herbert Fitzherbert[74], Tony Abbott[75], and of course James Bond[76].

But Charles Yelverton didn't have time to sit around basking in the glory of his minor decoration. He was still in the middle of a project even more epic than Fremantle Harbour; a project that would come to define him for generations to come; a project that finally made all those childhood hours spent gluing toilet roll holders together and flooding the kitty litter seem worthwhile: the Goldfields Water Supply Scheme.

---

72 At least I assume they did. That's what people back then did, right?

73 [shrug]

74 Royal Navy Admiral.

75 The well-known Governor of Montserrat.

76 Seriously.

The goldfields of Western Australia were booming at the time: thousands had flocked into the dry, dusty interior in search of riches, riches being very much in fashion at the time. Unfortunately, unlike most desperate fortune hunters, they lacked foresight, and upon discovering that the West Australian desert was one of those deserts without water in it, began to feel a terrible thirst coming on. What's more, in order to get supplies to the goldfields, and get gold out of them, you needed a railway, and steam trains can't run without water, for obscure scientific reasons.

Desert rain was scarce – indeed this is one of the first things you notice about deserts – water trains proved inadequate, and brief experimentation with drinking molten gold led nowhere good. Water availability was reaching crisis point in the regions of Coolgardie and Kalgoorlie, which may actually be the same place pronounced by two different people. There was only one solution: a pipeline. Fortunately, Premier Forrest had already put in the call for a man who had pipelines running in his blood. And more blood running within those pipelines. His veins were a real Inception-style scenario with a strong pipeline theme.

O'Connor finally felt the most electrifying sensation a man can experience: the feeling that he has at long last crossed paths with his destiny. His whole life had been spent looking at water and thinking, *my god, how wonderful it would be if that was over there instead of here*, only to look over there and find that there was already water there. Ever since he could remember, he had dreamt of pipes, big pipes and small pipes, straight pipes and curved pipes, pipes criss-crossing the world and connecting all manner of things and people – and those dreams had been stymied by the fact nobody needed the pipes that he felt born to provide. He had come to the point where he feared he might die without ever having scratched his pipe itch. Yet here he was, trembling with anticipation, about to finally fit the missing piece to the CY O'Connor puzzle. He could, at last, bring a gigantic quantity of fluid to a location where there wasn't any. Western Australia and O'Connor were about to complete each other.

Forrest had the utmost faith in his pal. 'Build me a pipeline, Charlie,' he said in his gruff, surveyor's way. 'Make the deserts bloom.' O'Connor took up the task with gusto, even though many in WA doubted the wisdom of their premier's insane plan. Politicians and journalists alike found the idea of Western Australia having the longest freshwater pipeline in the world absurdly unrealistic. The consensus was that the project was doomed to failure and that O'Connor might as well try building a flying-fox to Jupiter for all the good it would do anyone.

Furthermore, the thing was going to cost a hell of a lot, and there was a fear that the government would not be able to pay for it if the gold discoveries dried up. On the other hand, if the gold miners dried up, the economy would take quite a hit. There were arguments on both sides, although the arguments that recommended letting miners die of thirst did seem to be the meaner ones. When completed, the pipeline would transport water from the dam at Mundaring Weir on the Helena River more than 500 kilometres to a reservoir at Coolgardie. Five million gallons would be delivered every day, and the whole thing would cost £2.5 million[77].

O'Connor set to his work with all the zeal and passion of a true pipeline enthusiast[78]. Opposition, however, persisted: while Forrest and O'Connor saw their work as part of a grand plan to supercharge Western Australia's development by providing it the infrastructure it needed to become an economic powerhouse of the 20th century, others saw Forrest and O'Connor as a pair of jumped-up little wankers with ideas well above their station.

---

77 In today's money, $17.34.

78 Of which he's the only one there's been as far as anyone knows.

So it was that O'Connor found himself confronted by powerful enemies. This became a particular problem when his friend Forrest left state politics to join the Federal parliament in 1901: the engineer's greatest supporter was out of the picture, locally speaking, and the WA parliament embarked on a vicious campaign of smear and abuse against the hapless Irishman. The press was merciless: Perth's *Sunday Times* accused O'Connor of corruption and taking kickbacks from the companies contracted to build the pipeline. A brutal *Times* editorial of 9 February 1902[79] savaged O'Connor, accusing him of 'gross blundering or something worse', claiming he had 'robbed the taxpayer…of many millions', and referring to him as a 'crocodile imposter'. Meanwhile MPs were claiming the dam at Mundaring was unsound and set to crack, bringing a catastrophic flood down upon Perth[80].

O'Connor had support from myriad experts in his field, all of whom backed the soundness and excellence of his plan, but the voice of expertise was being drowned out by the agendas of self-interested politicians and vindictive sensationalist journalists. Thankfully such a thing could never happen nowadays.

As 1902 rolled around, Charles Yelverton O'Connor was overworked, under constant attack from political and press enemies, and suffering from depression, insomnia and neuralgia. He retained confidence in the pipeline scheme, but was in desperate need of a break from the work and the harassment. On 8 March, he had a victory: a test of the pumping mechanism over the pipeline's most difficult section was successful, proving his confidence well-founded. That night a small leak in the pipe was detected and plans were made for O'Connor to inspect the site on the 10th March.

79 My birthday – pretty eerie.

80 Well, relatively catastrophic: it would only have been Perth.

On the Monday morning, CY O'Connor prepared for his usual early morning ride, but first penned a short note. It read:

> *The Coolgardie Scheme is alright and I could finish it if I got a chance and protection from misrepresentation but there is no hope of that now and it is better that it should be given to some entirely new man to do who will be untrammelled by prior responsibility*

Having written the note, O'Connor rode his horse along Fremantle beach, past the harbour that he had built, and south to Robb Jetty, where he rode into the water, placed his revolver in his mouth, and pulled the trigger. Charles Yelverton O'Connor was 59 years old.

O'Connor gone, his work went on. By the end of 1902 the Goldfields Water Supply Scheme was complete. On 24 January 1903, the now-Federal MP Sir John Forrest turned the water on, naming O'Connor as 'the great builder of this work … to bring happiness and comfort to the people of the goldfields for all time'. CY O'Connor had, at long last, achieved his greatest dream, the mighty desert-dampening pipe that would turn dry to wet, barren to fertile, miner who died of thirst to miner who died later of something else.

CY O'Connor changed the face of Western Australia and revolutionised ideas of what was possible in a vast dry land like this one. The harbour he made possible when others thought it impossible still operates today. The ludicrously ambitious project that he brought to life against all odds reshaped a state. Kalgoorlie owes its very existence to O'Connor's vision, making him also a vital figure in the history of both the brothel and topless waitress industries in Western Australia.

A visionary, a pioneer, and a tireless worker for the betterment of humanity, CY O'Connor is perhaps more than anything else an icon for all those whose genius is held back by the small-minded and unimaginative. The downfall of the brilliant individual at the hands of the stupid masses is an all-too-common tale (for example, some people refuse to buy this book). O'Connor was a colossus beset on all sides by complete idiots, and sadly it is often the intellectual titan's fate to find him or herself outnumbered by the mental midget. O'Connor is an inspiration to those of us who suffer this fate. He is a salutary example that tells us: while it's perfectly natural, when nasty-minded cretins try to tear down your life's work, to feel like grabbing your gun and riding a horse into the ocean, just remember that a hundred years from now, they'll be reading books about you, while those carping halfwits will remain as anonymous as *Sunday Times* editor Thomas Walker, who nobody has ever heard of.[81]

CY O'Connor lives on in the annals of history: the perfect embodiment of the old axiom, 'Live fast, die middle-aged, and leave a gigantic water infrastructure project'.

FUN FOR YOU AT HOME: Discover what it was like to be CY O'Connor by building a pipeline to carry water from your bathroom to the backyard. For greater realism, force a younger sibling to sit in the yard digging holes and don't let them drink anything until you're finished.

81 He served in two state parliaments for a total of 32 years as well, and still nobody has the slightest idea who he was. Suck it, Walker.

CHARLES TAIT
Hitchcock of Collins Street

MENTION THE NAME 'Charles Tait' to most people, and they'll give you a blank look, and not just because beginning a conversation by abruptly announcing a random name with no context is an unusual way to behave. Charles Tait is not a household name in any but the most obsessively studious households. He is not a historical celebrity of the ilk of Kelly or Bligh or Somers. He tops no charts, is memorialised by no colossal monuments, promotes no cutting-edge hair replacement techniques, stars in no Carols by Candlelight extravaganzas. Today, in our disposable McChicken world, Charles Tait is not 'famous'. Yet he boasts an achievement that you or I or Grant Denyer never will, an achievement that frankly should make every one of us feel like tiny inferior scraps of refuse.

For Charles Tait was the writer and director of the world's first feature film. If you can name a single other person about whom you can say that, I'll be very surprised.

Charles Tait was born on 15 November 1868, in the goldfields town of Castlemaine, best known as the birthplace of Frank McEncroe, inventor of the Chiko Roll: yet in some ways Tait would go on to create something even more impressive than that. John Turnbull Tait, a Scottish tailor who had come to Australia in search of more challenging inside legs to measure, had nine children, including five sons, of whom Charles was the eldest. His brothers John, James Nevin, Edward and Frank would be his collaborators in various professional endeavours over the years, earning themselves the collective sobriquet 'the Tait brothers'.

From an early age, Charles Tait felt that he was destined for greatness. Where other urchins of his acquaintance would waste their days roaming the streets of Castlemaine, starting fights, kicking cans and tying cricket bats to the tails of stray dogs, Charles would be hard at work in his bedroom at home, building miniature theatrical sets and devising ways to convincingly simulate gunshot wounds. Why he did these things, he could not say, but he felt certain that someday the technological development would arrive that would make his bizarre bedroom experiments make sense. That day, he knew, would be the day that Charles Tait came into his own – that, too, being something he used to do a lot in his bedroom.

At the age of 11, Charles left school, which was the sort of thing you could do in the childhood utopia of 19th-century Victoria, and began working as an usher at Saturday night concerts in Melbourne. At 15 he got a job as a messenger at Allan & Co's musical warehouse, which was either a warehouse full of musical instruments, or a regular warehouse where the staff just liked to sing and dance a lot[82]. A bright lad whose megalomania was matched only by his greed, little Charles quickly rose through the ranks of the Allan organisation, going overseas with George Allan in 1893 and becoming manager of Allan's store in 1896. He was still officially with Allan's when in 1902, at the age of 33 and eager to make his mark before entering old age[83], he took

82 It should be obvious which one we're hoping for.

83 Life expectancies were low back then; so 33 was positively elderly, assuming you're someone who doesn't understand statistics and likes to make ignorant comments about historical life expectancies.

control of J&N Tait, concert promoters: the business that had been formed by his brothers John, Nevin and Frank, who knew that despite their ambition and drive, they were in no condition to run a business – they'd already forgotten to put Frank's initials in the name. Charles therefore oversaw the operations of J&N Tait as a kind of power behind the throne, à la Dick Cheney or Yoko Ono.

Nevin Tait ventured overseas to find acts for J&N Tait to promote, thus introducing Australian audiences to such renowned performers as the Welsh Male Choir, Haydn Wood, Dame Clara Butt[84], the Cherniavsky Trio, and, most hilariously of all, the Royal Besses o' th' Barn Band. The Melbourne public, incandescent with excitement at the prospect of some quality foreign entertainment that nobody had ever heard of, flocked to performances at the Athenaeum Hall on Collins Street.

Besides the music or the plays or whatever the Royal Besses o' th' Barn were getting up to, these concerts at the Athenaeum also included short film screenings, taking advantage of the new technology that was taking the world by storm. Moving pictures had only recently come into existence, building on previous inventions such as the zoetrope and the phenakistoscope[85] and the praxinoscope and various other comically-named contraptions. And so the world of entertainment, that had for millennia consisted of nothing more exhilarating than pig-baiting, suddenly exploded into a kaleidoscope of possibilities, making it ironic that the movies completely destroyed the kaleidoscope market.

The Tait brothers' short films were a popular success, which got the ever-savvy Charles thinking: if people would pay money to watch a short film, would they not pay even more money to watch

84 One of Enid Blyton's most memorable characters.

85 The first device in the world to allow people a full view of their own phenakisto.

a *long* one? This is a line of thinking that has subsequently caused the destruction of western civilisation, but at the time it seemed wonderfully fresh and exciting.

But was such a thing possible? Up to that point, cinematic art had been mainly concerned with a few well-established themes: horses running; girls having pillow fights; and trains rushing headlong at the audience and making them scream in terror because they were incredibly stupid. None of these would sustain a feature-length presentation: a horse race of more than a few minutes becomes tedious, girls don't have the stamina for hour-long pillow fights, and in order to have a lengthy movie about a train coming at you, you'd have to start with the train too far away to see. In order to keep film fans on the edge, or even nestled comfortably towards the rear of their seats, it would not be enough to simply elongate the filmic art: an entirely new storytelling paradigm would need to be generated.

Charles Tait was limited in the range of subjects available to him. Transformers, for example, had yet to be invented, ditto James Bond. And the concept of jaded professionals returning to their home town to gain a new lease on life among authentic rural folk was practically unknown. Instead, the world's first feature director looked to his own nation and its rich history for material, and found the perfect subject.

In 1906, Ned Kelly was still fresh in the memory of many Australians, given not much had been happening in the past 25 years. Charles himself had been four days short of his twelfth birthday when Ned met his end in a noose at Melbourne Gaol, and no doubt remembered the contemporary newspapers' lurid tales of Ned's daring adventures and amusing headwear. Here was a hero – handsome, rebellious, psychotically violent – tailor-made for the new medium of film. Little did Tait know how much his silver-screen exaltation of Kelly would influence future generations of filmmakers, with that simple template of 'man with metal head shoots people' recurring throughout the twentieth and twenty-first centuries: Terminator, Robocop, Iron Man, Dirty Harry, Mr Miyagi, etc.

Bushranging entertainments were extremely popular at the time, a combination of the public's hatred of authority and love of murder, and plays about bushrangers were doing brisk business around Australia: such as *The Importance of Being Ben Hall; Who's Afraid of Mad Dog Morgan?; Romeo and Captain Thunderbolt;* and *A Streetcar Named Frank Gardiner*[86]. Charles and his brothers were, therefore, tapping into an already-existing thirst, which they planned to slake by pouring gallons of celluloid down the public's throat. Charles had little to no experience with filmmaking, but correctly guessing that screenwriting and directing were extremely easy jobs that literally anyone could do, he gave it a red-hot go.

And so *The Story of the Kelly Gang*, Charles Tait's directorial debut and the world's first feature film, began shooting, with a budget of between £400 and £1000[87]. Much of the film was shot in Heidelberg, north of Melbourne, on the property of Charles's wife's family.

Fifteen-minute credit sequences having yet to be invented, the full cast of the movie is not known with any great certainty: the makers used friends and associates rather than professional actors, to keep costs down. Fortunately this decision did not detract from the film's quality much, as the role of actors in silent movies was basically to open their mouths as wide as possible and occasionally fall over. The cast members who have been identified by the

86 This should definitely be a Twitter hashtag game.

87 In today's money, between $13 and $7,000,000,000.

Australian National Film and Sound Archive[88] include:

- John Forde as Dan Kelly, Ned's sensitive-yet-uninteresting younger brother
- Elizabeth Tait as the stunt double for whoever played Kate Kelly (Charles Tait didn't want his wife to be an actress, but was comfortable with her risking her life in order to guarantee the safety of an actress)
- Frank Mills, father of Rob 'Millsy' Mills, as Ned himself.

The production was assisted by the Victoria Railways Department, which provided a train – the most crucial prop for a successful movie in these days when cinemagoers expected to irrationally fear for their lives on every outing. Genuine Kelly armour was borrowed from the aristocratic Clarke family, collectors of rare and severely dented metal.

The Story of the Kelly Gang is a tragic tale, of innocence lost and the ending of an era. In many ways it is the *Wild Bunch* of its time, although in other ways it's more like *The Goonies*[89]. The film begins with the malevolent Troopers, who discuss an arrest warrant for Ned's brother Dan, while one of their number is rebuffed by Ned's sister Kate, who like all Kellys has been raised to find the police sexually unappealing. The Troopers grow resentful of Kate's unwillingness to enjoy the pleasures of law-enforcing flesh, and vow to harass the family as hard as they can until Kate comes to her senses. Outraged at the treatment of his beloved Kate, Ned cries to the heavens for vengeance and shoots three cops at Stringybark Creek as punishment for their insolent refusal to stand still while being shot. Troopers Kennedy, Scanlon and Lonigan

88 Motto: 'Three *Crocodile Dundees* and Counting'.

89 Except that *The Story of the Kelly Gang* features dialogue you can understand.

are gunned down, and the dye is cast: Ned Kelly has murdered three policemen and now has no choice but to become a national hero. Next the Kelly Gang holds up Younghusband's station, holding Younghusband at gunpoint and making numerous rude jokes about his name. They also hold up a bank, marking a slightly mercenary turn in their activities. The gang proceeds to play cat and mouse with the police: the Kellys being the mouse and the cops a particularly dull-witted and slow-moving cat. The gang then kills Aaron Sherritt, a former friend of theirs who chose to betray them to the authorities, in line with narrative convention that a friend of the gang must always betray them to the authorities. The gang then tries to derail a train because, you know, what else are they going to do for fun around here, and finally engage in the climactic final shootout at the Glenrowan Inn, where the Troopers shoot Ned and 'thus falls the last of the Kelly gang', laid low by his inexplicable failure to make armour for his legs. At the end of the film Ned begs the Troopers to spare his life in a most undignified way. Poignant, to say the least.

The Story of the Kelly Gang may look primitive to modern audiences, raised on *Tron* and Dwayne 'The Rock' Johnson, but Charles Tait showed considerable filmmaking flair in his directorial debut – several scenes, including the legendary 'police shooting parrots' scene and the final battle when Ned looms out of the woods in all his tin-hatted glory, only to realise just how flimsy his trousers really are, were lauded by critics of the day as 'replete with dramatic tension' and 'looking like those are actual real people up on that screen thingy'. No doubt all the people who thought that train was going to hit them were thrilled to bits as they frantically ducked the bullets they assumed were flying around the theatre.

The Taits made their money back just on the trial screenings in country towns, and the film was a hit even before its Melbourne premiere on Boxing Day, 1906 – the premiere's date kicking off another grand cinema tradition. At the Melbourne screenings the film was accompanied by live sound effects – firing blanks for gunshots and clacking coconut shells together for hoof beats[90] – which greatly increased the verisimilitude of the viewing experience; and sometimes by a lecturer explaining the plot – which didn't.

Like most great films – e.g. *The Last Temptation of Christ*, *Uncle Buck* – *The Story of the Kelly Gang* sparked controversy. Some saw the movie as glorifying criminals, which was a harsh and accurate judgment. In 1907 the film was banned in those areas where the Kelly gang had plied their trade – presumably in case it encouraged the Kellys' ghosts to cash in on the movie's success. In 1912 Victoria banned bushranger films altogether, the wise government realising that the best way to dampen enthusiasm for popular products is always censorship. Nevertheless *The Story of the Kelly Gang* ended up making more than £25,000[91] for its producers: a spectacular rate of return given the original budget of around £1000. Charles Tait had not only become the world's first feature-film director, but the world's most successful feature-film director at the same time: a turn-of-the-century Michael Bay; you could mock him for his over-reliance on lurid violence and expensive special effects (many of the beards in the film were not real), but you couldn't deny his ability to please the public.

Charles Tait, with the help of his brothers and co-producers, had proven once and for all that people would sit in front of a movie for more than an hour at a time, and even if they needed to go to the toilet in the middle, they would come back in and keep watching. It was a major breakthrough in the field of keeping large numbers of people still in the same place for extended periods of time.

---

90 Yep, Monty Python ripped off Charles Tait.

91 In today's money, $26,000.

For many years *The Story of the Kelly Gang* was thought completely lost, until the 1976 discovery of several seconds of the movie. In subsequent years, further footage was discovered in collections, rubbish dumps and Blockbuster going-out-of-business sales, till at the time of writing, 17 minutes of the film have been restored by the National Film and Sound Archive. The extant footage provides proof of the artistry of Charles Tait and just how hard up for entertainment people were back then.

Charles Tait's career continued after the triumph of *The Kelly Gang*: he continued to make movies, starting with a series of his sequels: *Kelly Gang 2: Return of The Tin, K3LLY, The Kellys Take Manhattan, Kellys In Space,* and of course *Neddy Versus Jason;* before moving on to more original productions such as *The Train That Stopped, Dracula In Ballarat,* and *Carry On Canberra.* In 1911 the Tait brothers formed Amalgamated Pictures alongside *Kelly* backers William Gibson and Millard Johnson. A year later Amalgamated merged with its rival Australasian Films, leaving the Taits to focus on exhibiting and concert presentations. The main venue for these concerts was the Auditorium on Collins Street, built by the Taits in 1913. The brothers also oversaw a network of theatres across Australia and New Zealand, promoted tours by the world's leading artists, and even moved into the fledgling medium of radio.

The family business continued to operate all the way into the 1970s, providing Australians with theatrical and musical entertainment that for all any of the audiences knew was of a pretty high standard. But all their myriad and notable achievements pale in comparison to the indelible mark the Tait family left on the world of film, and the influence that Charles Tait's vision has caused to echo down the decades.

Charles was the first of the Tait brothers to die, on 27 June 1933, of hydronephrosis, or 'water in the kidneys', which doesn't sound too bad but there you go[92]. He was 64 years old and left behind four children – two daughters and two sons. But far more important than his uninteresting children was the artistic legacy he left: a movie that put Australia on the map, ignited an industry, and reminded everyone of just why we love forest-dwelling sociopaths. Few men can claim to have done more in their brief span of years.

FUN FOR YOU AT HOME: Make your own movie! If you have a large Milo tin at home, you can make it about the Kelly gang: otherwise, make a movie about another iconic Australian – some good suggestions are Dawn Fraser and Agro. You can use your phone to make your movie: think about how much harder it must've been for Charles Tait without a phone. Do you think *The Story of the Kelly Gang* would've turned out differently if it'd been shot on a phone? Think about whether this is an interesting question or not.

92 Aren't kidneys supposed to have water in them?

ALBERT JACKA
The Widowmaker

'GREATER LOVE HATH no man than this, that a man lay down his life for his friends.' So says the Bible, in John 15:13, one of the New Testament's many exhortations to devout Christians to commit suicide for the greater good. And it's been an article of faith over the centuries that the most beautiful act humanity holds within its power is that of sacrificing one's own life in order to save others. There is, however, another way in which one may demonstrate one's love of one's fellow man[93]: by killing large numbers of people.

Australia, as a modern, forward-thinking nation, has known many generous-hearted, public-minded killers, but perhaps none shed so much blood in as noble a cause as Albert Jacka, VC, MC and Bar[94]. This humble country lad, raised on tried-and-true Aussie values like mateship, hard work, and trees, grew up to display a facility for snuffing out life that drew admiration all around the world. Even more laudably, after discovering this rare talent, Jacka used it only for good and never evil, making sure to kill exclusively foreigners.

93 Or woman, in a pinch.

94 Pretty much any bar.

Albert Jacka, like so many legendary soldiers and/or dairy farmers, was born on a dairy farm near Winchelsea in Victoria. Whether he was born on this dairy farm because his parents lived there, or it was just one of those weird country traditions that when a pregnant woman went into labour she headed to the local dairy farm to give birth among the wholesome ambience of udders, we cannot be sure. All we know is that from the very first, Albert had a strong affinity with milk: some reports say he drank milk before every one of his kills, or at least within a three-to-four-week timeframe around them.

When Albert was five, the Jacka family moved to Wedderburn. Little Albert attended the local school, where he killed none of his classmates or any of his teachers, even though he absolutely could have taken them all down with one hand tied behind his back[95]. Albert had only a basic level of schooling: what he had, you can't teach. After learning to read and write and finger-paint or whatever people learn in schools, Albert got a job with his father in a case of sickening nepotism. He worked as a haulage contractor, but not very hard, because he was the boss's son and didn't have to. How he laughed at the poor fools who were unemployed because his father refused to hire on merit.

Albert didn't stay with his father for long, however – there comes a time in every young man's life when haulage no longer fulfils him. He moved instead into forestry, taking a job with the Victorian State Forests Department, where he worked day and night to ensure that Victoria's forests were safe. Or possibly that they were unsafe. The Victorian State Forests Department was a shadowy and mysterious body that either existed to protect forests, or to cut them all down. Which it was is lost to the mists of time, and there's no way to find out without doing research[96].

---

95 You only need one hand for a gun.

96 And I do not swing that way.

Jacka's talents were being wasted in forestry. No matter how many times he shot a tree, the tree refused to display any pain or distress. No matter how many woodland creatures he bayoneted, it did nothing to serve his country. 'Who am I?' he would ask wistfully, staring into a bubbling forest stream. Answer came there none, just the mournful hooting of the tawny frogmouth, who Albert absent-mindedly shot with no satisfaction.

Albert Jacka may have gone his whole life without realising his true calling, were it not for an extraordinary stroke of luck that came his way on 28 June 1914, when a Bosnian Serb revolutionary named Gavrilo Princip shot Archduke Franz Ferdinand of Austria-Hungary. This was what Jacka had been waiting for. I mean, not specifically this. Jacka hadn't been sitting around in Wedderburn saying, 'I wish that bloody Bosnian Serb would get off his arse and do the business.' But the direct consequence of Princip's action was World War One, famously the first and, according to some pundits, the best World War.

Albert saw the opportunity to be all that he knew he could be. On 18 September he enlisted in the Australian Imperial Force, a body that suffered from frankly appalling branding. Assigned to the 14th Battalion, 4th Brigade, 1st Division[97] – but with a bullet[98] – he went to Broadmeadows Camp for training: Broadmeadows, then as now, being the closest thing to a war zone that Australia had. He then headed to Alexandria, the 1st Division arriving in Egypt to defend the Suez Canal from Turkey, which had become a German ally during the straw-drawing process every nation had to go through at the beginning of the war to find out which side they were on.

In Egypt Jacka's 4th Brigade merged with two New Zealand brigades and the 1st Light Horse Brigade to form the New

97 Now known as the Premier League.

98 This joke works on several levels.

Zealand and Australia Division, in which New Zealand's name, to our everlasting shame, came first, even though even the most rudimentary map clearly shows that Australia is bigger. The division was under the command of Major-General Alexander Godley, an experienced British officer who had made his name heroically suppressing the rights of indigenous peoples in Africa[99].

Obviously Jacka was at this stage just a private[100]. Nobody in the division had any idea what a hero they had in their midst, although Albert's fellow soldiers did detect a certain difference in the way he carried himself, a certain *je ne sais quoi*, the kind of ineffable presence that says, 'Look at me funny and I will blow your frigging head off'.

Albert Jacka, finally placed in a situation where the termination of human life was not only permitted, but positively encouraged, was having the time of his life, but he didn't really come into his own until he joined what today we know as the Gallipoli Campaign, but what was at the time called 'Operation Dead-Turk Weekend'. The New Zealand and Australia Division arrived at Anzac Cove – named after the popular biscuits – on 26 April 1915, a day late to avoid traffic. The division occupied a position known as Courtney's Post, named for Lieutenant-Colonel Richard Courtney, who had recently had his mail redirected there.

It was at Courtney's Post that Albert Jacka, former forestry worker and disappointing student, would write the first chapter of his horrifically violent legend … in blood. In the early hours of 19 May 1915, the Turks launched a massive assault on the Anzac line. At 4am they fell on Courtney's Post and captured a twelve-yard section of trench, which doesn't sound like much but this was World War One, when on average about 50,000 men died for every

99 For several centuries this was Britain's number one industry.

100 The rank named for the realistic genitalia displayed on the shoulder.

yard of ground gained by anyone, under the novel new 'Stagnant Slaughter' warfare technique. Unfortunately for the Turks, one end of the section captured at Courtney's Post was defended by Jacka, and having been woken up so early, he was in no mood to not kill anyone.

First, Jacka took three comrades in an attempt to enter the trench in which the Turks were inexcusably squatting, but found his men sadly un-Jacka-like, as all three were wounded. Realising that his fellow soldiers weren't cut out for frontal assault, Jacka formulated an alternative plan, having them fire on the trench and throw bombs to distract the Turks while he circled around behind them.

This plan required Jacka to wander out into No Man's Land, a foolhardy move for less superhuman men. He casually strolled out into the death-ridden hellscape, climbed over the trench's parapet, and came crashing down upon the hapless Turks, who frankly never knew what hit them. On landing in the trench, Jacka shot five Turks dead, ran two more through with his bayonet, and struck a heroic pose as the rest fled the trench in abject terror of this vengeful human hurricane.

For the rest of that night, Jacka held the trench alone, enemies kept at bay by a combination of precise rifle fire, vigorous bayoneting, and the look on his face that told every Turkish soldier just what he had coming to him if he dared try to get into that trench. 'I managed to get the beggars, sir,' he told the first officer to come on the scene. At least that's what he was reported to have said – what he actually said was probably far more obscene and muffled by a mouthful of blood. That was the day that serious doubts began to appear in the minds of the Turkish people as to the long-term viability of the Ottoman Empire: if this crazy-eyed Australian ever gets to Istanbul, they surmised, we're stuffed.

As it happened, Jacka's assault on Istanbul did not come to pass: he had bigger fish to fry. The morning after his patriotic massacre, his platoon commander told him he would be recommended for his bravery, and indeed in due course he became the first Australian in World War One to receive the Victoria Cross. This was, and remains, the highest award of the British military honours system, and was also awarded to brave Australians in recognition of our country's role as Britain's submissive stepson.

Jacka's VC made him an instant hero in Australia, a young country with precious few heroes that had been struggling for years to find a man fit for the job. Ned Kelly had looked promising, but the murder got in the way. Then there was Breaker Morant, but again, murder made his heroism difficult to show unqualified enthusiasm for. So the relief at the emergence of Albert Jacka, a bona fide hero who was not, in a legal sense, a murderer, was palpable. His deeds were celebrated up and down and occasionally sideways across the country. Magazines put him on their covers, running popular profiles on Jacka's life, background, turn-ons and turn-offs, and Ten Top Tips For Dealing With Problem Skin In The Trenches. The government put him on recruiting posters, promising myriad other young Australians that if only they would sign up in the service of their country, they too could wade knee-deep in the blood of strangers with whom they had no personal quarrel.

In addition to the rewards and plaudits, Jacka won rapid promotion in the field, and occasionally back at the house. He became a corporal, a sergeant, and then a company sergeant major. None of these promotions meant he got to stop fighting, so you've got to question what good any of them were. Jacka stayed at Gallipoli, continuing to fight, shoot and stab Turks as hard as he could, while all around him, less robust and less Australian men dropped like flies. After nine months of this, and the campaign having gone, in official military jargon, 'thoroughly tits-up', the Allies withdrew from Gallipoli. They had been defeated on the battlefield, but they had at least died in phenomenal numbers without achieving any of their objectives, so it was a sort of moral victory.

It wasn't long before he found himself back in the trenches when his unit took up residence near Armentières. The motto of Armentières is '*Pauvre mais fiere*', which means 'Poor but proud', so that tells you how much fun it was being stationed there. Soon he moved on to the Somme with the 14th Battalion, assigned to the Pozières sector. Today the Australian flag flies over the town Pozières in recognition of the sacrifice of Australian soldiers at the Battle of Pozières, making it especially embarrassing that the Australian flag has another country's flag on it. But our nation's eternal shame notwithstanding, Australia suffered over 5000 casualties at Pozières between 23 July and 7 August 1916, capturing the village at horrific cost.

It was on the morning of 7 August that Jacka wrote his name into the annals of legend again, making a total of two entire annals that had his name in: a high number of annals by anyone's standards. At dawn, Jacka was in his dugout when a mob of Germans – known as the 'Turks of the North' – stormed the Allied line. Two Germans threw a bomb into the dugout, killing two men and making the always-fatal error of annoying Albert Jacka.

As he burst from his dugout, gun blazing and the words 'I am SO pissed off' on his lips, he found the Germans, in their petty Teutonic way, taking 40 Australians prisoner. Only seven of Jacka's men were in fighting condition after the attack, but seven men was more than enough for Albert. He called them to his side and charged like a buffalo in heat. Some of the Germans, who obviously knew who they were dealing with, threw down their weapons at once. The rest, idiotically, chose to fight, and therefore suffered the excruciating fate of having a huge Jacka-shaped hole punched straight through their guts.

As the enraged second lieutenant fell werewolf-like upon his antagonists, the imprisoned Australians turned on their captors and fought back à la the end of *Indiana Jones and the Temple of Doom*[101]. In the brutal hand-to-hand fighting – which despite its name probably involved quite a lot of guns and knives[102] – every member of Jacka's platoon was wounded. Jacka himself received seven wounds, including two head injuries and a bullet through the shoulder, but if anyone thought that seven wounds was enough to prevent Albert Jacka kicking arse without even stopping to take names, that person had not been paying attention up to this point. Fifty Germans were captured, and Jacka killed between twelve and twenty himself, proving that he was just as good at killing Germans as he was at killing Turks and silencing those critics who had suggested he might be a one-race wonder.

Legendary military historian and Charles Hawtrey impersonator C.E.W. Bean called Jacka's counter-attack 'the most dramatic and effective act of individual audacity in the history of the AIF': even better than the time Major G.P.W. Meredith shot several emus in Western Australia[103]. In recognition of courage that by now had tipped well over the edge of what would by most people be called insanity, Jacka was awarded the Military Cross, the medal given to soldiers who are pretty good but not, as Elaine from *Seinfeld* might put it, Victoria-worthy. Many believed that Jacka should've received

---

101 It's pretty easy to imagine Albert Jacka ripping out someone's heart and showing it to him.

102 Truth be told, anyone fighting with just their hands copped it pretty badly.

103 Now THAT was heroism. Those emus are tough buggers.

a second VC, an honour bestowed on only three men in history[104], but it was not to be. Two theories have been advanced to explain this failure to fully recognise Jacka's exploits at Pozières:

1. The fact that Jacka's gallantry was only made possible by his failure to ensure the security of his platoon's position, allowing the Germans to waltz casually in in broad daylight, means a few of his points for bravery were deducted for incompetence.
2. The snobbish military establishment of the time were disgustingly bigoted towards unpolished larrikins from the rough Aussie bush like Jacka, and their hideous class hatred disfigured the honours system by denying a true hero his due.

Which of these theories is correct? Who knows? But the second one sounds pretty good, so let's go with that. It'd be just like those English bastards, wouldn't it?

Following the triumph of Pozières, Jacka was evacuated to England, despite his protestations that his wounds were 'just some harmless little holes, honestly' and that 'the Army will never get by without me'. On 18 August 1916, he was promoted to lieutenant, but on 8 September, tragedy struck: Albert Jacka was reported dead. The news was devastating to all on the Allied side, and its impact was only slightly ameliorated by the fact that it wasn't true. Albert was not, in fact, dead, and provided near-conclusive evidence of this fact by attending an investiture ceremony on 29 September, where King George V handed over his Victoria Cross, remarking admiringly on how alive Albert looked. In November Jacka returned to his unit in France, and resumed his work killing every German on earth. By March 1917, he had been promoted to

104 Two of them weren't even real soldiers, but doctors. Didn't kill a single person, if you can believe it.

captain and was predicted, if the war did not end soon, to reach the rank of Prime Minister by mid-1920.

In early 1917, the German army had retreated to the Hindenburg Line, a defensive position constructed entirely out of zeppelins, behind which they thought they'd be safe. Had they learnt nothing of the ways of Jacka? On 8 April, Our Bert led a party into No Man's Land to inspect German defences. After slipping through the wire in two places, he made his report, then went back out to lay tape to guide the attackers. On the way, he captured a two-man German patrol, just for fun and to keep himself fit[105]. For this he was given a Bar to his Military Cross, denoting that he had been awarded a second MC. He still didn't get another VC though: *bloody* English!

By this time, the German military machine was beginning to crumble, crippled and exhausted by the remorseless assaults on it by Albert Jacka. Things were not about to get any easier for the Kaiser: given command of D Company, 14th Battalion, Jacka secured victory at the Battle for Messines Ridge in June 1917, taking out numerous machine-gun posts and capturing a German field gun. Jacka received no medals for this action, because people were getting so used to it by now. Much as Don Bradman's average during the Bodyline series was seen as disappointing despite being an excellent number for most batsmen, because of the incredibly high standards The Don had set, Jacka had performed so many ridiculously gallant actions that ordinary heroism wasn't enough to impress anymore. Not that I'm comparing the courage of Bradman to that of Jacka: Bradman had to do his job without a helmet.

In July Jacka was shot again, and went to hospital to sign autographs for the doctors. Returning to action in the Battle of

---

105 Capturing Germans is fantastic cardio.

Polygon Wood[106], he led an assault on German pill-boxes that resulted in the liberation of huge amounts of enemy medication. For this he was recommended for the Distinguished Service Order, but passed over. Jacka, however, was not in this business for the awards: he was in it for the killing; and he went on diligently carrying out his task until May 1918. It was then that he was gassed outside Villers-Bretonneux, and shot through the throat.

Evacuated again, Jacka was expected to succumb to his injuries by naïve fools who had yet to learn that Albert Jacka was not like other men. Bloodlust still fizzing through his veins, he recovered again, only to find that, tragically, the war was over. Jacka's ferocity had been so effective that Germany had been forced to surrender. With mixed feelings – glad that he had won the war for the forces of good, but disappointed at his enforced hiatus from bloodshed – Jacka went home to Melbourne, where he was received as a hero, something that some believe would have been quite unlikely had he stayed with the Forests Service.

Jacka's activities after the war were neither particularly patriotic or of any real interest to anyone, but in case you care, he co-founded the electrical goods import-export business *Roxbugh, Jacka & Co.* He also married, and adopted a daughter, who grew up with a thorough knowledge of how to bayonet a fully-grown man from any continent. In 1929, Jacka was elected to the St Kilda City Council, and in 1930 became the mayor. While on the council he gained a reputation for social justice, working to assist the unemployed, defend evictees and developing public works projects to provide jobs for the poor. Which is all very nice, but doesn't really compare to 'killed 20 Germans in one morning', does it?

It was around this time that the Great Depression swept across the world. In 1931, Jacka's business collapsed, and later that year, so

106 Named for the lush crop of geometry teachers grown there.

did Jacka. On 14 December, the former war hero was admitted to hospital after a council meeting. On 17 January, 1932, nephritis did what bullets, bombs, gas, bayonets, muddy trenches, malnutrition and the combined Turkish and German armies never could: kill Albert Jacka. He was 39 years old, and 6000 people lined the streets to watch his body be carried to St Kilda Cemetery.

Today Jacka is memorialised in an annual service at his grave, organised by St Kilda's Council, as well as an inscription on the Victoria Cross Memorial in Alfred Square, St Kilda. His name is borne by, among others, Jacka Park in Wedderburn, Jacka Boulevard in St Kilda, and the suburb of Jacka in Canberra. The Australian War Memorial holds his Victoria Cross, the everlasting tribute to one man's ability to kill in service to his country.

Albert Jacka was the kind of hero that comes along but rarely in history: a man who refused to allow fear to be his master, and who would bear any hardship, face any peril, and most importantly, shoot any foreigner square in his ugly face, for the sake of honour, glory and the ideals of the British Empire that today we so justly revile. Perhaps more than anything, he showed Australians that they could compete on the world stage in something more important than cricket: indeed, in the most important game of all, the game of geopolitical violence. We were a young country, still a-wobble on our lanky coltish legs, but with men like Albert Jacka, we need not simply tag along behind the big boys, bowing and scraping to our venerable elders: we were perfectly capable of taking the lead, standing front and centre in the thick of battle and hacking the enemy to pieces as well as any more ancient nation. Albert Jacka gave Australia a soul: the most beautiful, blood-soaked soul it could ever have hoped for.

FUN FOR YOU AT HOME: Learn what it was like to be a soldier in the World War One! Dig a trench in your backyard, half-fill it with water, and ask your friends over to shoot at you. If they come too close, stab them. Now you're living like a real war hero!

CHARLES KINGSFORD SMITH
The Boy Who Hated Gravity

NOWADAYS, AIR TRAVEL is a simple matter of cramming hundreds of people into a massive metal tube which then hurtles through the air at terrifying speeds in total defiance of the laws of physics. But there was a time when flying was a difficult, even dangerous practice, back when technological advances like complimentary headphones and body-cavity searches were but a dream. It was in these days that Charles Kingsford Smith carved out his place in history, as one of the most notable members of an exclusive club that might be called 'men who, by any objective standard, made recklessly bad decisions in life', thereby providing inspiration for generations of Australians who dream of a life spent among the clouds in a patently inadequate vehicle.

Charles Kingsford Smith was born in Brisbane on 9 February 1897[107], the youngest of seven children of William Charles Smith and Catherine Mary, nee Kingsford. Even as a tiny tyke, Charles was fascinated by flight. He would sit playing at his mother's feet in the family garden, gazing up at the mighty geese flapping across the wide blue yonder, and he would ask his mother:

---

107 Exactly 82 years before the birth of the author of this book, so, you know, there are two reasons to celebrate that date.

'Mama, how do birds fly?'

And his mother would look lovingly on the child, and gently reply, 'I don't know, Charlie, why don't you ever shut your stupid neck?'

Charles would nod in wonder, but his curiosity could not be sated. 'Can people fly, Mama?' he would ask, eyes wide and shining as they turned upward and followed the dazzling rosellas across the sky.

'Yes, Charlie,' she would answer with sweet patience. 'For example, soon I will smack your arse so hard you'll fly right over that fence.'

It was around this time that the Wright Brothers made their historic breakthrough in heavier-than-air flight, flying 120 feet at 10 feet above the ground. Even at six years old, little Charles almost certainly said, 'I reckon I can beat that.' Probably most people around the world did: it was a very unimpressive flight.

It was after his family moved to Sydney that Charles first demonstrated his aviational proclivities: while attending St Andrew's Cathedral Choir School, he repeatedly voiced his disgust that the choir spent all its time singing and none engaging in heavier-than-air flight. Moving on to Sydney Technical School, 'Chilla', as he was nicknamed due to his ability to keep lettuce fresh, won plaudits for his essays, including 'Birds: The Prime Ministers of the Sky'; 'Fifteen Ways in Which Bats Are Better Than Humans'; and 'How I Plan To Surgically Transform Myself Into An Owl'.

At the age of 16, young Charles was apprenticed to the Colonial Sugar Refining Company, and a glittering future in sugar beckoned, but the teenager was restless, feeling there must be something better out there, something more savoury and aerodynamic. It wasn't until World War One broke out that that something better happened along.

For a high-spirited, adventurous young man like Charles Kingsford Smith, the war was a splendid chance to travel, see the world, and kill strangers of various ethnicities, which was at the time known as 'the Great Australian Dream'[108]. Indeed, many young people found that although World War One had its dark side, it also provided many excellent career opportunities, and is recognised today as one of the most useful world wars ever in terms of personal development.

Charles saw action at Gallipoli, a campaign that must have had a powerful effect on the young man, illustrating as it did the terrible dangers of staying on the ground. Indeed, many military historians today believe that if Gallipoli had been fought in the air, casualties may have been as much as halved – not least due to the increased difficulty of digging trenches three hundred feet above the earth. And so, in October 1916, Charles Kingsford Smith finally embraced the destiny that had been his ever since his infant days scowling enviously at passing moths, and joined the Royal Flying Corps.

Receiving his wings in 1917 – a process which involves qualifying as a pilot and not, as the original draft of this book stated, having feathers sewn onto his arms – Charles served in France as a fighter pilot and immediately knew he had found his calling. 'I have discovered one thing about flying,' he wrote to his parents, 'and that is that my future, whatever it may be worth, is bound up with it.' His parents were naturally shattered that their son had thrown away his bright future in sugar, but at the same time were pleased that he was so happy in his new, insanely dangerous career. It's easy to imagine how overjoyed Mr and Mrs Kingsford Smith must have been: just think of how ecstatic *you* would be to find

108 The 'Great Australian Dream' in the modern day refers to becoming a contestant on *My Kitchen Rules*.

out that your child was careening around the skies of France in a flimsy assemblage of wood and canvas, being shot at by homicidal Germans.

And they really *were* flimsy: in World War One, fighter planes were not so much sleek, exquisitely engineered fighting machines as billycarts with wings. Besides the fact that the bodies of the planes were about as resilient as the average cheese toastie and provided as much protection for the pilot as a fairy-floss raincoat, they were also fitted with machine guns designed to fire *through* the propeller. The guns were synchronised so as not to hit the propeller while it was spinning, so it was perfectly safe except when it didn't work. So the two main risks of being a World War One fighter pilot were:

1. Having your plane shot to pieces by the enemy.
2. Having your plane shot to pieces by your plane.

That is, if you didn't count the fact that planes had only been invented 14 years ago and the technology of flying in general was still at the 'only to be undertaken by the suicidally deranged' stage[109].

Still, everyone in World War One who wasn't in a plane was sitting in a muddy hole eating weevils and watching their own feet rot off, so the mad, brief life of a pilot did hold some charm. At least you got some fresh air before you were killed.

Charles Kingsford Smith got plenty of fresh air in his war days, during which he shot down four enemy planes in his first month, and did sterling work attacking ground targets and hostile balloons[110]. Unfortunately, he also found himself in a spot of bother, when he was shot down himself, with both his plane and his foot

---

109 This is the stage that Twitter is at right now.

110 And I'm sure you'll agree, a hostile balloon is pretty much the worst kind of balloon there is.

filled with bullets. The foot had to have three toes amputated: the plane, sadly, was put to sleep. As Royal Flying Corps regulations at the time specified that active pilots must have no fewer than ten toes[111], Kingsford Smith was removed from combat duty, made an instructor, and given the Military Cross[112] for his gallantry in battle and missing appendages.

Historians are divided on just how great an influence Kingsford Smith had on the outcome of the war, but it seems likely that if Germany had managed to keep those four planes in the air, they would have won. Hence, we can see that Kingsford Smith, like every other Australian in the war, won it singlehanded.

After the war, Charles worked in a number of different jobs, although they all involved flying planes, so they were all the same job, really: if we're honest his life did have a pretty one-note character to it. For a while he partnered with his friend Cyril Maddocks in a joy-riding service in the north of England, a region notable for its urgent need of joy. He also travelled to the US, where he worked as a barnstormer, performing shows for audiences around the country. Barnstormers engaged in daring stunts such as nose dives, loop-the-loops, barrel rolls and flying through barns – this last giving the profession its name, after 'Cowsplattering' was rejected as too graphic. Barnstormers also performed tricks like stunt parachuting and wing-walking – some even put on displays of dancing or tennis on the wings of planes in mid-air, while others took the more direct route of simply gathering a large crowd to watch them shoot themselves in the face.

However, Charles knew that his destiny lay not in short-form aerial suicide, but in the burgeoning field of staying in the air

111 And no more than 16.

112 A third-level decoration: you have to lose a whole foot to get anything higher.

for far longer than necessary. With this in mind, in 1927 he and fellow pilot Charles Ulm flew all the way around Australia in ten days and five hours. It is said that this achievement was especially praiseworthy because it was done 'with minimal navigational aids', but really, as long as you make sure the sea stays on one side of the plane and the land on the other, navigating your way around Australia should be pretty simple. It's the minimal toilet facilities that actually make the trip so impressive.

In 1928 Kingsford Smith truly etched his name in history, when in a three-engined Fokker F.VII monoplane[113] he had named the *Southern Cross*, he flew from Oakland, California to Brisbane, beginning the flight on 31 May and completing it on 9 June. Only 83 and a half hours of that was actually spent in the air, however, so there was a lot of slacking off on this voyage.

Kingsford Smith was not alone on his trans-Pacific journey. Besides relief pilot Ulm, the *Southern Cross* carried radio operator James Warner and navigator Harry Lyon. Of course, you've never heard of these men without whom Kingsford Smith could not have achieved such a feat, which just proves that life is cruel and unfair and that working hard and fulfilling your dreams is probably a waste of time. Or at least that history is written by the guy with the best publicist.

This flight made Charles Kingsford Smith a true celebrity. He was awarded the Air Force Cross[114] – despite the fact that, even by the most generous of interpretations, he was not in the Air Force – and appointed an honorary squadron leader, although records indicate the honorary squadron achieved little in the years to come. More importantly, he was cemented in the public consciousness as

113 From the Greek 'mono', meaning 'one', because the monoplane had just one wing, making it incredibly dangerous.

114 Q: How do you get the Air Force Cross? A: Divert funding to the Navy.

a genuine national hero, and granted the highest honour that can be bestowed on an Australian: a dull, unimaginative nickname. Henceforth, Charles Kingsford Smith would be forever known as 'Smithy', a quintessentially Australian sobriquet in that it expresses nothing of significance while also not making it particularly clear who you're actually referring to when you say it.

'Smithy' had achieved the very greatest heights of the Age of Impractical Aviation, but never having been one to leave well enough alone, he just kept getting into planes and zooming off to god knows where. Just a few months after the Pacific crossing, he flew from Point Cook to Perth in the first non-stop trans-Australian flight. He followed that up a month later with a flight from Sydney to Christchurch, proving once and for all that air travel was possible even to places that nobody wanted to go. At the end of this flight, 30,000 New Zealanders turned out to welcome him and the event was broadcast live on radio. Kingsford Smith and Charles Ulm – still hanging on to those coat-tails for dear life – were then taken on a triumphant tour of New Zealand, which took almost the whole afternoon.

Smithy's star was in the ascendant, but even the most in-the-ascendant star can be shot down by the space-cannon of public controversy, and his public image took a hit in 1929 during the 'Coffee Royal Incident', an incident involving tragedy, scandal, and dark conspiracy theories deserving of a slightly more serious-sounding nickname than 'Coffee Royal Incident'.

It began when Smithy decided to fly to England, determined as he was to explore all the uncivilised regions of the globe. The flight began well, with the plane staying up in the air; but quickly turned sour, with the plane not being up in the air anymore. Forced by bad weather to land on the mudflats of Western Australia, Smithy and his poorly publicised pals waited for help to arrive, passing the time by drinking a coffee and brandy blend dubbed 'Coffee Royal' – hence the name of the incident. Some thought the incident could've been called the 'Plane Crashing Incident', or even the 'Men Stranded in the Middle of Nowhere Because They Were Dumb Enough to Try to Fly to England Incident', but the media thought 'Coffee Royal' was snappier.

Where the incident got controversial was when two men who had set out to search for Smithy's party crashed their own plane and died, which can't have come as that great a surprise to them, but still, it was a shame. Some accused Kingsford Smith of having staged the incident for publicity, which would've been a pretty good stunt, I suppose, although you'd think if a fellow only wanted publicity, actually completing a flight to England would've done the job. The point was, that if he *had* staged the whole thing, it would've all been in terribly poor taste. Then there was the fact that one of the dead men, Keith Anderson, was a former business partner of Smithy's, who had unsuccessfully sued for what he claimed was his rightful share of the prize money from the trans-Pacific flight.

So, I mean, I'm sure there was nothing in it, but if you *were* to write a devilishly clever murder mystery novel about a devious and greedy aviator, this'd be a pretty good plot, right?[115]

The public's faith in Kingsford Smith's perfection had been somewhat dented, as often happens when national heroes act slightly douchey, despite the fact that a pretty impressive percentage of our national heroes have literally been murderers. Despite the opprobrium, he pressed on with his grand life's work of flying places and then flying back again. Later in 1929, he did complete the flight to England, in a new record time: 12 days, 18 hours. Imagine doing that with your knees pressed up against the meal tray and the drinks cart banging your elbow every five minutes. It must have been hell.

115 Actually, nobody write that: that idea is mine. Okay?

In the 1930s, having launched his own airline, Australian National Airways, Smithy kept busy by crossing the Atlantic from east to west, and then flew solo from England to Darwin, breaking the record for that journey that had previously been held by Bert Hinkler, a pilot who had previously been thought as pretty special, but who was now exposed by Smithy as a pathetic failure.

Despite continuing to humiliate his peers, Kingsford Smith was flying into severe turbulence[116]. The Great Depression, combined with the loss of one his planes in the Snowy Mountains, hit Australian National Airways hard, and he wasn't helping his business prospects with his stubborn insistence on jumping in a plane and gallivanting off somewhere new every couple of weeks. Throughout 1931 and 1932 he spent an inordinate amount of time whizzing all over the world picking up people's mail for them, a practice that had deleterious effect on his health and also made everyone think he was a bit weird, the way he was constantly babbling about getting Christmas cards to London.

In 1932, Kingsford Smith was knighted for services to aviation, but just about broke – and no matter what you've heard, knighthoods don't come with large cash prizes, so I don't even know what's the point of having one. He was back to selling ten-bob[117] joyrides, but still trying to make a killing in the mail business. It wasn't catching on, though: the New Zealand government knocked back his pitch to conduct mail services between Auckland and Singapore. 'Why not give the whole mail business a rest, Charlie?' the Kiwis said. 'It's not as interesting as you think.'

At the end of 1933, Smithy's cloudy skies cleared somewhat, with a solo flight from London to Wyndham in Western Australia earning him a £3000 grant from the Commonwealth government,

116 This is an aviation metaphor, you see.

117 In today's money, $500,000.

which was inexplicably still incredibly impressed by this kind of thing. He'd been doing it for years by now, but still governments kept clapping their hands like toddlers and handing over the cash. What taxpayers thought of so much of their money being thrown at this goggle-clad weirdo is not certain.

In 1934 Smithy achieved another first by flying from Brisbane to San Francisco: the first west-to-east crossing of the Pacific. Which, as he'd already crossed it from east to west, was fairly underwhelming, but people still seemed to think it was a big deal. In 1935, a dream was realised when he was authorised to begin a trans-Tasman airmail service. It was then quickly un-realised when on the first flight, a propeller broke and Kingsford Smith's co-pilot had to climb out and take oil from a dead motor to top up another one. This co-pilot's name was PG Taylor, but you don't know his name – you know the name of the guy who stayed safe in the cockpit the whole time, because history doesn't give two shits about fairness.

That same universe was, by this stage, dropping some fairly heavy hints in Kingsford Smith's direction. But the significant looks and pointed coughing of the Fates would not deter the brave airman. Smithy's ambitions were finally to prove his downfall. On 6 November 1935, he and JT Pethybridge – who naturally you've never heard of – took off from London in an attempt to fly to Australia and break some record or other. But the only record they broke was that of Saddest Inter-Hemisphere Flight Ever. Flying at night towards Singapore, the plane plunged into the sea off Burma. Smith and Pethybridge were never seen again: their bodies remain unrecovered; so I guess it's technically possible that they're still alive. If you see them, tell a policeman.

It was a tragic end to a life of spectacular accomplishment. At the same time, it wasn't exactly the least predictable end a life ever had. But it definitely proved that getting into planes is a bad idea.

Kingsford Smith left an incredible legacy from his short life. He stands proudly in the pantheon of legendary aviators alongside all the other brave pioneers who conquered the skies before plummeting out of them. In recognition of his efforts to spit in the face of God, his name is now borne by Sydney's airport and the electorate surrounding it, several streets, a couple of schools, and two airliners. His own plane, the *Southern Cross*, is on display at Brisbane Airport, where visitors may marvel at the primitive technology of early aviation and lie to themselves that they will be any safer in their own flying deathtraps.

That misplaced confidence is perhaps Smithy's greatest bequest to the world. If he only knew just how many people are risking their lives in planes every day, thanks in part to his own tireless efforts, he would, I think, smile.

FUN FOR YOU AT HOME: Build your own plane! Using items from around the house such as toilet paper rolls, old ice-cream containers, and stolen truck engines, see if you can construct a working model of Charles Kingsford Smith's *Southern Cross*. Take it down to the local park for a test flight. Take notes to help you figure out what went wrong.

MAKING OUR MARK

IN THE EARLY YEARS of the 20th century, Australia had fought hard to establish its national identity: in fact we'd just fought hard in general. Much blood was shed and a generation left dead in the mud of Europe in the interests of defining what it meant to be Australian, and when you put it like that it really does seem colossally pointless. Still, the war criminals and corpses of Australia's early days as a nation, combined with the political independence and cultural confidence that had boomed at the turn of the century, had given the whole country a wonderfully smug feeling. It was great to be Australian, we decided, and the future was looking bright, especially if we kept having regular wars to remind us what the point of us was.

Identity built, Australians began looking more and more toward the outside world in the middle years of the 20th century, or more particularly, began striving to get the outside world to look more and more toward them. By this time, the international community had a vague idea of what Australia was: a nightmarish desert in the middle of the sea filled with snakes and parrots and criminals. But they had little idea of *who* Australians were. If you'd fought against or alongside Aussies, you might have had an impression of what they were like in battle: i.e. the perfect killing machine; but beyond that, not much. Ned Kelly was hardly a household name in the salons of New York, and one could say the same about Caroline Chisholm on the French Riviera.

But Australia the country was young, energetic, and looking to make its mark, and Australians the people were exactly the same. In the fields of sport, science, the arts, politics and warfare, the inhabitants of the great southern land were determined to make the rest of the world sit up and take notice. By the latter stages of the century, the world would be in no doubt that Australians could hold their own in any field of endeavour: we were spreading across the globe, and we planned to conquer it.

The job was done by a plethora of men and women of extraordinary ability: men and women who took the people of the world on at their own game and won. Whether making world-changing scientific breakthroughs, entertaining or inspiring millions, or standing up for their own against the bullies of the superpowers, these people were letting everyone know Australians were here to stay. These are their stories.

ANNETTE KELLERMAN
Billion Dollar Barracuda

WHEN AUSTRALIA MADE its momentous move to Federation, Annette Kellerman was just thirteen years old, and even at such a tender age, her legs were almost normal. To many people, having normal legs may not seem like an achievement of great note, but for Annette Kellerman, the attainment of relatively run-of-the-mill legs represented a triumph in itself. As a little girl she had suffered from a condition that rendered her legs unnaturally weak, and had been forced to wear steel braces on them from the age of six. As her nation achieved independence, she achieved mobility, and both had displayed the courage and determination that would see them amaze the world in the decades to come.

Had little Annette never had dysfunctional legs, she might never have embarked on the career that made her famous: with regular strong pins she might just have followed in her parents' footsteps; her father a violinist and her mother a pianist; ironically both professions that can be done without legs. But Annette was born to swim – or if not 'born', at least severely damaged, in order to prod her in that direction.

It was in Marrickville that Annette was born, that Sydney suburb with a reputation for producing sporting legends, from Jeff Fenech to Bob Simpson to Trisha Noble. But no legend of

Marrickville forged a legend more legendary than Annette Kellerman. Enrolled in swimming classes to help her overcome her disability, the youngster turned out to be something of a prodigy. Less than two years after Federation, those relatively normal legs had helped her not only master every stroke, but win the New South Wales championships in the 100 yards and mile – something that, thanks to the metric system, not even Ian Thorpe ever achieved. She was also, at the age of 15, already giving public displays of diving, a remarkable activity in those days for one so young who was not also a horse.

Moving to Melbourne with her parents, Annette combined her school studies with her burgeoning career in doing unusual things in water, swimming with fish twice a day in a glass tank at the Exhibition Aquarium. These shows were incredibly popular, though no historian has ever quite managed to figure out why[118]. She also performed a mermaid act, but modern experts believe it is unlikely that she ever was an actual mermaid. In 1903, still only 16 years old, Annette performed in the play *The Breaking of the Drought* at the Theatre Royal, stunning the crowds with her high dives back in an era when the theatre industry had the creative vision and guts to have young girls leap recklessly into pools on stage: a far cry from the moribund, barren, pool-less theatre landscape of today.

It is perhaps difficult for modern minds to comprehend the impact that Annette Kellerman had on the Australian public. Nowadays we have a million entertainment options and can see myriad varieties of water sport on TV[119], and we've become jaded, unable to feel wonder anymore. But back in the early days of the twentieth century, people could still be excited by the simple sight of a girl swimming with

118 It may be related to the fact that people back then had few sources for teenage girls in bathing suits. It was an austere age.

119 And on some extremely compelling websites.

fish. Or even a girl swimming by herself. To be honest, just the fact of there being a big box of water that you could see through was enough to wow the audiences of the day. These days people are a lot less impressed by the existence of swimming, and that might be our mistake: after all, human beings can't breathe underwater; how nuts do we have to be to keep going there?

Annette Kellerman was quite nuts indeed, and her love of the water could not be contained. In 1905, the 18-year-old Kellerman was one of the first women to attempt to swim the English Channel, and in another pioneering move, was one of the first women to fail to swim the English Channel. It may have been Kellerman's brave effort that was the origin of the popular phrase, 'swimming the English Channel is pointless'.

But Annette didn't have to swim the English Channel, or indeed any channel, to impress people. All she had to do was dive into a pool and splash about for a bit. It was hardly surprising that her phenomenal aquatic charisma could not be confined to Australia for long: people in other countries were just as desperate for something to take their minds off their lives, and just as keen on seeing fit young women get moist. Indeed, some things never change.

Kellerman crashed onto the international stage in 1907 with the force and urgency of a crazed dugong escaping its enclosure. At the New York Hippodrome – previously known only for its spectacular staging of hippo races – she performed the world's first water ballet, something people had said could never be done after looking at a regular ballet and noticing that the shoes weren't waterproof. It is said that by performing the ballet, Kellerman helped popularise synchronised swimming, which has led some to dub her history's greatest monster.

If her role in promoting synchronised swimming speaks poorly of her moral compass, she may be redeemed by something else she popularised in 1907 – getting arrested for public indecency. The arrest occurred on Revere Beach in Massachusetts and was a result of Kellerman wearing a one-piece bathing suit. She had for some time been advocating the right of women to wear one-piece suits, as opposed to the gigantic contraptions that passed for acceptable swimwear at the time. It was widely considered obscene for any woman to enter the water without looking like she'd been thrown overboard from a cruise ship in the middle of a ballroom dancing tournament, and Kellerman's bold attempt to ease restrictions on women who wanted to swim without being dragged to the bottom of the ocean by the weight of their skirts was akin to a woman in the 21st century demanding to pin oversized photographs of her vulva on the walls of a kindergarten. The bathing suits in which Annette Kellerman used to perform were of course less revealing than the average giraffe onesie, but in 1907 Queen Victoria had been dead less than a decade and her grim, disapproving visage still sulked over much of the western world.

Obviously, Annette's desire for greater freedom in swimwear placed her on the right side of history, and it was no surprise that once she started trotting around beaches in her one-piece, the tide of public opinion turned. Dr Dudley Sargent of Harvard University conducted a study of 3000 women in 1908, determining Annette Kellerman to be 'the Perfect Woman' in terms of physical dimensions. Sargent's criterion for awarding this title was Kellerman's similarity to the Venus de Milo, which casts doubt on the whole process: the Venus de Milo has no arms, whereas Kellerman's success in both freestyle and butterfly events strongly suggests that she did. Just how much thought Sargent put into putting Kellerman top of his list is unsure, but it was almost definitely less thought than he put into working out how he could get a funding body to pay him to stare at thousands of women's bodies. On hearing she'd been named the Perfect Woman, Kellerman quipped, 'Only from the neck down': it's really annoying when people can't take a compliment, isn't it?

Whatever the academic merits of Sargent's study, it was clear proof that Kellerman's figure was easy on the eye, which made her as ideal a model for the promotion of the one-piece bathing suit as Queen Victoria herself would've been inappropriate for the same purpose. But the Marrickville Maverick was not going to stop there, either in terms of scandalising the public or her rapidly growing fame.

As a world-famous swimmer, underwater ballerina and indecent exposure proponent, it was only a matter of time before Kellerman became a movie star, because in those days the movie business was still in its infancy and would pretty much put anyone in a film: swimmers, carnival folk, Germans; whoever stumbled onto the lot.

Annette Kellerman was not one to do things by halves, so naturally she did not so much dip her toe into the movie world as do a cannonball into it. In 1916 she became the first major actress to appear nude on screen, beating Helen Mirren by 53 years. The film was *A Daughter of the Gods*, the first American movie to cost more than $1 million, most of which went on waxing. In the movie, Kellerman played the titular[120] god's daughter, the target of a sultan who agrees to help the Witch of Badness[121] destroy her if the witch will bring his son back to life. Somehow that ... well for the sake of argument we'll call it a 'plot' – somehow that was stretched out to three hours, which would be a bit much even now, let alone in 1916 when people were still getting used to the idea of a movie being longer than six minutes.

---

120 As it turned out, VERY titular.

121 That is what the character was called. Take a look at yourself, Silent Movie Era.

No copies of *A Daughter of the Gods* are known to exist, which is a tragedy for all lovers of old-timey smut. Still photographs do exist of Kellerman, showing off the form that made her Dr Sargent's Perfect Woman and made millions want to watch her splashing around in a tank. Sadly, in the photos much of her body is obscured by her long hair, which is a bit of a cheat really. Nevertheless, you can see why people might've been willing to sit through three hours of sultans and witches.

Kellerman was a ground-breaker throughout her film career. Before her contribution to the study of anatomy in *A Daughter of the Gods*, she had starred in *Mermaid*, in which she was the first actress to wear a swimmable mermaid costume. What's more, Kellerman designed her own mermaid costumes, making her unique among Australian film stars – Bryan Brown, for example, has never designed a mermaid costume in his life.

Other entries in the Kellerman filmography include *Siren of the Sea, Queen of the Sea, Venus of the South Seas,* and *Neptune's Daughter*, and it has to be said there was an element of typecasting that crept into her career. She also appeared in 1917's *National Red Cross Pageant*, a film that raised a lot of money for the Red Cross but really wasn't worth it. One of the most striking elements of Annette's acting career was her willingness to do her own stunts, which included such feats as a 92-foot[122] dive into the sea, and a 60-foot plunge into a pool filled with crocodiles – the latter raising the question: it's all very well for Kellerman to do her own stunts, but why was it necessary for the crocodiles to do theirs as well at the same time?

Miraculously, throughout her Hollywood career, Annette did not drown, break her neck, get eaten by crocodiles, or succumb

122 Meaning the measure of distance – she wasn't wearing dozens of prosthetic feet.

to a crippling cocaine addiction. By the 1920s it seemed as if she could not put a foot wrong, which is a valuable skill in swimming, particularly for kick-turns. She had conquered the world of competitive swimming, conquered the vaudeville stage with her aquatic shows and diving demonstrations, and even stormed the barricades of Hollywood – something undreamt of for Australians of the day, let alone Australians of the day who were swimmers and not actors.

With an appetite for achievement that apparently could not be sated even by accomplishments that would inspire deep and bitter hatred in millions of justifiably jealous fans, the tireless Annette continued to scoop the world out of its shell and slide it down her throat. Having found that swimming had worked quite well for her, she sought to take the message of swimming as a route to physical perfection to the masses with her book *Physical Beauty, How to Keep It*. This volume, published in 1918, was an invaluable guide for anyone who wanted to attain peak fitness, or just to feel terrible about themselves, and is seen as the forerunner of today's *The Biggest Loser.* Annette also wrote *How to Swim*, which the Australian Dictionary of Biography refers to as 'partly autobiographical': that seems like a fairly superfluous description, doesn't it? Her authorial dabblings also extended to children's literature: in 1926 she published *Fairy Tales of the South Seas*, a book of stories for children who weren't allowed to see her movies.

Having toured the world with her stage routine, which incorporated swimming, diving, wire-walking, dancing, acrobatics, singing and male impersonations[123], Kellerman later travelled throughout Europe and America in the capacity of lecturer, speaking on health and fitness to crowds eager to learn and hopeful that she'd finish the lecture by stripping down to her one-piece.

123 I can't imagine.

Annette Kellerman's phenomenal energy did not flag as she grew older. In World War Two she worked for the Red Cross and entertained the troops back in Australia, while at her home in California she ran a health food store, but I think given her service to the war effort she can be forgiven for this. All her life, Annette was a teetotaller and vegetarian, yet somehow retained her Australian citizenship.

Possibly the greatest tribute to be paid to the life and exploits of Kellerman came in 1952, when the film of her life, *Million Dollar Mermaid*, was released. Starring Esther Williams as Kellerman, the film was one of the most factually accurate biopics Hollywood has ever made, inasmuch as it got Annette's name right and correctly identified her as a swimmer. Other elements, such as the boxing kangaroo, the spinal haematoma, and Victor Mature, were less rigorous. But it was still a lot more faithful to history than *Night and Day*, the movie about Cole Porter not having sex with men.

In 1970, Kellerman returned to Australia; she died at Southport, Queensland, in 1975. Her ashes were scattered in the Great Barrier Reef – as if it's not polluted enough. She had no children, because frankly she had more important things to do. She is commemorated by Kellerman Close in Canberra, a star on the Hollywood Walk of Fame, and a swimming centre in Marrickville.

Today Australian movie stars are a dime a dozen, or even cheaper if it's Rebel Wilson. But in Annette Kellerman's day, the idea of a little girl from Marrickville becoming the toast of Hollywood was utterly absurd. She made the impossible possible and showed that Australia, the rugged brown land famed for covering people in dust and spiders, could also produce beauty, glamour and frontal nudity. To smash athletic records, entertain the masses, win acclaim around the world, and break new ground in sport, entertainment and gender equality, all in the span of one lifetime, is simply astonishing. It's all the more so from a girl who started life with dodgy legs, although when you think about it, these stories all start off like that. Once Annette Kellerman made a splash, the world was in no doubt that Australia had something extraordinary to give the world.

FUN FOR YOU AT HOME: Set up a diving board in your backyard! See how high you can raise it and test yourself diving from different heights. Once you've mastered the dive, put in a swimming pool. Does this make a difference to the experience? Make notes.

PHAR LAP
A Horse That Ran Fast

THERE ARE MANY kinds of heroes. Heroes who wear capes, heroes who wear tights, heroes who wear metal suits, heroes who wear cleavage-enhancing catsuits: the list goes on. But sometimes a hero comes along who isn't quite like other heroes. A hero who does not fight crime, or save lives, or actually help anyone in any way whatsoever, but rather, a hero who inspires people to be their best selves through great deeds and spectacular example. A hero for the masses, a hero who gives hope to the hopeless, joy to the joyless, and an intangible temporary sense of illusory wellbeing to the people who don't have one of those. Every now and then, a hero comes along who you can bet on – not in a figurative sense, but literally. What I'm saying is, sometimes a hero is, in a nutshell, a horse.

Australia has had many hero horses over the years, from Black Cavalier to Mugabe Diva, but every great horse who emerges in this country lives in the shadow of the greatest of them all: Phar Lap.

Phar Lap. Big Red. The Wonder Horse. Red Terror. Bobby. Ol' Horsey Legs. The Fast Runner. Galloping Sam. Lord Saddled-Up. Racewinner Von Jockeychair. He went by many names. But call him what you like, the one thing you couldn't call him was slow. Because that would be a lie. He was quick.

How quick was he? Well, put it this way: if you and Phar Lap were to go head-to-head in a 100-metre race, the International Association of Athletics Federations would declare the race un-sanctioned, and neither of your times would count. But rest assured that although the IAAF would refuse to allow the result to stand, Phar Lap would definitely beat you. It wouldn't even be close – you're not really in great shape anyway, are you? Be honest.

In today's world, when we revere fast horses far too much, it's hard to imagine how Australians of the 1930s revered Phar Lap slightly more than that. To understand the effect of this magnificent beast on the national psyche, it is necessary to first understand the Great Depression, a terrible time when everybody was unemployed but still had to wear hats in public to avoid being called a communist. The stock market had crashed on 29 October 1929, on what became known as 'Black Tuesday' due to systemic racism.

Australia, which even back then had a strict federal policy of doing whatever America did, threw itself into the Depression with gusto. Unemployment lines grew to giant-snake-from-the-end-of-*Aladdin* proportions. Men left their families to travel the land seeking any work they could find. Everywhere you looked, there was another poor soul with a piece of cardboard hanging around his neck, reading, 'Wanted: A decent job' or 'Will work for food' or 'Please give: spent all my money on cardboard'.

To sum up, the Great Depression was, no fooling, bloody depressing. Not just in hindsight – people remarked at the time on how big a downer it was. There are few things more disheartening than becoming the subject of award-winning black-and-white photography, and this was the fate of many during the Depression. What the people needed was something to cheer them up. I mean, what they really needed was money, but failing that, something to cheer them up would be nice too. Australians were crying out for a spirit-lifter. 'Please God,' they pleaded, 'send us a horse, that we might smile again!'

Their salvation was already at hand: on 4 October 1926[124], in the little town of Seadown on New Zealand's South Island, a foal was born to Entreaty, a black mare who had had one race, for no place – typical of the sexism of the time. The foal's father was Night Raid, a leading sire named after the movie *Meatballs*, who was very much in-demand as a sire at the time. Since retiring to stud in 1924, Night Raid's sperm had taken New Zealand by storm, and was named Gamete of the Year three years running at the annual Kiwi Gonad Awards.

The fact that Phar Lap was born in New Zealand has caused some to question whether he was a true 'Australian' hero. However, Australia has a proud history of producing talented New Zealanders: Russell Crowe, the Finn brothers, Derryn Hinch, Marcia Hines, Manu Feildel – these are just a few of the stars who have 'come across the Dutch' to find that while New Zealand is a decent enough place to be born in, you have to come to Australia to really live.

Phar Lap's migration to the big brother of the Antipodes occurred earlier than most other celebrities: he was only one at the time, younger even than Jay Laga'aia when he came. He was purchased by the American businessman David J. Davis, who had channelled all his resentment at his parents' choice of his name into becoming wealthy enough to buy horses. He made his money in photography and dinnerware imports and was known popularly as 'The Flashbulb and Gravy Boat King'. Or at least, would've been known popularly if photography and dinnerware were popular things to do.

---

124 The very day, ironically enough, that former general Rodolfo Gallegos led an uprising in southern Guanajuato. Funny coincidence.

Davis was taking the advice of his trainer, Harry Telford[125], but regretted it when young Phar Lap arrived in Australia. The colt hardly looked like a future champion: he was gangly, awkward, and had a face covered with warts. But then, so was Audrey Hepburn when she started out, and look how well she did. Phar Lap would prove to be the Hepburn of his day, although only after Telford placated the outraged Davis by offering to train him for free, the trainer not wanting to lose one of his few remaining owners through what racing industry insiders had taken to calling 'Harry's balls-ups'.

The name 'Phar Lap' was given to the horse by Telford, from an idea by medical student Aubrey Ping, Telford apparently being the kind of horse trainer who hung around universities waiting for students to name horses for him. Ping suggested 'farlap', a word which in the Zhuang and Thai languages means 'lightning'. Telford liked the idea, but changed the initial 'F' to a 'Ph' because Melbourne Cup winners had frequently had seven-letter names and he was also the kind of horse trainer who thought that would make a difference: which was why he didn't have many remaining owners.

Telford also gelded Phar Lap, believing this would help the horse focus fully on racing and also because he just liked doing that to animals. He was a weird guy, Harry Telford, but one hell of a trainer. Or rather, he probably wasn't that great a trainer really – he hadn't won much before he met Phar Lap, and his subsequent success may have had more to do with having a particularly good horse in his stable rather than any innate ability on his part to transform ordinary horses into champions. Though let's be fair: that's basically the case for every trainer ever, and maybe trainers should stop acting so superior all the time just because they remembered to feed the horse and buy a stopwatch.

---

125 The trainer he employed, I mean – Telford wasn't training *him*.

Still, at some point after Harry cut Phar Lap's balls off, the facial warts cleared right up, so maybe there was something there.

The newly eunuchised Phar Lap finished last in his first race, which must have made his owner want to shoot him in the head right there and then – I know I would have. Luckily, David Davis restrained his bloodlust long enough to see his gangly, awkward, wart-faced freak not come last in his next three races. Consulting his 'How to Own Horses' guide, he found that not coming last was an improvement on coming last, and was filled with renewed hope. This was rewarded on 27 April 1929, when Phar Lap stormed home to win the Maiden Juvenile Handicap[126] at Rosehill. As it was a maiden race, he was competing only with other horses who had never won a race, but every champion has to start somewhere, and Phar Lap's new status as Fastest Loser was indeed a start.

Having broken through for a win, the eccentric genius Telford immediately stopped Phar Lap from racing. Several months went by before he returned to competition, and began making a name for himself[127]. A second place at Randwick in September put him on the racing world's radar, and the public felt a sudden upsurge of wellbeing. 'There's always the risk of a major global financial disaster next month,' they told each other, 'but that horse coming second makes the prospect seem a lot less frightening.' He followed that second with wins in the Rosehill Guineas, the AJC Derby, and the AJC Derby Plate, and pundits could deny the facts no longer: Phar Lap was a horse that could run fast, and he had hardly any warts any more. A shiver went down the spines of the other horses in the Australian racing scene: this was because they were terrified of the tiny men who kept hitting them, but if they'd had any idea

126 These were ableist times.

127 'Phar Lap'.

what was going on in their lives, that shiver might well have been fear of Phar Lap's looming dominance.

A few days after Black Tuesday, Phar Lap won the VRC Derby, feeding off the misery of the nation as if he were running an equine hedge fund that had shorted several failed stocks. Immediately, the poverty-stricken populace smiled in relief and murmured, 'It's going to be all right' to each other. Three days later, he came third in the Melbourne Cup, aka the 'race that stops a nation'[128], serving notice that this was one young horse that was going places fast, and in circles.

Phar Lap was going from strength to strength, and occasionally even to strength again: from March to May 1930, he won nine races in a row, and people were starting to think that the Great Depression wasn't so bad, really. Especially with Don Bradman hitting hundreds and Walter Lindrum scoring thousands and Hubert Opperman riding a bike and all. The correlation between economic misery and Australian sporting success was so great that the government was forced to give serious thought to maintaining a state of permanent Depression, just to keep the country's self-esteem up.

Phar Lap, of course, was completely ignorant of such matters. In fact, he was completely ignorant of most matters, being – and this bears repeating – a horse. His attention was focused on one thing, and one thing only: running fast enough to make the man stop hurting him. Another sensational winning streak in the 1930-31 season included the prestigious Cox Plate, and he was now hot favourite for the Melbourne Cup.

There were still obstacles to overcome, however, and by 'obstacles' I mean 'bullets'. So profound had been the mighty chestnut's impact on the country that a gang of criminals tried to shoot him on 1 November 1930. What was the reason for

128 I.e. white people.

the attempted assassination? Perhaps Phar Lap threatened their investments in his rivals. Perhaps it was purely a personal matter: Phar Lap may have insulted one of their wives. Or maybe it was the racecourse vet, having double-booked himself on race day, attempting pre-emptive euthanasia so as to avoid any embarrassment.

In any case, the incident didn't worry Phar Lap much, because he was a horse and he didn't know the shots were aimed at him: for all he knew it was just normal weekend gunplay. He won the Melbourne Stakes later that day, and three days later lined up in the Melbourne Cup, a testament to his resilience, and the lack of follow-through common to the criminal gangs of the day. The Underbelly guys wouldn't have given up so easily.

The 1930 Melbourne Cup was a day of destiny for Phar Lap, whose entire four years of life had been – unbeknownst to him because he was a horse – leading up to this. The *Sydney Morning Herald* said that the horse 'had become nothing short of an obsession in the public mind', and that public mind was bent on Flemington Racecourse, where the object of this quite unhealthy obsession was ready to take the final step into immortality. On his back he carried 63kg, most of which was a young jockey named Jim Pike, who had himself sacrificed much – food, for example – in his quest to sit on the nation's greatest horse. Sixty-three kilos isn't heavy for a grown man, but it's a hell of a lot for a horse to carry on its back, especially when the horse has skinny legs. According to the *Herald*: 'The question was not which horse would win, but "Can Phar Lap carry the weight? Can he do what no other horse before him has done?"' Which seems a very similar question to 'Which horse will win?' if you ask me, but I am no turf expert.

Whatever question you cared to ask, Phar Lap answered it with head held high. He smashed his opposition, carrying those 63kg as lightly as if they had been 61.5kg. He had been the shortest-priced favourite in history at 8/11, and was the only favourite to win at odds-on, thus defying the odds by performing exactly as the odds had predicted.

It's difficult today, when people have very few economic concerns and sport is never used as a distraction from more important matters, to picture the amazing scenes when Phar Lap bolted home in the Cup. If 'the race that stops a nation' had been mostly marketing spin previously, it certainly wasn't now: everyone stopped. Strong men wept with joy. Strong women laughed at the strong men. Weak people of both sexes smashed windows and set fire to each other out of sheer exuberance. Delighted punters rejoiced in their extremely meagre winnings due to the winner's incredibly unsporting odds. If the Melbourne Cup wasn't already a public holiday, and if public holidays weren't meaningless anyway because nobody had a job, it would've been as if everyone took a holiday to celebrate Phar Lap's victory.

The 1930 Melbourne Cup was part of a 14-race winning streak for Phar Lap. In all he won 37 times from 51 starts: and from 1 March 1930, when he won the VRC St Leger Stakes, to his final race on 20 March 1932, he won 32 of 35, which seems pretty decent. Freakish, even: and more amazing when you consider that in every one of those races, he was competing against other horses, which are pretty fast.

Australia was now simply too small for a talent as gigantic as Phar Lap: it was time to take Big Red international. Davis shipped Phar Lap, and stable foreman Tommy Woodcock, to North America, and with them went the dreams of a nation, who lined up at the soup kitchens with that hope burning in their breasts that every Australian feels every day of their lives: the hope that some other Australian will validate their existence by achieving something significant overseas.

First stop for Phar Lap was Mexico, where he was entered in the Agua Caliente Handicap, the richest race in North American racing, which seems a bit odd, don't you think? I mean, Mexico? Twenty years before this they were all fighting the Wild Bunch, and now they were offering big money to horses, more than Kentucky or Massachussetts or Delaware or any of those people? Mexico is full of surprises[129].

Anyway, Phar Lap won the Agua Caliente Handicap, obviously. As an Australian[130], he was always going to be no match for the feeble American horses, raised on hot dogs and prone to hyper-obesity. It sent a message to the whole North American racing establishment: the only thing standing in the way of Phar Lap's total world domination was the possibility of sudden, mysterious death. In retrospect, this message was dangerously specific.

Phar Lap's first North American win would turn out to be his last. The world's most famous five-year-old[131] fell ill on 5 April 1932, at a stable in California, and haemorrhaged to death that day, which is a pretty awful way to go, even for a horse. Immediately a suspicion arose that Phar Lap had been poisoned, based on the suddenness of the death and the fact that that was exactly the kind of thing Americans would do. An autopsy revealed inflamed stomach and intestines, a conclusion refined by specialists examining the results in 2000, by which time you'd think everyone was over it, but there you go. These specialists opined that Phar Lap died of duodenitis-proximal jejunitis, a severe inflammation of the duodenum and upper jejunum, which are I believe things that horses have in their tummies.

The studies did not end there, however: in 2006 scientists at the Australian Synchrotron, who one assumes had no more pressing

129 Few of them as fun as this one.

130 Sort of.

131 A title now held by former Liberal MP Wyatt Roy.

tasks to attend to, declared that Phar Lap was almost certainly poisoned with a huge dose of arsenic. However, Sydney vet Percy Sykes – if for some reason you're interested in his opinion – believes the horse was not poisoned, noting that arsenic was a common ingredient in tonics of the time, for both horses and humans, which if nothing else proves how stupid people in the past were.

As it was apparently common practice among the idiots of the day to feed champion racehorses regular drinks of arsenic to keep them fit and healthy, it's hard to determine just how the poison got into Phar Lap's system. A further analysis of his mane in 2007 revealed that he had ingested a massive dose of arsenic in the couple of days prior to his death. Whether it was put there by nefarious intent, or by someone who thought he looked peaky and decided to pep him up with some nice fresh arsenic, it's impossible to say. Tommy Woodcock said Phar Lap was never given any arsenic-based tonic, but the probability of Tommy Woodcock being a hopelessly naïve young idealist is high: Harry Telford definitely gave his horses arsenic from time to time, as any responsible trainer of the 1930s would.

So we can't know conclusively whether Phar Lap was brutally murdered by ruthless American gangsters scared of what his astonishing feats would do to their revenue from illegal bookmaking, but nevertheless, let's be honest, that's definitely what happened. If he wasn't poisoned by gangsters, this story becomes much less interesting, and who wants that?

His death was tragic, but already in his five short years on earth, Phar Lap had achieved more than most people who aren't lower animals forced into servitude for the entertainment and enrichment of humans. His legacy was greater than any horse before or since, pretty much all of whom are a big disappointment in comparison. He was an inaugural inductee to the Australian Racing Hall of

Fame and the New Zealand Racing Hall of Fame, and statues of him stand in both Melbourne and his birthplace of Timaru. His likeness graced a postage stamp, along with a caption explaining who it was because otherwise it's just a random horse.

The affection the public had for Phar Lap – who was, to reiterate, a horse – is perhaps best shown by what happened to him after he died: unlike most horses, the people loved Phar Lap so much they split him into several pieces and took them to various places – we can only hope that someday someone loves us enough to dismember us. At the Melbourne Museum, you can see Phar Lap's stuffed body, staring eerily at you with his dead, glassy eyes, a faint air of accusation in his face: 'see what you have done to me,' he seems to say. Meanwhile, visitors to the National Museum of New Zealand in Wellington can see Phar Lap's skeleton, the absence of which might be why the stuffed skin in Melbourne looks so moody. And his heart, that huge heart that weighed almost twice as much as an average horse's, the heart that beat for us all and drove him on to accomplishments hitherto unprecedented for a horse, is to be found at the National Museum of Australia in Canberra.

Unless it doesn't. The heart in Canberra has been declared a fake by journalist Peter Luck: a TV interview Luck conducted with the daughter of the vet who performed Phar Lap's first post-mortem contained the claim that the heart was destroyed in the autopsy and the museum's organ is of an anonymous draught horse. But museum visitors get to see a really big horse's heart, and who can ask for anything more? Let's hold on to the myth – let's not allow Peter Luck to ruin our happiness any more than he already has.

The provenance of a heart is hardly important anyway, of course: the main thing is that this beautiful, gentle animal continues to capture the public's imagination in ways that border on the disturbing.

Phar Lap came along at a time when Australia needed a lift. Spirits sagging, morale plunging, we were craving a hero, and we got one. In just five years he won the hearts of millions and turned the sport of racing into something more than just a vortex of despair for gambling addicts and a front for organised crime. If the Great Depression placed the country in the grip of the black dog, it was the chestnut horse who proudly kicked that dog to death. And he did it all without ever once having the slightest clue that he was doing it, a much more selfless career than all the so-called 'role models' whose success is tainted by self-awareness. Truly, no hero has ever been purer, or nobler, or more quadrupedal, than the testicularly challenged champion they named 'Lightning'.

FUN FOR YOU AT HOME: Buy a horse! Head to the Yearling Sales and bid on a horse of your choosing. Try to get the best one you can for what you can afford. Take the horse home. Regret buying it? This is very common.

HOWARD FLOREY
Sweatin' to the Mouldies

HAVE YOU EVER really looked at mould? Try it now: go look at the mould on the bread in your kitchen. Take a look at the mould in your bathroom. Examine the mould growing on your walls and ceilings. You probably never paid much attention to this mould before, but now you're looking more closely, you'll probably realise something quite interesting: your house is disgusting.

What you *won't* realise is how to use that mould to save millions of lives, because you are not a farsighted scientific genius. Thankfully for the rest of us, Howard Walter Florey, Baron Florey, OM[132], FRS[133], FRCP[134] *was* such a genius, and when he looked at mould, he saw all sorts of possibilities that had nothing to do with your squalid living arrangements.

The Howard Florey story[135] begins, as practically no other great story ever has, in Adelaide[136]. It was here that young Howard, son of an English boot-maker, first developed his love of putting

132 'Old Man'.

133 'Frigging Rad Scientist'.

134 'Friendly Rabbits Call the Police' – a useful mnemonic.

135 Handy rhyme, there. Why hasn't there been a musical about Florey yet?

136 A city that to this day has more giant pandas per capita than any other Australian metropolis.

unpleasant substances into people to see what would happen. Stories abound[137] of the lad finding stray cats or dogs or slow-moving classmates, and force-feeding them various fungi and expired food, while taking meticulous notes on the results. Who knows how many died to sate Florey Jr's grisly curiosity? Yet in the end the benefits of an inquiring mind would amaze the world.

Florey's iron-willed determination to interfere with human bodies led him to study medicine at the University of Adelaide[138], where he met Mary Ethel Hayter Reed, a fellow medical student and aspiring millstone. He was immediately attracted to her keen, inquiring mind and coquettish way of repeatedly contracting pleurisy, and romance soon bloomed between the students. From 1920 to 1926, Howard would write Mary Ethel 153 letters, but she ignored the blatant red flag that this dangerously obsessive behaviour was throwing up, and eventually they were married and embarked upon four long decades of making each other miserable. The marriage was soured both by Ethel's poor health – as well as her pleural problems, she suffered from otosclerosis, an abnormal bone growth in the middle ear that gradually sent her deaf – and by Howard's intolerance, which was sort of understandable: it's not a great look when you win a Nobel Prize for Medicine but your wife's at home coughing up a lung and replacing the batteries in her hearing aid. Also, he found that living with a woman is a much bigger hassle than writing letters to one, especially when she keeps taking up all the blankets.

But before Florey was married, he went to England to take up a Rhodes Scholarship[139] at Oxford University, chest swelling

137 Mainly made up by me, admittedly.

138 Motto: 'Ample parking'.

139 Founded by Cecil Rhodes in order to win a bet against a friend who claimed he couldn't possibly get more racist than he already was.

with pride at having achieved the same thing that Tony Abbott would one day. At Oxford he received his BA[140] and MA[141], and learnt many useful medical facts such as what a pancreas does and how to bandage a head. From Oxford he went to Cambridge, an unforgivable act of betrayal, and attained a PhD[142].

After completing his stint at Cambridge, Florey spent time in America before moving to London, driven by his gnawing terror of going back to the constantly-coughing Ethel. His plans were foiled when Ethel took it upon herself to come to London, and they were married in 1926. From that point on, Howard really threw himself into his work, realising there wasn't much point doing anything else. Ironically, in all his years of incredible medical breakthroughs, he never did figure out a way to make Ethel better, and while I'm not implying anything, if you find that suspicious I can't stop you.

In 1927, Florey began lecturing at Cambridge, while working on his doctoral thesis on the flow of blood and lymph. If successful, he hoped to answer once and for all the great question of modern medicine: what is 'lymph'? Is it an organ? A tree? A spice? It was while he was at Cambridge that a momentous event, that would change Florey's life forever, and with which he was completely uninvolved, occurred at St Mary's Hospital in London.

Sir Alexander Fleming had served in World War One, where he had seen many men die and reached the conclusion that this was a bad thing. Subsequently he had dedicated his life to fighting bacteria, which on the surface seems an unfair fight – Fleming was, after all, much bigger than the bacteria – but it needs to be remembered that the bacteria outnumbered him by millions. It's like the old conundrum: would you rather be attacked by a single

140 Baracus.

141 Massachussetts.

142 Phantastic Doctor.

elephant, or by 50 weasels? It's impossible to choose definitively, although it probably depends on the terrain.

After Fleming's advice that antiseptics used to treat battlefield wounds were making things worse rather than better was roundly ignored by wartime doctors who lacked his puritanical desire to see his patients not die in agony, he had continued his work at St Mary's, spending his time investigating mucus and wondering whether it was all worth it.

The date 28 September 1928 was notable as being the day that, according to Fleming, 'I certainly didn't plan to revolutionise all medicine'[143]. Yet in one of those funny twists of fate that happen almost every day, his plan to not revolutionise all medicine went hopelessly awry, and he ended up revolutionising all medicine instead – a complete reversal of every previous day, when he *had* planned to revolutionise all medicine, but then accidentally didn't. Having left a stack of cultures of staphylococci lying around like the messy pig he was, Fleming found that one of them had become contaminated with a fungus, which had apparently destroyed the staphylococci colonies closest to it. 'That's funny,'[144] said Fleming, who was notorious for his terrible sense of humour, and went on to grow the fungus, finding that it killed some kinds of bacteria. He named the substance released by the mould 'penicillin', having rejected his original name, 'mould juice'[145], and satisfied that he had finally done enough to earn the knighthood that would make the name 'Sir Alexander Fleming' seem less inappropriate, he went on to do not very much for many years. He had discovered penicillin, but like the man who invented the frankfurter but had to wait for the invention of the hot dog bun, it would be up to others to make real practical use of his discovery.

143 Genuine quote. Write it down.

144 Another one!

145 Seriously, he called it mould juice for months. What a knob.

Enter Florey. Driven by his twin passions of scientific discovery and working long hours to avoid his wheezy deaf wife, the plucky young Australian was making great advances in experimental pathology, although his quest to identify the nature of lymph remained fruitless. In 1935 he was made professor of pathology at the Sir William Dunn School of Pathology at Oxford – named after Sir William Dunn, 1st Baronet of Lakenheath, one of the most prominent of the famous 'Uninteresting Men' of the 19th century – and began assembling his dream team of pathologists.

The most important among these was Ernst Boris Chain, a German-born biochemist who had pursued a scientific career after discovering that he looked a bit like Einstein and figuring there was no point fighting destiny. Chain had left Germany to dodge the Gestapo, and history has vindicated this decision. His judgment of matters scientific was just as good as his judgment of the advisability of fleeing secret police forces, and Chain formed a superb team with Florey, despite what was described as the German's 'difficult personality': Florey was well experienced with difficult personalities anyway, having been raised in Adelaide. In the remarkable discoveries that were to follow, Chain played an integral part, but often goes unnoticed because, unlike Florey, he was not Australian, and therefore not as good.

Florey began his work on penicillin in 1938 when he read Fleming's work regarding the miraculous mould and decided it'd be a bit of a laugh if he took a bit of this mould and started sticking it into people. Obviously this was a ridiculous idea, but they were starved for amusements down at the School of Pathology and had to make their own fun.

The first person he stuck it into was a man named Albert Alexander, a police constable who had scratched his mouth on a rose thorn[146] and suffered a horrific infection as a result. When he came to the attention of Florey's team, his face and scalp had swollen grotesquely à la Jeff Goldblum in David Cronenberg's *The Fly* – he had had an eye removed[147] to relieve some of the pain of the abscesses covering his head.

Florey and Chain had been concerned about the possible side effects that large doses of penicillin might have on a human patient, so they were quite happy to find one in such a bad way that there was literally no chance of them making him any worse. As it happened, the old mould juice worked a treat, dropping the constable's temperature and beginning to heal his infection. Unfortunately, Florey's team then discovered they didn't have enough penicillin to keep treating him, and Alexander died: his last words reportedly, 'Oh, you are KIDDING me.'

The tragic end of Albert Alexander was very encouraging to Florey and Chain, cold-blooded sons of bitches that they were. As Florey himself once said:

> *People sometimes think that I and the others worked on penicillin because we were interested in suffering humanity. I don't think it ever crossed our minds about suffering humanity. This was an interesting scientific exercise, and because it was of some use in medicine is very gratifying, but this was not the reason that we started working on it.*

How cold is *that*? There's your hero, Australia: he never cared about you. He never cared at all. Where is your god NOW, science fans?

---

146 Your guess is as good as mine.

147 Please remember this when you're deciding how grateful you should be to Howard Florey – people without penicillin got a scratch from a rose and had to have their eyes removed *to relieve pain.*

Anyway, the point is, the fact that the penicillin had, to some extent, worked, was a good sign, but the fact there hadn't been enough to actually save the guy's life was chalked up as a negative. With the difficulty of producing penicillin in mind, Florey decided to concentrate on treating children, who needed less penicillin to treat them, and whose bodies would be easier to hide if things went wrong. These treatments, however, were a success, and Florey's experiments did not result in mass child-murder, although as the man himself stressed, he wouldn't have really minded if they had.

Florey, Chain, and whoever the other nobodies on the research team were kept working, intent on making it possible for penicillin to be produced on a large scale. Major mould production was, to the surprise of everyone who knew how damp their houses were, beyond the capabilities of British industry, but in what had become a bit of a theme in World War Two, the Americans stepped up to the plate[148], and by 1945 penicillin was being produced for the treatment of war casualties. The results were stunning: penicillin was hailed as a miracle drug as it saved what would, over the subsequent years, become millions and millions of lives.

Florey's greatest work, his medicinal masterpiece, was complete: he had achieved his dream of undertaking an interesting scientific exercise without any interest in how it could benefit anyone else. The world of science looked in awe upon him, as a titan who had changed the world irrevocably in ways that frankly he found rather tedious.

For his brilliantly selfish work, Florey was awarded the Nobel Prize in Physiology or Medicine[149] in 1945, sharing the honour with

---

148 Irritating many patriotic Britons who would've preferred a cricketing metaphor.

149 For Christ's sake, pick ONE, Nobel guys.

Ernst Chain, and also with Alexander Fleming, who really did some serious coat-tail-riding here.

The awards and honours kept flowing for Florey[150], although none of them were really as impressive as the Nobel: he was appointed a Knight Bachelor in what most observers saw as a deliberate slap in the face to Ethel; in 1947 the Royal Society of Medicine awarded him a Gold Medal in the mistaken belief that medicine is an Olympic event. Before this, in 1945, he had won the Lister Medal, an award given by the Royal College of Surgeons to recognise the practitioner whose contributions to surgical science most remind one of Lister from *Red Dwarf*. In 1946 he gained France's Legion of Honour, and in 1948 America's Medal of Merit. In 1958 Florey became president of the Royal Society, and in 1962 Provost of The Queen's College, Oxford, a position that mainly required him to lock up at the end of the day and call a plumber when the shower broke. In 1965 he was appointed a life peer[151] and gained the title Baron Florey of Adelaide and Marston, County of Oxford, which all seems a bit over the top if you ask me.

During these years he also played a major role in establishing the Australian National University – of which he became chancellor in 1965 – and during his tenure as Royal Society president he reorganised the society and expanded its research-professorship program. All this while he authored or co-authored two hundred scientific papers and played tennis into his fifties – many historians believe Howard Florey's tennis career gets nowhere near as much attention as it deserves, just like Andre Agassi's work in biochemical engineering.

Florey's achievements guaranteed him scientific and historical immortality, but literal immortality remained just beyond his grasp,

---

150 As did the mould juice.

151 A more desirable honour than the dreaded Death Peer.

a fact that became starkly apparent with a fatal heart attack in 1968, two years after Ethel passed away and one year after he married his research assistant Margaret Jennings, the old waiting game having finally paid off for Our Howard. Might Florey's death have been avoided if he had tried harder to find the right kind of mould to rub on his heart to stop it attacking itself? We'll never know.

Florey kept on piling up honours in his typically greedy way even after he died: from 1973 to 1995 his face was on the fifty-dollar note (1995 being the year when the Australian government decided that saving 82 million lives wasn't really that big a deal), and his name is carried by the suburb of Florey in Canberra, the Florey Institute of Neuroscience and Mental Health[152] at the University of Melbourne, the Florey Lecture Theatre at the University of Adelaide, and the Lord Florey Student Prize, given by the Australian government to outstanding school-leavers[153]. In England, the Royal Berkshire Hospital contains a Florey Unit, and the University of Sheffield's Faculty of Medicine has a Lord Florey Chair. To put it bluntly: the guy's name is just freaking everywhere today, nearly 50 years after he died, and that says something.

Florey's legacy is enormous, and not in that slightly fake way that we have to pretend other people's legacies are after they die even though actually they barely have any legacy at all. Like, when some guy dies who was Agriculture Minister about a million years ago and people are all like, 'he made a lasting impact on Australian parliamentary government' but actually he never did anything. Florey wasn't like that guy at all: not only was he never Agriculture Minister, he actually did a huge, huge thing; and if it's true he had

---

152 I'm not sure what Florey has to do with mental health, unless it's something to do with Ethel.

153 I'd rather give awards to kids who STAY at school, but nobody listens to me.

lots of help from other brilliant people, it's also true we see no reason to give a shit about any of them.

Sir Robert Menzies said, 'In terms of world well-being, Florey was the most important man ever born in Australia', and Menzies did not say this lightly: he was quite aware of the existence of Bert Newton. It's hard to even fathom the massive effect Florey had on the world: in making an effective drug out of Fleming's accidental mould, he saved millions of lives and made antibiotics a thing, which led to some pretty terrible consequences down the road but was probably a pretty good result all in all. This passionate, inspired, hardworking, impatient, grouchy, somewhat insufferable man, born in humble circumstances in sleepy Adelaide, ended up having a more profound effect on the twentieth century than almost anyone else who didn't actually commit genocide, and the fact he did it despite not being especially interested in doing it makes it even more admirable, in a way, and less admirable in another way. So it all balances out.

FUN FOR YOU AT HOME: Do you have mould in your house? Collect as much of it as you can and eat it. Make a chart to record which bits of mould provide fantastic medical benefits, and which ones don't. You can use coloured cardboard!

ERROL FLYNN
The Heterosexual Blade

IN THE 1930s, an Australian movie star was an unusual sight. Annette Kellerman had set a precedent for Aussies in Hollywood, but a career in film remained an absurd thing for most Antipodean youngsters to dream of. In the suburbs of Hobart in Tasmania, locals would have reacted with scornful and slightly cruel laughter if you'd suggested that anyone from those parts would become a legend of the silver screen. If you'd claimed that a Hobart boy would not only find fame in Hollywood, but also become the world's greatest sex symbol, their laughter would become even more derisive. If you'd then asserted that the same lad would one day be charged with statutory rape, they'd probably have stopped laughing and said, 'Yeah, that sounds more like Hobart'. Still, as a whole, the story would seem pretty unlikely.

Yet it is all true: Errol Leslie Flynn, born in Hobart in 1909, grew up into a fine strapping lad who thrilled millions of moviegoers and bedded almost as many women in his short 50 years of life. No Tasmanian has ever been so famous, and besides David Boon, no Tasmanian has ever been so handsome. So remarkable was Flynn's career that when you read that he came from Tasmania it's worth checking to see whether it was a typo.

Contemporary depiction of Bennelong; latter-day historians dispute the picture's accuracy, citing evidence that Bennelong had a neck.

Sheep-obsessive John Macarthur after winning the All-Sydney Highest Stiffest Collar Championship.

Statue of John Batman in Melbourne, showing the pioneer engaged in his favourite hobby of Sudoku.

Henry Parkes sighs with frustration at the length of that year's 'Naughty List'.

Caroline Chisholm plans her next assault on fragile masculinity.

Mary MacKillop showing off her famous ‘come hither eyes’.

Albert Jacka, VC. Not shown: pile of dead Turks.

Climactic scene of *The Story of the Kelly Gang*, remade years later as *RoboCop*.

Land rights activist Vincent Lingiari wondering who the weird old white guy who keeps following him around is. *Image by A.K. Hanna.*

Annette Kellerman in her bathing suit, avoiding the collapse of moral fibre that would be occasioned by bare calves.

Errol Flynn, pictured here thinking about vaginas.

Prime Minister John Curtin. Out of shot: middle finger directed at Winston Churchill.

Educated in Hobart, then London and Sydney's Shore School, Flynn was expelled from the latter for theft and, according to him, for having sex with a laundress – an early example of Flynn's willingness to flout social conventions and make up ridiculous lies. Gaining a job as a clerk with a shipping firm, he was fired for stealing from them as well, and a pattern of behaviour was starting to emerge that did not augur well for a future career in acting: although sport still seemed a viable path.

Knowing that he risked throwing his life away on petty crimes, young Errol realised that the only way to save himself was to go immediately to Papua New Guinea. It worked: historical records show that after his stint in New Guinea, Errol Flynn rarely if ever stole from either schools or shipping companies.

In PNG Flynn was trying to make a living in tobacco and metals, but it soon became clear how unsatisfying this would be to anyone reading his biography in future years, and he returned to Australia to plant the seeds of a legend. In 1933, he appeared in the film *In The Wake of the Bounty*, based on the famous American movie that was made two years after it, in a hitherto-unexplained case of cinematic time travel. Flynn played Fletcher Christian, an apt role as he too was a good-looking rebel who would travel around the world committing crimes. Finding that he enjoyed acting even more than theft, he went to England, the Papua New Guinea of the North, and joined the Northampton Repertory Company, one of Britain's foremost producers of little-seen, poorly-staged plays. After working and training at Northampton for seven months, he was dismissed, not for stealing, but for throwing a female stage manager down the stairs, which showed versatility if not exactly progress.

Free of the stiflingly repressive, anti-assault atmosphere of Northampton, Flynn headed for Warner Bros's London studios and won the lead role in *Murder at Monte Carlo*, a mystery thriller now classified as a 'lost film', meaning for all we know it never even existed. But if it did, it seems likely that it involved a murder, and that the murder occurred in Monte Carlo. Flynn played a journalist who doesn't want his fiancée to come to Monte Carlo, but she comes anyway because women are incorrigible, and she ends up solving the murder and making Flynn look a right old duffer. Upon which, Flynn steals her wallet and throws her out a window. Probably. It's a lost film, we can make up any plot twists we feel like really.

Having not only become a leading man, but cunningly arranged for the film to become lost, therefore preventing anyone from knowing if he was any good, Flynn headed to America, with a contract with Warner Bros and a dream in his heart. The dream had nothing to do with acting and involved large numbers of nude teens, but it was definitely in his heart.

Flynn's first lead in Hollywood was in *Captain Blood*, the swashbuckling tale of Richmond footballer Jack Dyer – or according to some cinephiles, a movie about a doctor who becomes a pirate. The role of Doctor Peter Blood, an innocent Irishman forced into wrongdoing by the corruption of the Crown, was originally meant for Robert Donat, but Donat turned the role down due to his asthma[154]. This health-conscious but career-sabotaging decision was to be the making of Errol Flynn as a movie star, and may be one of the main reasons why today, you have no idea who Robert Donat is. In the role of Blood's beautiful love interest, Warner Bros chose Olivia de Havilland, then just 19, and so began a fruitful on-screen partnership. De Havilland and Flynn would co-star in eight movies, and fall in love, although de Havilland claimed the relationship was not consummated due to Flynn's marriage, a story that anyone who has ever heard of Errol Flynn will find incredibly

154 He actually did. Ventolin wouldn't be along for decades yet.

unconvincing – all available evidence indicates that Errol Flynn never had a relationship with a female that he didn't consummate, and that is not necessarily restricted to the human species.

Not that Flynn wasn't keen on marriage – he was married three times in all, and apparently enjoyed it, especially given the total lack of restraint his marriages imposed on his sexual activities. His marriages – to actress Lili Damita from 1935-1942, actress Nora Eddington from 1943-1949 and actress Patrice Wymore from 1950-his death – made it clear that he definitely had a 'type'. Some people think that type was 'actresses', but actually it was 'women with a detectable pulse'[155].

Captain Blood was a huge success. The combination of Flynn's good looks, thrilling action sequences, and then those two things a few more times, made for a cracking adventure romp – just what America was looking for to cheer it up amid the hardships of the Depression and the hideously ugly faces of its own young men.

Flynn specialised in exhilarating on-screen sword fights. If World War One had taught the world that Australians were better at fighting than anyone else, Flynn was quickly teaching the world that they were also better at pretending to fight than anyone else, except Basil Rathbone – but he was: a) not as handsome as Errol; and b) called 'Basil', which is a terrible name for a swordfighter no matter how good he is. After *Captain Blood*, Flynn teamed up with that film's director, Michael Curtiz, again in *The Charge of the Light Brigade,* in which he played a courageous British officer who overcomes his low body mass to stick swords into evildoers from India to Russia. Curtiz and Flynn kept up the derring-do with *The Prince and the Pauper,* in which Flynn played a courageous British nobleman who overcomes a confusing plot to stick swords into other, less courageous British noblemen.

155 Although he was willing to be flexible on that requirement if need be.

Curtiz and Flynn, realising that they were onto a good thing with each other – Flynn's ability to waggle a sword and cause feminine dampness perfectly complementing Curtiz's ability to point a camera in the correct direction – decided they had reached that point in every creative artist's career when he needs to make a timeless classic beloved of people of all ages forever. There was only one option open to them: *The Adventures of Robin Hood.*

Often when Australia's contribution to the world of cinema is discussed, it's overlooked that while yes, Heath Ledger was an amazing Joker, and yes, Nicole Kidman was pretty good as the lady with the big nose, and yes, Isla Fisher was fine in *Arrival*, Australia also gave the world its definitive Robin Hood. There may have been better actors in the world than Errol Flynn, but there's never been a more Robin Hood-ish one. *The Adventures of Robin Hood* is, frankly, one of the most awesome movies ever made, and even today it still stands up as a magnificent adventure, as long as you have decent taste in movies. It's one of those movies that is so incredibly cool it manages to completely transcend all the bits of terrible writing and acting in it. Like magic.

The Adventures of Robin Hood is the tale of Robin of Locksley, a noble Saxon whose passion for justice leads him to turn outlaw in rebellion against the evil Normans and their snivelling leader Prince John. In this he is aided by his Merry Men, including the statuesque Little John, the rotund, frog-voiced Friar Tuck, the talentless human blobfish Much The Miller's Son[156], and Will Scarlet, who is just sort of there. By the simple expedient of shooting arrows, having swordfights, and carrying deer on his back in a particularly witty way, Robin manages to overthrow John's wicked regime, and slay

156 And nobody's ever answered to my satisfaction the question: is he the son of a miller called Much; or is he a man called Much whose father is a miller; or is it as simple as an excessive example of a miller's son?

the evil Guy of Gisborne and his creepy hooded eyelids. Moreover, he wins the heart of the fair Maid Marian (played by his good platonic friend de Havilland), who starts the movie as a big Norman fangirl, but turns to the Saxon side after discovering how good Robin is with his blade. Not that Guy *isn't* good with his blade – he was played by the aforementioned swordmaster Basil Rathbone – but his receding hairline is no match for Errol Flynn's figure-hugging tights. In the end, justice prevails over tyranny and the good people of England are free to enjoy the benevolent stewardship of King Richard the First for the six months of his ten-year reign that he was actually in England. This was just one of the millions of historical facts that *The Adventures of Robin Hood* ignored, because when you have a star as sexy as Errol Flynn who gives a shit about history?[157]

Flynn had defied all those who claimed that an Australian could never effectively portray an English icon, and although this would lead years later to the tragedy that was George Lazenby as James Bond, it was still a mighty blow for Aussie pride and all the Australian children who dreamt that they may one day transcend their origins to swing on a vine and sass Claude Rains.

Funnily enough, Flynn didn't tend to refer to himself as Australian, preferring to call himself Irish. His father had been a professor at the Queen's University of Belfast, although this seems a pretty flimsy reason to claim ancestry – my father used to be a photographer at rodeos but I don't go around calling myself a cowboy. Flynn's fellow Australian icon Ned Kelly also called himself Irish, of course, but unlike Kelly, Flynn has not been portrayed in numerous biopics by actors doing bad Irish accents.

Robin Hood cemented Flynn in the pantheon of Hollywood legends, but he did not rest on his laurels. In *The Dawn Patrol*, he

157 Seriously: who? I want to know.

played a courageous British fighter pilot forced to get up early. In *Dodge City*, he played against type, departing from his usual courageous British roles to depict a courageous Irishman who shoots as many people as possible and ends up sharing yet another hearty handshake with Olivia de Havilland. In *The Private Lives of Elizabeth and Essex*, he returned to his comfort zone as a courageous British Earl who bangs an old Queen and then gets his head cut off. In *The Sea Hawk* he played a courageous British pirate who sticks it up some Spaniards good and proper.

Flynn's career was going from strength to strength, and he was now amassing sexual partners at an estimated rate of sixteen women for every dollar grossed by one of his films. The only dark cloud on the horizon was World War Two, although as he was in the movie business it wasn't that dark: it gave screenwriters some fantastic new material to work with. To this day, movies are being made about World War Two, to the point where if it hadn't happened, Warner Bros would've had to stage it.

Flynn became a naturalised American citizen in 1942, taking his place in a long and proud tradition of great Australians who are ashamed of their own nationality. He also attempted to enlist in the army – in 1937 he had travelled to Spain as a war correspondent during the Spanish Civil War, and had there developed a powerful thirst for making recklessly poor choices – but ran into an obstacle, in that physically speaking he was an utter disaster area. His physical examination revealed chronic back pain, multiple heart problems including at least one heart attack – bear in mind that he was 33 years old at this time – chronic tuberculosis, recurrent malaria contracted in Papua New Guinea, and a multitude of venereal diseases which could not have surprised anyone. Essentially Errol Flynn was the real-life analogue of Mr Burns from *The Simpsons* when he goes to the doctor and is informed 'you have everything':

and like the elderly cartoon billionaire, the only explanation for Flynn even being alive seems to be that all his illnesses were balancing each other out. Not that I'm a doctor, but having malaria, tuberculosis, heart disease and multiple-VD does not seem like a recipe for sustained metabolic processes. And that's before we get to the fact that he was self-medicating for his back pain with morphine and, later, heroin.

It's easy to look aghast at Flynn's physical state and be shocked at the self-destructive lifestyle that had led him to this point. But if you know of any other consumptive malarial syphilitic junkie heart attack sufferers managing to make a decent living as action movie stars, name them. Plus, with all those horrendous health problems, he was still cutting a stunningly athletic swathe through Hollywood's female population. I think any fair-minded person would, if they could, give the man a high-five. Before assiduously washing their hand, obviously.

Although Flynn's physical decrepitude was a big plus for him, inasmuch as it prevented him from fighting in World War Two, which most sources indicate was one of the more dangerous wars to be in, it had a downside in terms of publicity. Warner Bros had invested quite a lot in positioning the Taswegian Tyro as a swashbuckler: a dashing, rollicking, rope-swinging, rapier-wielding, quick-witted rake, with muscles of iron and the strength of 10 tigers. He was, in summary, presented as the platonic ideal of manhood, a physical specimen without peer. Wide public knowledge of the amount of opiates being pumped into his system to help his bad back, and the unruly mob of deadly diseases milling ominously around his internal organs, was not likely to be an asset in the promotion of this image.

Luckily, all this was happening in the 1940s, when it was still possible for celebrities to live a lie in peace. If studios could avoid letting the public know about the several hundred of their stars who were gay, Warner Bros wasn't about to let Errol Flynn's disintegrating body cause trouble. They simply didn't tell anyone, and if the movie-going public wondered why Flynn wasn't fighting in the war while so many of his fellow movie stars were, the movie-going public could suck it up and watch the pretty pictures.

Possibly more damaging to Flynn's public reputation was the charge of statutory rape levelled at him by Betty Hansen and Peggy Satterlee in 1942. His romantic screen persona was slightly dented by the allegation that he made a habit of seducing schoolgirls, although his most passionate fans never lost faith in him: the American Boys' Club for the Defense of Errol Flynn, or 'ABCDEF', was just one of the organisations – albeit the one with the objectively worst name – formed to stand up for Flynn's good name. In the end Flynn was acquitted, thanks to his attorney's good work in portraying his accusers as the bad kind of schoolgirl[158].

Thanks to the efforts of Flynn's fellow Australian supermen at Tobruk, Kokoda and various other places, World War Two was eventually won, and Flynn celebrated by writing a novel. Titled *Showdown*, it was a romantic adventure based on his experiences in New Guinea, and its cover depicted a handsome young man carrying an unconscious woman while Flynn's gigantic smiling head floats in the air next to him. Judging from this, it can safely be assumed that it is about a heroic man who travels to New Guinea to help fight the female fainting epidemic, but is plagued by a handsome giant head that follows him everywhere he goes. The working title was *Charlie Bow-Tie Proceeds*, so we can also assume that there was a certain element of incredible stupidity involved. For the novel, he earnt $184,000, which equates to over $2 million in today's money, a statistic that probably makes all aspiring novelists

158 Or the good kind, depending on your point of view.

feel really good about the strong sense of justice that has always been innate to the publishing industry.

It was a good time for Flynn to be raking in some big bucks – his book deal was followed by a 15-year contract with Warner Bros worth $225,000 per film. In hindsight this seems like a pretty reckless move from the studio, which not only failed to account for changing tastes in movies, but also for the extreme improbability of Flynn living for another 15 years. Had anyone at Warner had the slightest capacity for foresight, the deal would not have been made, but to Flynn's delight, it was, and yet again a plucky young Australian got one over on the fat cats.

The foolishness of Warner Bros quickly became apparent, as the American public, shaken by the war and haunted by the corruptibility of mankind, developed an interest in gritty realism and film noir[159]. Suddenly Errol Flynn, a suave rogue who specialised in playing historical heroes with a line in damsel-rescuing and villain-skewering, was decidedly passé, as tastes shifted to unshaven creeps doing dubious things in shadows and mild-mannered everymen turning to a life of crime on the basis of dames with hair over one eye and gams that went all the way up.

The irony, of course, was that in real life, Errol Flynn *was* a creep doing dubious things in shadows. You could make a great film noir about him, but he was terrible at playing moral ambiguity, and the late 40s fashion for men to not hold swords was death to his popular appeal. He tried to reinvent himself as a complex man of shady motivations in movies like *Cry Wolf* and *Uncertain Glory*, but his success in this can be gauged by a quick assessment of whether you've ever heard of those movies.

It was at this point that Flynn's tendency to forego restraint started to tell against him. Much as he couldn't just have malaria

159 French for 'Black films', e.g. *Boyz N The Hood*, *Big Mama's House*, etc.

and tuberculosis, but had to pile venereal disease and heart attacks on top, he now also demonstrated that he could never be satisfied with simply declining as a box-office draw: he felt the need to compound the problem by also becoming a complete pain in the arse to everyone he worked with. It's possible the dip in public adulation was bringing out the bad old Errol, the one who liked to steal things and throw people down stairs. Whatever the reason, his behaviour during filming worsened to the extent that studio boss Jack Warner[160] released him from his contract.

Washed-up, riddled with disease, and with both his savings and his access to nubile starlets drying up, Flynn sunk into the deepest of funks. He had made millions as a movie star, but lost much of it through poor investments such as *The Story of William Tell*, a film in which he planned to star and to that end ploughed $430,000[161] into its production. Flynn hoped to re-establish himself as a major star in the role of Tell, the Swiss hero who inspired his countrymen by skilfully not shooting his son in the head; but the production fell victim to the one ironclad law of Hollywood: to make a hit movie, you must first make a movie. *The Story of William Tell* was never completed, which put a major crimp in plans to release it, and Flynn did his dough.

And so, his career as a heart-throb basically over, Flynn embarked on a new career as a sad fat old drunk. Spending his days sailing in his yacht, the *Zaca* – a former Navy vessel that, like its owner, had once been of much more use to society – his new lifestyle saw him add hepatitis to his dizzying array of ailments. In

---

160 Whose position on the moral high ground had been established by his serial philandering, and then consolidated by his destruction of the careers of screenwriters who he named as Communist sympathisers to the House Un-American Activities Committee. A solid citizen.

161 In today's money, $431,000.

1958 he went to Cuba to make *Cuban Rebel Girls* and met Fidel Castro, becoming an enthusiastic supporter of the Cuban revolution in a development which kind of took everyone by surprise[162]. His last acting work was *Cuban Story: The Truth About Fidel Castro's Revolution*, a short which he narrated in 1959.

That same year he died in Vancouver, British Columbia, while on a trip to negotiate the lease of his yacht to stave off financial disaster. After complaining of severe back and leg pain, he passed away in Vancouver General Hospital, with 'heart attack' winning the competitive sweepstake as to what would end up killing him. The greatest swashbuckler Tasmania had ever produced was gone, aged just 50.

Into a relatively short life, Errol Flynn packed more living than most could manage with twice as long, particularly if 'living' is here considered synonymous with 'being in movies and banging chicks'. In an era when rock music didn't even exist, he led a life that would've made Mötley Crüe emit low whistles of admiration – heavy drinking, chain smoking and drug abuse combined with an epic volume of sexual conquests. His rumoured partners included Lupe Vélez, Marlene Dietrich, Dolores del Rio, and almost every other woman who passed within a hundred feet of a movie set in the 30s or 40s. One of his biographers also claimed that he had numerous affairs with men, but in all fairness it should be pointed out that he probably made this up. It was also claimed, by the son of L. Ron Hubbard, founder of Scientology, that Hubbard and Flynn enjoyed many happy hours of drug smuggling and sex with underage girls together, a story that is just insane enough to be entirely in character.

After Flynn's death, his autobiography, *My Wicked Wicked Ways* was published. It was a compellingly blunt depiction of old

162 Flynn's support, that is. Although, the revolution itself also.

Hollywood, an unflinching stripping of the veil from Tinseltown to reveal the sordid reality behind the glamour. *Newsweek* described Flynn's book as 'unsparing of himself or anyone else': overall it seems to have been better-received than *Showdown*, despite lacking the giant head or Charlie Bow-Tie. As the final testament of a legendary pants man, it seems an apt note to leave on.

Errol Flynn never fought in a war, made a scientific breakthrough, or made landmark achievements in human rights. He is rarely listed among Australia's greatest artists: but if he was not the world's greatest actor, no man has ever more perfectly epitomised the concept of 'movie star'. For a boy from Tasmania to grow up to light up the big screen and electrify audiences around the world is a fairytale worthy of one of Flynn's movies: once Errol had been in town, nobody could deny that Australians could sell movie tickets and lift skirts with the best of them. The phrase 'in like Flynn' sums up his exploits as a womaniser: to sum up his legacy as an actor, one need only note that thanks to him, in the mind's eye of the world, Robin Hood will forever be Australian.

FUN FOR YOU AT HOME: Make your own Robin Hood costume. Stage your own archery contest. Steal from your own local government authorities. Foment rebellion amongst your own neighbours. Flee to the woods to live as a criminal. Reflect on the inaccurate impressions movies can instil in us.

JOHN CURTIN
The Iron Curtin

AT FIRST GLANCE, John Curtin doesn't necessarily seem like an Australian hero. Looking at a photo of the former Prime Minister, you're most immediately struck by his resemblance to a particularly pedantic vice-principal, or the grandfather you always hated visiting and compared unfavourably to your other grandfather, the *fun* grandfather. Few men in Australian history have looked less likely to be fun than John Curtin.

But no matter what Peter Helliar tries to tell you, there's more to being Australian than having fun, and John Curtin has a decent claim to not only being the greatest Australian prime minister of all time – yes, even better than Chris Watson – but maybe the greatest Australian of all, if we were to judge greatness by guts, integrity and uncompromising determination to put one's own country first, to never allow the exploitation of your people for the advantage of outside forces.

Curtin's emergence as a giant of history was not inevitable, or even predictable. He had left school at the age of thirteen, and his first foray into politics was a bid for the position of secretary of Brunswick Football Club. He was defeated, and a lesser man would've given up politics at that stage, as would a more realistic man. But Curtin was a dreamer: later he became Secretary of the

Timber Workers' Union, which wasn't as interesting as a football club, but did offer opportunities for advancement.

Curtin was in this position when World War One broke out, and like a skilful screenwriter of his own biopic, he foreshadowed the high principles and refusal to buckle that he would display in World War Two, by actively opposing attempts to impose conscription. He refused to attend a compulsory medical examination, despite knowing he would fail due to his bad eyes. For this bolshieness, he found himself thrown in gaol, earning him the famous nickname, 'the Derryn Hinch of the Great War'. Meanwhile he stood for election in 1914 as the Labor candidate for Balaclava, a failed bid which did not dissuade him from public service as logic may have dictated it should.

During this period, the stress of being a convicted criminal, political loser and short-sighted unionist drove Curtin to drink heavily. His drinking would be a recurring problem throughout his life, but also helped reassure those who doubted his patriotism – there's nothing more Australian than alcoholism.

When Curtin was spending his time fighting for the right of Australian men to refuse to go to war, it probably couldn't be foreseen that he would become the steeliest of wartime leaders. But then it probably couldn't be foreseen that he would become a leader of any kind – in 1925, in Western Australia, he stood for the seat of Fremantle and lost again. In 1928, either too stubborn or too drunk to know when to stop, he tried again, and amazingly won. When Labor took government in 1929, he was in contention to be named to the Cabinet, but Prime Minister James Scullin kept him on the backbench as a result of his drinking habit. In a happy bit of karmic justice, Scullin was then punished for his puritanism by the arrival of the Depression, which most Australians blamed on the government because they were horribly uneducated.

Curtin was kicked out of his seat in 1931 as part of the anti-Scullin backlash that saw Labor electorally obliterated, and then got back into it in 1934 as part of the anti-anti-Scullin backlash that saw Labor slightly un-obliterated. When Scullin resigned as Labor leader, the unions backed Curtin to a surprising victory, on condition that he stop drinking, which was an odd stipulation for unions to make, but this was decades before Bob Hawke.

As Opposition Leader Curtin proved effective, steadily gaining ground on the sarcastically named United Australia Party. The government of Robert Menzies was in turmoil in the early days of World War Two, suffering leadership tensions due to Menzies having not yet become the hard-nosed inflexible bastard he would later become. While in Britain sucking up to Churchill and writing creepy erotic poetry to the Queen, Menzies was deposed as UAP leader and replaced by former prime minister Billy Hughes, a popular patriot whose only drawback as a leader was the fact that he'd technically been dead for twenty years. With this in mind, Hughes was persuaded via Ouija board to allow the prime ministership to go to Arthur Fadden, leader of the Country Party, the junior partner in the ruling coalition.

In modern terms: it's as if after Malcolm Turnbull resigned, the Liberal Party replaced him with John Howard, but he was so old that they let Barnaby Joyce be prime minister. The situation was so untenable that the Fadden government's only hope of remaining in power was a widespread appreciation for comedic performance art among the general public, and it was no surprise to anyone when the parliament's two independents switched their allegiance from the coalition to Labor, and Curtin became prime minister on 7 October 1941. His first act was to announce harsh economic sanctions against the Brunswick Football Club, and his leadership only got stronger and more decisive from there.

As often happens with prime ministers, Curtin's career entered its most notable phase after he became prime minister. Unlike most prime ministers, however, Curtin gained the top job in the middle of a world war, which adds to the degree of difficulty, although at least it gives you an excuse when people accuse you of neglecting superannuation reform. Just two months after Curtin got the top job, Japan rather cheekily bombed Pearl Harbour, causing Curtin to make the solemn announcement to the nation on the radio:

> *Men and women of Australia ... we are at war with Japan. This is the gravest hour of our history. We Australians have imperishable traditions. We shall maintain them. We shall vindicate them. We shall hold this country and keep it as a citadel for the British-speaking race and as a place where civilisation will persist.*

This speech struck a chord in the Australian people, whose hearts were stirred and uplifted by Curtin's eloquence, although they agreed that that bit about the 'British-speaking race' seemed a bit racist. (Mind you, researchers have determined that it remains only the 674th most racist thing ever said by an Australian prime minister.)

It was the outbreak of the war in the Pacific that was to transform John Curtin from ordinary politician to immortal statesman. Up till then, Australian policy with regards to warfare had been fairly consistent: on the beginning of any war, the Cabinet would meet and undertake urgent talks for several minutes before ringing London and asking them what we should do. It wasn't that Australia was a puppet state of Britain, exactly: it was just that the United Kingdom's favourite party trick had always been getting Australia to talk while it drank a glass of water.

After the declaration of war with Japan, Curtin implemented a complete overhaul of this policy. Realising that war in the Pacific meant a direct threat to Australia itself, he told President Roosevelt that Australia would 'gladly accept United States commanders in the Pacific area' to prevent Japan's advance southward. His New Year's message of 1941 stated that 'I make it clear that Australia looks to America, free of any pangs as to our traditional links or kinship with the United Kingdom', stressing that although Britain was facing its own fairly hefty challenges at the time, 'we know … that Australia can go and Britain can still hold on.' In essence, Curtin was telling Britain that it had been a blast, but we'd found someone new, and he was sure that Britain would get over us in time.

Curtin obviously came in for some criticism over his stance, from the many Australians who had long considered Britain to be 'the mother country', and America to be an unbearably vulgar upstart fit only for cowboys and diabetics. Yet two facts could not be denied about America: it had a huge bloody army; and it had an interest in keeping the Pacific free of Japanese rule. Britain, meanwhile, as nice and cosy and liable to hand out Werther's Originals as it was, was quite heavily preoccupied at the time by fighting Germans, and the Pacific was a very long way away.

Nevertheless, the flak flew thick and fast for Curtin: other Australian politicians criticised him for abandoning Australia's special relationship with Britain; Churchill reacted angrily to the news that he'd been friend-zoned; and Roosevelt himself, despite Curtin's clear attempt to butter him up, said that the New Year's speech 'smacked of panic'. But as the old saying goes, better to panic during a speech than while the Japanese are actually swarming over the Harbour Bridge. The possibility that Australia might actually be invaded hadn't been taken seriously till then: Curtin's speech and policy pivot ensured that it would be, and the nation was galvanised to give due attention to its own defence.

As Curtin reoriented the foreign policy settings, his government passed the Statute of Westminster Adoption Act of 1942, an act which formally allowed Australia's governments to act independently of the British government, something that always comes in handy when trying to run an independent nation.

Curtin continued to forge his own path with respect to Australia's defence, determined that nothing would guide his decisions but a commitment to the safety and security of his homeland. The great test of Curtin's defence of the nation came with the fall of Singapore, on 15 February 1942. Singapore was Britain's main military base in South-East Asia, and Japan's invasion of it was cataclysmic for Allied operations in the Pacific. The entire Australian 8th Division was captured – more than 15,000 men – and a huge barrier to Japan's conquest of the Pacific, and a potential invasion of Australia, was removed. If the threat had not hit home starkly enough to the average Australian, this was remedied on the 19 February, when Japan bombed Darwin. This was the first and largest of 97 attacks by Japanese forces on Australian territory, with 242 aircraft taking part and 235 Australians killed. The threat was real, and the attitude that had prevailed in times past, of unshakeable faith that nobody could ever want to attack a country as open and friendly and full of loveable larrikins as us, was no longer sustainable.

Churchill's response to the fall of Singapore was divert the Australian Army's I Corps to reinforce British troops in Burma. Curtin's response to Churchill doing this was to tell him to go fornicate himself. Pointing out that Australia was actually under threat of invasion by the Axis powers, and that the whole point of having an army was to use it to defend your country, the Aussie PM stared down the drunken jowls of his UK counterpart and demanded that the I Corps return to Australia.

John Curtin had done what no previous prime minister had: firmly and unmistakably asserted Australia's right to put its own interests ahead of the old ties of Empire. His position aroused controversy, to be sure, but it was popular: in the 1943 election Labor won what remains its most crushing victory, with a two-party-preferred vote of 58.2 per cent and a 17-seat swing. The Coalition held only 19 seats federally, and the message of the Australian people was clear: we would prefer a government that sticks up for Australian independence than a complete rabble without the faintest idea what it's doing. Interestingly enough, in the twenty-first century the message of the Australian people has evolved to become essentially the exact opposite.

Not that it was only wartime considerations that made Curtin so popular. In a time when he could be forgiven for concentrating solely on the possibility of the forces of totalitarian brutality running rampant through the streets, he still managed to enact progressive reforms to improve the lives of Australians beyond the base standard of not dying in a forced labour camp. Curtin's government introduced pensions for deserted wives and widows, and established the Women's Employment Board that increased women's wages during the war. Curtin also increased Aboriginal entitlements to welfare, raised old age pensions, and extended maternity allowances, in a wild orgy of compassion and consideration for the lives and wellbeing of those less fortunate that frankly verged on Stalinism. Nowadays Curtin would be called out for class warfare, since none of these reforms were balanced by subsidies to coal miners or tax breaks for major corporations. They did, however, involve a Child's Allowance for children dependent on invalid pensioners; exemption from income tax for widow's pensions, pharmaceutical benefits, and eligibility for pensions for Aboriginal people, Pacific Islanders and Asians who were British subjects. It should be noted once again that the government that enacted these and other socially progressive reforms was actually one of the most popular in the nation's history, and was at no point thrown out of office by an electorate furious that retail workers were being paid too much on Sundays.

Curtin's prime ministership had been an unalloyed triumph, one that could scarcely have been suspected back when he was losing multiple elections and drinking himself to death. But on a personal level, the demands of leading a country during wartime were taking their toll. You might suspect that World War Two was a bit of a breeze for the leaders of combatant countries, but actually it was quite hard: Hitler himself was looking a bit haggard by the end of it. John Curtin had also had to battle ructions within his own party, caused by opposition to his change of heart on conscription – in the heat of war and not personally having to go fight, Curtin had abandoned his lifelong opposition to it.

Having endured attacks from within and without, and carried the nation on his shoulders during its most terrifying days, Curtin's health began to deteriorate. He did not live to see the end of the war: on 5 July 1945, 41 days before Japan surrendered, he died at The Lodge. A Catholic priest who came to minister to Curtin was turned away by the Prime Minister, who had been raised a Catholic but as an adult had never once even entered a Catholic church – in religion as in foreign affairs he preferred to stand on his own two feet than rely on outdated alliances. He was just 60 years old. More than 30,000 people crowded into the cemetery for his burial in Perth, with more on the streets outside: in 1945 it's uncertain whether that many people even lived in Perth. Such was the love and affection that Curtin's people had for the man who had guided them through their darkest days.

John Curtin occupies a special place in the hearts of patriotic Australians. In a world in which Australia was seen as a bit player subject to the whims of powerful overlords, he forced other nations to sit up and take notice of a country that would put its own people first and refuse to be pushed around. He kept Australia strong and united throughout the war, and managed to establish a welfare state and a social safety net for millions at the same time. If he failed to epitomise the traditional Australian values of hedonism, apathy and good eyesight, he made up for it in the areas of grace under pressure, steadfast advocacy for his own people, and booze. He was a true Australian hero, even when not judged by the incredibly low standards of the average prime minister.

FUN FOR YOU AT HOME: Hold a mock election among you and your friends. Decide which of you will be an ardent isolationist, which of you will be a depressive alcoholic, and which of you will be the corpse of Billy Hughes. Find out whether democracy is, in fact, a good idea.

WEARY DUNLOP
Practically Perfect in Every Way

IT MAY BE TRUE, as George Patton said, that wars aren't won by dying for your country, but by making the other bastard die for his. But it's also true that there's more to war than making bastards die: indeed there is more to war than winning. The history of warfare is filled with stories that speak of things beyond victory or defeat: the terrible clash of civilisations awakens something in the human spirit beyond base feelings of triumph and humiliation. When mayhem and slaughter spread across the globe, we see the worst of humanity, but every now and then, we also see the best. Which makes it all worth it really, I think.

The story of Sir Ernest Edward 'Weary' Dunlop AC[163] CMG[164] OBE[165] is one that has inspired generations of Australians and cemented the principles of selflessness, compassion, mateship and courage as traditional Australian values that, thanks to men like Dunlop, we can convince ourselves are somehow unique to our own country. More than perhaps anyone in the history of Australian military engagement, Weary Dunlop illustrates the truth that even the bloodiest of global conflicts can, with a bit of

163 Air Conditioned.

164 Catch My Gonorrhea.

165 One Big Egg.

perspective, become the feel-good story of the year.

Many young people today think that Weary Dunlop was the inventor of the Dunlop Volley, a stupid and disrespectful belief that makes me feel I am totally justified in loathing young people, the ignorant little creeps. In all his life, in fact, Weary Dunlop never once designed a sandshoe, and it never held him back one bit. So there is more than one way to be a success in life.

Though not in the field of footwear manufacture, Weary's achievements did include success in the sporting field as well as that of medicine. He was something of a polymath (from the Greek for 'many maths', denoting a man who can count to surprisingly high numbers), and even without the humanitarianism that made him a national icon, would likely have gone down in history as one of this country's most prominent citizens, although not one that you'd necessarily bother putting into a book, which is the true measure of a person's worth[166].

Ernest Edward Dunlop was born in 1907 in Major Plains, a tiny town in Victoria named after a chronic shortage of ideas. Upon finishing school, he began an apprenticeship in pharmacy, reasoning that when you come from Major Plains, your only chance of a fulfilling life is learning how to make your own drugs. He studied at the Victorian College of Pharmacy, learning how to type the little labels, before moving on to the University of Melbourne, gaining a scholarship in medicine. In 1934 he graduated with honours in pharmacy and medicine, meaning he could both prescribe and dispense his own medication, setting him up nicely for an extremely relaxed life.

While at university, Dunlop did as all honourable, decent men do, and took up rugby union[167]. A talented forward, he quickly rose

166 The REALLY valuable people WRITE the books.

167 Aka 'the good sport for smart handsome guys'.

through the ranks, representing Melbourne University's first XV, then his state, and finally his country. He was the first Victorian-born player to make a Wallaby team, a testament to his iconoclastic nature and a powerful reminder of what a rubbish state Victoria is for never having properly appreciated rugby.

Dunlop, incidentally, was already by this time going by the nickname 'Weary', a nickname bestowed on him for reasons that are at best dubious and at worst positively irritating. Basically the logic goes like this: his name is Dunlop, like the tyres; 'tyre' sounds like 'tire'; another word for 'tired' is 'weary'; hence, Weary Dunlop. It's depressing the amount of spare time these people must have had. We could all have great nicknames if we could afford to sit around all day constructing flowcharts to work them out: some of us have jobs.

Speaking of jobs, Weary was in need of one, since he lived in the era when rugby union was a purely amateur sport and there was no money to made from it. Therefore Dunlop enlisted in the army in 1935, gaining a commission as a captain in the Australian Army Medical Corps, the part of the army that fixes up the wounded and de-incentivises combat personnel by giving them a safety net. To really motivate soldiers, it would be smarter to eliminate all medical care, so everyone knew that if they got even a minor wound they would probably just have to lie down and bleed to death. Fortunately for Weary Dunlop this sensible idea had not taken hold in the Australian Defence Force of the 1930s, and the mollycoddling of the troops provided him with a career path. In 1938 Weary sailed to London and attended St Bartholomew's Medical School, even though he'd already been to medical school and finished it – it's uncertain whether the administrators realised that he was trying to double-dip. In London, Weary met the eminent George Grey-Turner and Sir Thomas Dunhill, famous surgeons with much great wisdom to impart to an up-and-comer like himself, such as, 'always check that you haven't dropped your keys in before you close up' and 'if the patient's head falls off, you've cut too far'.

Due to unforgivably poor planning, Dunlop found himself in the army when World War Two broke out. He was dispatched to medical headquarters in the Middle East, where he developed the mobile surgical unit, later to be immortalised in the TV series *M*A*S*H*, starring Alan Alda as Weary. He then moved on to Greece, and later to Tobruk, where Weary worked as senior surgeon to the famous 'Rats', who were in dire need of veterinary treatment.

Weary's work at Tobruk ended when the Australian Divisions were withdrawn as a result of Prime Minister John Curtin's unprecedented plan to use its defence force to defend itself. On the journey home, his troop ship was diverted to Java in an attempt to help stem the Japanese tide currently sweeping through South-East Asia like an especially terrifying broom. He was placed in charge of the No. 1 Allied General Hospital in Bandung and promoted to temporary lieutenant-colonel, while the permanent lieutenant-colonel was off with the mumps.

The attempt to strengthen defences on Java was not effective. The Japanese, as part of their ongoing drive to make the Third Reich look generous and cuddly, slammed into Java in March 1942, capturing Bandung, the hospital, and Weary, in that order.

Weary Dunlop was now a prisoner of war, something that seems like it would be a lot of fun when you watch *Hogan's Heroes*, but in reality, was often an almost difficult experience for many. Few of Japan's POW camp commandants were either wacky or comically incompetent, and Weary found that life as a prisoner was quite hard work. In fact, it made him extremely 'weary', hahaha! He used to tell that joke himself to his patients and they always laughed, because when you're in a Japanese POW camp, almost anything seems funny in relative terms.

Weary was put in charge of prison camps in Java, as he was not only seen as the perfect man to command a large group of physically and emotionally shattered husks of humanity, but he was trusted by both prisoners and captors, which seems a bit suspicious to me, but there you go. I mean to say, do you really want a commanding officer whom your captors are happy to have be a commanding officer? But anyway, doesn't matter. I'm just saying, it's a bit dodgy, don't you think?

Later that year Dunlop and the prisoners under his command were transferred to Changi, in Singapore, a camp notorious for its harsh conditions and surrealist musical numbers[168]. In January of 1943, he was moved to Thailand, although there are some historians who believe this was not entirely his own decision. In Thailand he commanded 'Dunlop Force', a detachment of Australian soldiers working on the notorious Burma-Thailand railway.

This railway, also known as the 'Death Railway' by those who have clearly abandoned any pretence at unbiased reportage, ran for 415 kilometres between Ban Pong in Thailand and Thanbyuzayat in Burma and was constructed to aid Japan's forces in the Burma campaign. The railway was built by forced labour, with 60,000 Allied prisoners of war joining more than 200,000 civilian workers in an early version of the Work For The Dole program later adapted so popularly by the Australian government. During the railway's construction, 12,621 POWs died, including 2802 Australians, though the civilian death toll was even more staggering: up to 90,000 South-East Asian labourers died, most of whom had been coerced into employment on the railway, with many others having been promised pay and working conditions that failed to materialise: a management model later copied by 7-Eleven.

---

168 This joke is a real deep cut.

It's clear that working on the Burma railway was no picnic, but that probably doesn't properly convey the reality: after all, working on a normal railway is no picnic either, but it's still not such a terrible job. In fact, apart from professional picnickers – a tiny minority in most countries – very few people could describe their working lives as 'a picnic', yet they would probably admit that drawing parallels between their employment and the Burma railway would be quite insulting.

Life was, as you can imagine, not all beer and skittles, but it might have been even less beer and fewer skittles without one Weary Dunlop there to make life, if not exactly bearable, at least slightly more possible. Food was scarce, medical supplies were non-existent, disease was widespread and brutal beatings by the sadistic guards were common, as they pushed their weak and sick captives to achieve impossible productivity targets. Yet amid the exhaustion, illness, starvation and violence, Dunlop was a tower of strength, putting to work all of his medical skills, as well as all his leadership ability and love of his fellow man. One of his men described him as a 'lighthouse of sanity in a universe of madness and suffering', a slightly mixed metaphor that really fails to convey a strong or coherent message: clearly a lighthouse would provide little benefit in the context of an entire universe. 'A lighthouse of sanity on a coastline of madness and suffering' would be better, I think we can all agree[169].

Inept imagery notwithstanding, Weary Dunlop became a legend for his dedication to helping his men, often at enormous risk to his own life. The eminent British plastic surgeon Maurice Kinmonth, who served alongside Dunlop at the Bandung POW

---

169 Other possibilities: 'an oasis of sanity in a desert of madness and suffering'; 'an empty space of sanity in a Christmas Eve carpark of madness and suffering'; 'a toilet in a music festival of suffering'.

camp, recalled a patient of his by the name of Billy Griffiths, who had been blinded and had both of his hands blown off in combat. The Japanese intended to bayonet Griffiths, but were stymied by Weary, who placed himself between Billy and his captors, until the soldiers backed off. There is only one word for this kind of courage: idiotic. When observing a situation wherein a man is about to be impaled by a homicidal maniac, believing that to stand between them is a viable solution requires a level of self-delusion rare even in prisoners of war suffering the delirium of malnutrition and exposure. Yet Colonel Weary would not stand by and watch a man in his care be murdered, even if the only action he could take was almost certain to simply end in his murder as well as the wounded man. And whether it was the bravery of the surgeon that stunned the Japanese, or they were just afraid that doubling their bayoneting quota for the day would trigger their carpal tunnel, it worked. Sometimes ridiculous courage has ridiculous results: they could well have inscribed that on Weary Dunlop's tombstone.

As mentioned, many thousands of men died building the Burma railway – indeed more than 100 Japanese officers were tried for war crimes for their part in the project, and 32 were sentenced to death. The construction was nothing less than cold-blooded mass murder. But it is a matter of record that casualties among Australian POWs were among the lowest, and survival rates among the highest, and this was at least in part due to the fact that they had in their camp a man of Weary Dunlop's calibre. Weary Dunlop saved many lives during the war, not purely through his surgical skills, but through the heightened morale that his leadership and defiance of the Japanese tormentors provided. He gave hope to the sick and wounded, instilling in his men a belief that survival was both possible and desirable, which isn't all that easy a thing to believe even when you're not in a POW camp.

Weary was not the only hero of the Japanese camps, but he became one of the most famous, bestriding the railway charnel house like a colossus, providing the starkest contrast possible between the inhumanity of war and the humanity that it can reveal. He was such a spectacular example of genuine heroism that the only emotion it is possible to feel when contemplating his extraordinary life is deep shame and self-loathing for the shallow, selfish existence you have been wallowing in.

One might have thought that Dunlop's days of making the majority of the human race feel hopelessly inferior would have ended with the war, but Dunlop wasn't going to let the cessation of hostilities keep him from his life's work of setting unfeasible moral standards. Instead, after the war, he steadfastly refused to hold a grudge against the Japanese who had caused him so much suffering. 'In suffering, we are all equal,' he said, eloquently recognising that in the tragic farce that is human warfare, there are victims on all sides; that in our humanity we share more similarities than differences.

At least, he refused to hold a grudge in public. It's possible he went home every night and screamed obscenities while throwing darts at a portrait of Hirohito, but to the world he presented a face of endless forgiveness, which is something to stand in awe of. I struggle to forgive people who take too many items through the express checkout: forgiving people who enslaved me and killed a bunch of my friends would be, I fear, a little beyond me. Then again, I've never had the chance to find out, and it's a lot easier to be a war hero when you have the good fortune to be in a war – we should be careful not to let Weary Dunlop's POW privilege blind us to his faults, of which there are none.

That's the problem, really: this guy was basically perfect. After returning from the war, he continued practising as a surgeon, served on the board of what is now known as the Cancer Council

Victoria, and as president of the Australian Drug Foundation. To rub it in he also campaigned for the welfare of former prisoners of war, and for better relations between Australia and Asia, which was fair enough, given the state of those relations during his first trip to Asia. Nowadays Australia has not been technically at war with any Asian nation for over 40 years: is this a direct result of Weary Dunlop's work? Of course not, but it was still nice of him.

Weary Dunlop's shining example was recognised in his lifetime by a dazzling array of honours. These included:

- Companion of the Order of St Michael and St George, which allowed him to accompany Michael and George on outings.
- Knight Bachelor, a title that definitely seems to be making some kind of insinuation.
- Companion of the Order of Australia, which is like the Michael and George one except for the whole country.
- Knight Grand Cross of the Order of St John of Jerusalem, awarded for his success fighting in the Crusades.
- Knight Grand Cross of the Most Noble Order of the Royal Crown of Thailand, because even Thailand has knights now.
- Honorary Fellow of the Imperial College London, a slightly insulting honour that implies he's not good enough to be a real fellow.
- Honorary Fellow of the Royal College of Surgeons of Edinburgh, and the hits keep coming.
- Honorary Life Member of the Returned and Services League of Australia, and seriously, what's going on here? Just make him a life member, RSL: what would it hurt?
- Life Governor of the Royal Women's Hospital and the Royal Victorian Eye and Ear Hospital, in which capacity he promoted awareness of eyes, ears, and women, to the point

where today any one of these can be treated by most doctors relatively comfortably.

Perhaps most prestigiously, Weary Dunlop was named Australian of the Year in 1976 – although on reflection, I might have meant 'least prestigiously'. Still, it does place Dunlop on a roll of honour that includes both John Farnham and The Seekers, and Weary wasn't even that great a singer.

Ernest Edward Dunlop passed away in 1993, finally going to a well-earnt rest after a lifetime being Weary. Dunlop was 85 years old and still nobody could find a bad word to say about him, apart from the occasional complaint that the warm golden glow that radiated from his body at all times could contribute to eyestrain.

Weary Dunlop was, to put it bluntly, the very best of us. There are those who say he epitomised everything great about the Australian spirit, but this is inadequate: it's truer to say that he was what the Australian spirit wished to be. Many people go through great hardship in life, and many do whatever it takes to survive their ordeal. Rarer are those who, given choices, will at every turn choose the more difficult, the more dangerous or the more painful course, if by so doing a benefit can be granted to their comrades. Such a rarity was Weary Dunlop. If you want to feel your life has been well-spent, I advise you to forget all about him immediately.

FUN FOR YOU AT HOME: Construct a miniature model of the Burma railway. Build tiny supply trains and craft detailed figurines representing workers, POWs and Japanese soldiers. Make a realistic jungle from coloured paper. Rig up a motor to make the miniature railway operate just as it did in real life. Take a good look at your work. Do you feel like you wasted your time? I don't blame you.

A COMPLICATED NATION

NO COUNTRY IS PERFECT, as is often pointed out by people trying to find a way to argue that there's nothing actually wrong with their country and no changes need to be made. And the fact that Australia is objectively *better* than every other country doesn't mean there aren't some bits that could maybe do with a bit of improvement.

Australia has never been perfect, obviously. But having gone through the long, painful process of becoming a nation, then discovering a national identity and finding a way to make the rest of the world take notice of us, Australians had devoted precious little thought to the nation's failings and contradictions. But in the post-war period we had a little time to stop and reflect, and to mull over the ways in which Australia, though having so much that was wonderful and positive to offer the world, also had a fair bit to feel guilty for.

The issue of the relationship between white Australians and the original inhabitants was perhaps top of this list: there are bound to be tensions when two peoples are forced to coexist with vastly different cultures and priorities; especially when one of those peoples spends a significant portion of its time trying to exterminate the other one. To this day Australia has not reconciled the darkness at the heart of its foundation, the brutality upon which the nation was founded: but in the relative prosperity that most of Australia enjoyed in the post-war years, serious thought was at last being devoted to it, and recognition of the struggles of Aboriginal Australia was starting to break through.

This was symptomatic of the increasing intellectual complexity of Australian culture. Great artists were exploring not only what it meant to be Australian, but how to turn that identity to the greater good. Even as Australians continued to make their mark on the world stage, the sophistication that comes with national maturity was causing the country to look at itself with a more sceptical eye. No longer could the simple fact of high achievement be used as an all-forgiving veil for the sins of either an individual, or a nation. The feet of clay of Australians were exposed by the gently lapping waters of inquisitorial analysis, resulting in the wet ankles of patriotic ambivalence. Meanwhile, others were fighting to redress the wrongs of the past and find justice for the marginalised, and the innocence of this young nation was threatened not just by recognition of a problematic foundation, but by tragedy and heartache in the present moment.

In this time, men and women of good heart and bad emerged to question and quarrel, to excel and exploit, to inspire and infuriate. They helped bring Australia into a new era of self-awareness and maturity, with all the wisdom and pain that necessitates. These are their stories.

JOAN SUTHERLAND
A Diva You Can't Sweat Out

SHE WAS *LA STUPENDA* – The Stunning One. The extraordinary voice that conquered the world, the Sydney girl who grew up to put her larynx to the noblest of purposes: thrilling and enchanting all of the minuscule segment of the world population that can afford to go to operas. She was one of the loudest women in history, whose titanic songs echoed across the oceans and allowed her to live the Australian dream, i.e. not living in Australia.

Many young people of today probably only know Joan Sutherland as 'Mum' from the smash-hit movie *Dad and Dave*[170], and would be surprised to know that before she began leaning silently on doorframes in art-house cinema, she had a long and distinguished career screaming to music.

To truly understand Joan Sutherland's life and work, one must first truly understand opera. Unfortunately nobody does, but we will do our best.

Opera, which is an Italian word meaning 'work' – raising quite reasonable questions as to how Italians manage to discuss their employment without everyone assuming everyone else is a professional singer – is defined as an art form in which singers and

170 Total box office estimated to be over $150.

musicians perform a dramatic work combining words (or 'libretto') and music (or 'music'). Traditionally opera features two types of singing: recitative, or speech-inflected, and arias, the more melodic style. What opera doesn't include is talking, known to opera lovers as 'the imbecile's song'. Opera incorporates many elements of regular theatre, although obviously not including spoken words or being understandable. The form was invented in the 16th century by Jacopo Peri, an Italian composer who had no idea what he was doing. The opera was called *Dafne*, and told the story of Apollo falling in love with the nymph Daphne, who is then killed by a hit-and-run driver played by comedian Greg Fleet[171].

Fairly quickly, the idea of telling a story via a medium that nobody understands caught on, and through the work of legendary operatic artists like Giuseppe Verdi, Richard Wagner, Andrew Lloyd Webber and the Marx Brothers, the art of opera became a popular way of demonstrating that you were not only rich, but judgmental. It was into this tradition that Joan Sutherland burst with explosive intensity in 1947, when as a young girl of 20 she made her concert debut in Purcell's *Dido and Aeneas*. This came after a childhood of intensive training, wherein little Joan would imitate her mother's singing exercises in what started as an attempt at cruel sarcasm, but developed into a love of music that followed her throughout her life. Joan's mother had herself taken singing lessons, but had not pursued a professional singing career, possibly because of the way her daughter kept undermining her confidence with impersonations.

In 1951, having already surpassed her mother's mediocre achievements with her role in *Dido and Aeneas*, Sutherland was cast in *Judith* by Eugene Goossens, playing the title role: a beautiful

---

171 References. You can't beat 'em.

young woman who learns some bittersweet lessons about life when she gets a man drunk and decapitates him.

Her role in *Judith* followed her 1949 triumph in Australia's most prestigious operatic competition of the time, the Sun Aria at the Sydney Eisteddfod. The *West Australian* reported that Sutherland won £300[172] and that 'Mr Harold Williams, who judged the contest, said that Miss Sutherland had a really fine soprano voice and he thought that she should do well in opera'. Which was lucky really, because that was sort of the direction she was thinking of going in already.

Having won the prize, young Joan popped over to London to study at the Royal College of Music: these being the days when you pretty much had to study in London if you didn't want to spend your life being viewed as a slack jawed provincial imbecile. Under the tutelage of the distinguished English singing teacher Clive Carey CBE[173], Sutherland learnt how to sing really loudly and breathe through her nose and so forth, and came on in leaps and bounds. In 1952, the Royal Opera in Covent Garden hired her as a utility soprano, a technical operatic term for a soprano who can also play fullback or midfield. She debuted at Covent Garden in October that year as the First Lady in *The Magic Flute*, a Mozart opera about a woodwind instrument that comes to life and takes terrible violent revenge on the humans who had enslaved it. This was followed by performances as Clotilde in *Norma*, the prequel to *Psycho*, and her first leading role at the Royal Opera House: Amelia in *Un ballo in maschera*[174].

At this time Sutherland was training to be a Wagnerian soprano, meaning a singer with both a high vocal range and troublesome racial

172 In today's money, $67.42.

173 Certainly British, Everyone.

174 Literally, 'a ball of mascara'.

views. However, she diverted from this pathway after marrying the conductor and pianist Richard Bonynge.

Bonynge convinced Sutherland that Wagner was not her ideal *Fach*, an operatic term derived from German and meaning one's area of vocal specialisation[175]. 'Get yourself a new *Fach*, Joanie,' Bonynge advised his bride, and Sutherland fortunately took this in exactly the right way. Bonynge noted Joan's ability with high notes and *coloratura* – an Italian word meaning 'colouring in' that applies to singers who can keep inside the lines – and suggested she try *bel canto*, another Italian term that means 'beautiful singing' but which in opera basically refers to anyone doing pretty much anything[176]. In this way Sutherland eventually became a dramatic coloratura soprano, or in German, a *Dramatischer Koloratursopran*, which means the thing I just said.

As a dramatic coloratura soprano, Joan Sutherland found herself with not only an oversized business card, but a bright and burgeoning career. She was making a name for herself as one of the world's greatest exponents of extremely loud, extremely high-pitched singing while in fancy dress. At the Royal Opera House in 1958, she received a ten-minute standing ovation after singing 'Let the bright Seraphim' from Handel's oratorio *Samson*, which must have really brought the whole show to a grinding halt and annoyed a lot of people who were sitting respectfully in their seats waiting for the next song. Still, despite having gained a reputation for singing that would cause audiences to unforgivably disrupt the performance, Sutherland continued to get work.

Sutherland's nickname, *La Stupenda*, came, of course, from Italy, because being an opera singer, she just couldn't get herself a

175 As in, 'Hey Wagner, go *Fach* yourself'.

176 These opera people just make up all these terms to confuse us, you realise.

nice decent Australian nickname. Plenty of people back home were quite willing to call her 'The Joan Ranger' or 'Suthering Heights' or the plain, classically Aussie 'Sutho'[177]. But in the snobbish world of opera, nothing's worth anything if it's not in German or Italian. So, *La Stupenda* it was, even if it made her sound a bit like an alcoholic magician.

In 1960 Sutherland's album *The Art of the Prima Donna* won the Grammy Award for Best Classical Performance – Vocal Soloist. Over the next decade, Sutherland took on all the great roles of her range: Violetta, Amina, Elvira, Cleopatra, Madonna, LaToya, Agnetha, Anni-Frid, Lady Gaga, Beyoncé. From Covent Garden to La Fenice, from La Scala in Milan to the Met in New York, and at the Dallas Opera – something that quite unexpectedly exists – she was an unqualified triumph. All around the world, when people thought of Joan Sutherland, they said one thing: 'that lady can sing quite well'. It seemed as if *La Stupenda* could do no wrong – little did she know that there was a dark cloud on the horizon, a cloud filled with mildly distressing rain.

In the 1970s the voice that had thrilled the most hyper-privileged subsection of the world for the first time started to hit the odd speed bump. The 70s was a time of great upheaval in music: the rise of disco, the revolutionary call-to-arms that was 'Piano Man', and the decline of the Sutherland voice. The star began to attract criticism for her imperfect diction, which seems a bit harsh: if you wanted to hear someone sing words that you could clearly understand, why did you go to the opera in the first place?

Working hard on her diction, Joan recovered clarity, but by the late 1970s, her voice was in decline, her vibrato loosening and her status as the world's greatest soprano coming under pressure from hungry up-and-comers like Leo Sayer. Yet, much as the ageing

177 Or for real opera nerds, 'Joan of Fach'.

Stephen Waugh compensated for his slowing reflexes with grit, determination and experience, Sutherland continued to handle the major roles with aplomb despite the increased difficulty of controlling her voice, and so truly earnt her famous nickname, 'Tugga'. Now in her fifties, Joan expanded her repertoire, adding roles such as Anna Bolena, Amalia, Adriana Lecouvreur, Anne of Green Gables, et al.

In 1979, Joan Sutherland was granted the title of Dame Commander of the British Empire in the New Year's Honours, and from that time on was permitted to refer to herself as 'Dame Joan', a title of immense prestige that still somehow comes off sort of insulting. Like the song, 'There Is Nothing Like A Dame' – I don't know if that was what they were going for. But Dame Joan she now was, and Dame Joan she would forever be, and that's more than Marina Prior can ever say.

Dame Joan's last full-length performance was as Marguerite de Valois in *Les Huguenots*[178] at the Sydney Opera House in 1990: her final public performance was on New Year's Eve of that year, at Covent Garden, when she sang in a gala performance of *Die Fledermaus*[179] with her old friend Pavarotti, as played by John Rhys-Davies. Sutherland was 64 years old, had been singing for half a century, and frankly had a very sore throat.

Having made the decision to never sing again, Dame Joan threw herself into the pursuit of her other interests: acting, writing, and racism. This last she indulged in a speech to Australians for Constitutional Monarchy in which she complained about coming into contact with Asians when renewing her passport. There was great controversy over these remarks, but critics of Dame Joan ignored two very pertinent facts: 1) when making her complaint,

178 Literally, 'The Huge Knots'.

179 Literally, 'Die, Flying Mouse!'

she had specifically said, 'I'm not particularly racist', so anyone accusing her of being particularly racist looks pretty foolish now, do they not; and 2) it was really just an illustration of the famous axiom, 'You don't get to be an internationally-renowned singer without picking up a fair bit of racism along the way'. The fact is, Sutherland was from a different time, and judging her by the standards of modern times completely misses the point of Australians for Constitutional Monarchy.

Dame Joan was not solely concerned with revulsion for unfamiliar skin colours in her later years: she also dabbled in cinema and became an author, penning *The Autobiography of Joan Sutherland: A Prima Donna's Progress*, which received mixed reviews (although critics appreciated Dame Joan's candour and sense of humour, they also noted that most of the book was about opera and should be approached with low expectations).

In the 21st century Dame Joan continued to enjoy a quiet private life at her home in Les Avants, Switzerland, emerging into public only occasionally to complain about how rubbish opera singers were nowadays. On 11 October 2010, at the age of 83, *La Stupenda* died at her Swiss home of cardiopulmonary failure. Tributes poured in from dignitaries including Opera Australia artistic director Lyndon Terracini, who said, 'We shall not see her like again'; and Prime Minister Julia Gillard, who said that Sutherland 'showed a lot of quintessential Australian values', such as singing in Italian and living in Switzerland. Or maybe she just meant the racism.

Dame Joan Sutherland left a massive mark on both international opera and Australian culture. By proving that in the elite, competitive, snobby, insufferable, repellent world of opera, even people from the filthy backwater of Australia could achieve great things.

Dame Joan's voice is still remembered as one of the greats: described variously as 'silvery'. 'golden', 'warm' and other words that don't provide very much useful information. Music critic John Yohalem writes that her voice was 'like molten honey caressing the line ... her lower register was a cello register, Stradivarius-hued', adding that 'On my personal colour scale ... Sutherland is among the "blue" sopranos'. From these descriptions we can discern beyond a shadow of a doubt that John Yohalem is out of his tiny little mind. What Joan Sutherland's voice was like, on the other hand, is anyone's guess: as a warm golden silvery honey-like voice that sounded like a blue cello, I would guess that it sounded pretty good. If you like that sort of thing. Which, according to all reliable music sales figures of the last century, hardly anyone does.

In the pantheon of great Australian artists, Dame Joan stands tall, and belts loud. Terracini was right: we shall not see her like again. But we've got recordings of her voice, so there's no need for us to see her like again really, is there?

FUN FOR YOU AT HOME: Build your own opera house! Using items found around your house – toilet paper rolls, discarded boxes, pipe cleaners, aluminium foil – construct a convincing replica of La Fenice, the Met, or the Sydney Opera House. Stage your own operas in your new theatre! For a really authentic experience, make sure you charge prices nobody you know could possibly afford.

LES MURRAY
Rhyming for no Reason

THERE ARE FEW names that command such instant respect and affection among Australians as that of Les Murray. His wisdom, humanity and wit have illuminated generations of Australians' lives, and many would rank him as this country's greatest-ever football commentator. Unfortunately, though, this chapter is about Les Murray the poet. As one of the most critically-acclaimed and internationally-renowned giants of Australian literature, Murray the poet's place in the history of this country's cultural development is a major and vital one, but we should not let that distract us from his main purpose in life: to make high school students' lives miserable.

Born in 1938 in Nabiac, a town on the north coast of New South Wales that is probably another town spelt backwards, Murray grew up in nearby Bunyah, which is where he still lives. The man just flat-out refuses to move, it's kind of weird really. I mean, would you want to spend your whole life in Bunyah? I know some people probably have no choice but to spend their whole lives in Bunyah, but Murray could surely have left if he'd wanted to, what with all those rivers of poetry money flowing in.

Attending Taree High School, Murray, like all students, was forced to study poetry against his will – this is simply one of the terrible trials that children have to go through, like puberty and alcohol poisoning. Teaching poetry in schools is the education system's way of preventing people from liking poetry as adults, and Murray was put through the process the same as anyone. But unlike the rest of us, who learn to move on and put the trauma behind them in favour of making a positive contribution to the world, young Les resolved to take out his resentment on future generations. No doubt there was something about the poetic form that struck a chord within him, some aspect of the versifier's art that opened up possibilities hitherto undreamt of. As he sat in the primitive chipboard shack that probably served as a classroom at Taree High, if my mental picture of Taree is as accurate as I find it convenient to assume it is, little Les must have come to the thrilling realisation that here, in the world of poetry, lay a way that he could make literally millions of people miserable for decades to come.

Murray's plan began to take shape at the University of Sydney in 1957, where he undertook an arts degree in order to prepare for a life of minimal usefulness. After completing his degree, Murray became a translator at the Australian National University, good training for the poet's calling of being incomprehensible. During this period of youthful hijinks, Murray immersed himself in the Australian cultural milieu, mixing with fellow students and future luminaries such as the late[180] speechwriter and political agony aunt Bob Ellis and the magical talking currant bun Clive James. While hitch-hiking around Australia, Les stayed for a time at the 'Sydney Push'[181] house of Brian Jenkins, where he learnt how to

180 Late now, I mean – obviously he wasn't late when Les met him.

181 The Sydney Push was an intellectual coterie of the 1960s that included James, Germaine Greer, Robert Hughes and Lillian Roxon among others, and had a profound effect on something or other at some point that nobody really remembers much. Anyway Les Murray knew them a bit, which is exciting.

be pretentious and act superior to people with real jobs. He was married in 1962, and after his translating stint, went gallivanting off around Europe for a while.

In 1971 Murray, back in Australia, quit his job to write poetry full-time. Can you even imagine doing that? Who writes poetry *full-time*? What sort of person thinks to themselves, 'no need for a job, I'll live off poems'? It's the mindset of either an egomaniac, or just an ordinary maniac. Yet somehow, it worked, which seems suspicious to me. What kind of scam was this dude running? He must've been selling Amway or something on the side.

Murray's first published collection as sole author was 1969's *The Weatherboard Cathedral*, an achingly emotional suite of verses pleading for improved structural integrity in religious edifices. This was followed by *Poems Against Economics*, an attempt to replace the international monetary system with a global currency based on rhetorical flourishes; and then *Lunch and Counter Lunch*, an anthology of every poem Murray had ever written about his habit of eating two meals for every one consumed by the general public. A major landmark in his career was the follow-up, *Selected Poems: The Vernacular Republic*, which came out in 1976 and established Murray as one of the most selective young poets of the new wave, bringing a whole new approach to poem-selection that had never been seen before. A review of the volume stated that Murray was 'a master of the art of potent rhetoric and memorable images' while also declaring him 'a little too self-satisfied' – and when a poetry reviewer calls you self-satisfied, you must be VERY self-satisfied.

That collection included such famous poems as 'Driving Through Sawmill Towns', 'The Fire Autumn', and 'Vindaloo in Merthyr Tydfil': the latter a salutary warning of the dangers of Welsh curry that stands as one of the finest examples of poems that you wish didn't exist in Australian history. Murray would go on to write of other gastric crises in other small, difficult-to-pronounce towns, but the jury remains out on whether he has ever regained the heights of 'Vindaloo in Merthyr Tydfil'.

Murray did not restrict himself to simply writing poetry that children everywhere would have to read: he was also an activist in poetry circles, if you can imagine such a terrible concept. A major figure in what poets called the 'poetry wars' of the 1970s, he championed more traditional forms against the so-called 'New Poetry' that was in vogue at the time.[182] Murray claimed that post-modernist poetry was confining the form's readership to a narrow group of intellectuals. He fought for poetry to be more accessible to a wider audience, which many believe to be his greatest crime.

While on furlough from the poetry wars, he drank to blot out the terrible memory of those he had killed and those he could not save from the awful blood storm of poetry. He also worked as the editor of *Poetry Australia* magazine from 1973-79, and as poetry editor for Angus and Robertson from 1976-91. He became literary editor of *Quadrant* in 1990, Australia's foremost magazine for middle-aged men who think whining about *Media Watch* makes them a rebel, and has edited several poetry anthologies. It's clear that throughout his career, Murray has not only disseminated poetry himself, but acted as an enabler for others.

In his poetry, Murray has generally taken a nationalistic bent, writing in praise of traditional values, the Australian bush, and, for some reason, pig-killing; and against modernism, feminism, and people in cities. The poem 'Sydney and the Bush' is a good representation of Murray's views on the urban-rural divide, which can be summed up as: everyone in cities is a dead-eyed idiot and

182 Or at least, as 'in vogue' as poetry ever gets.

everyone in the country is basically a god. It's possible Murray was influenced in this view by his formative years in Bunyah, a town which is liable to make anyone go a bit funny in the head. Living in the country often does strange things to people, and Murray was no exception. His rural spawning led to all sorts of erratic behaviour later in life, such as: converting to Catholicism; claiming that he'd seen Manning Clark[183] wearing the Order of Lenin[184]; and moving back to the country even though he knew full well that cities existed.

Murray also participated in the founding of the Australian Commonwealth Party, which may have been his most eccentric act of all. He composed the party's manifesto, which read in part:

> *The Australian Commonwealth Party is an entirely new political association, non-authoritarian, non-elitist, bound together by the mutual loyalty and common commitment of members. [The party] represents a rising of sensitivity and a restoration of grace. It seeks to reinstate qualitative values in the world in order to counter and, in the end, overcome the entrenched tyranny of quantity. It is thus the sworn enemy alike of divisive political techniques, of the mass solutions of doctrinaire economics and of rule by threat. As against all these, it espouses the higher pragmatism of vision.*

It is a complete mystery how this inspiring gibberish did not secure majority government for the Australian Commonwealth Party, although it may have had something to do with the fact that they only had one candidate, and his nomination was refused.

Although his political career has not necessarily been stellar, Murray has nevertheless enjoyed the admiration and even friendship

183 A minor Australian historian.

184 An early discarded draft by JK Rowling.

of many politicians, especially the ones who hate the fact that most writers are bleeding-heart green commie types and are overjoyed that Australia's most famous poet is more Tim Fischer than Tim Flannery. But how did he attain that status? What places Les Murray, in the words of the *New Yorker*, 'among the three or four leading English-language poets'?

I don't think it would be an exaggeration to say the answer to these questions is 'his poems'. Without these semi-random collections of what might loosely be called words, jammed down the unwilling gullets of generation after generation of innocent children, it is doubtful whether anyone would ever have heard of Les Murray, or at least whether they would have heard of two of them. It is therefore instructive to take a look at these poems and see exactly what the big freaking deal is.

From 'An Absolutely Ordinary Rainbow', his poem about how unimpressed he is by colours:

The traffic in George Street is banked up for half a mile
and drained of motion. The crowds are edgy with talk
and more crowds come hurrying. Many run in the back streets
which minutes ago were busy main streets, pointing:
There's a fellow weeping down there. No one can stop him.

Here Murray is sending a powerful and timely message: don't cry, it just annoys people and holds everyone up.

From 'Noonday Axeman', his poem about a guitarist who is scared of the dark:

Here, I remember all of a hundred years:
candleflame, still night, frost and cattle bells,
the draywheels' silence final in our ears,
and the first red cattle spreading through the hills

Here Murray puts his finger on the most pertinent aspect of his existence: he is very, very old.

From 'Sydney and the Bush', his poem about a young boy's struggle with puberty:

When Sydney ordered lavish books
and warmed her feet with coal
the Bush came skylarking to town
and gave poor folk a soul.

Here Murray is saying something or other, who can tell really. Something about global warming maybe, or B&S Balls? I think the main thrust of the poem is that books suck and poor people should burn the city down.

In any case, these examples showcase the depth and profundity of Murray's poetry, the way in which he uses rhyme and rhythm, metaphor and imagery, pomposity and an overwhelming superiority complex, to paint pictures of ordinary Australian life that seem hauntingly familiar and yet at the same time indefinably forgettable. In the webs of wordery that Murray wove like an enormous over-educated spider, he traps we unwary literate flies with the sticky strands of his descriptions of everyday existence. Murray's elaborate verbal constructions make the commonplace seem remarkable, even magical, in a way that can best be described as 'dishonest', because the commonplace is by definition not magical at all.

Whatever you think of Murray's work – whether you find it moving, evocative, and some of the most powerful representations of this nation and its people to enter the literary canon, or you consider it a pile of condescending old wank that Mr Evans should never have forced you to do a presentation on in Year 10

English[185] – it cannot be denied that he is an artist of enormous accomplishment. Many have tipped him as a future Nobel Prize winner – for literature presumably – although debate still rages as to whether he has reached a level of distinction to match that of Sully Prudhomme or Bjørnstjerne Bjørnson. A Nobel would be one of the few honours he has yet to acquire (in poetry, that is: there are hundreds of honours in better things that he's failed to land): already he has been named one of Australia's 100 Living Treasures[186], won the Kenneth Slessor Prize for Poetry twice, taken out the Queen's Gold Medal for Poetry, the Petrarch Prize and the Grace Leven Prize for Poetry, and been named an Officer of the Order of Australia, among others. So next time you're feeling good about the fact you're a better writer than Les Murray, remember you've won none of these awards and feel a little bit worse about yourself.

But the soccer Les Murray – he's *really* good. Look him up.

FUN FOR YOU AT HOME: Write a poem. There, that wasn't so hard, was it? What's the big deal, am I right?

185 That one is the right one though.

186 A list which also contains Kylie Minogue and Dick Smith, so take that for what it's worth.

HAROLD HOLT
Prince of Tides

THERE HAVE BEEN some colourful characters inhabiting the Lodge throughout the years: the first Australian prime minister, Edmund Barton, caused scandal in early 20th-century society by refusing to wear a beard; Billy Hughes, the seventh prime minister, lived until he was six hundred years old and spent almost the whole time trying to force young men to shoot at each other; and then there's Malcolm Turnbull, who owns more than one jacket. But few prime ministerial tales are as wondrous and life-affirming as that of Harold Holt, an oft-underrated but undeniably courageous and loveable character who left a lasting impact on Australia that no other PM can possibly hope to match.

Many young Australians today probably pass by the Harold Holt Memorial Swimming Centre in Melbourne without even knowing the story behind the pool's name. What sort of man, they might wonder, could merit such an honour? What kind of accomplishment earns someone immortality in the shape of a Brutalist public bathing establishment? It never even occurs to those young Australians that the Harold Holt Swim Centre might have been given its name as a sick joke.

Certainly the early stages of Harold Holt's life provided no clue to the heights he would eventually scale: scholars are agreed that the young Holt's life was almost preternaturally boring. Born in Stanmore, New South Wales, highlights of Harold's youth included the death of his mother, a singing performance at school to which none of his family went, and his mother's funeral to which he didn't go. Despite his attempts to spice up his life with crushing sadness and loneliness, he remained surprisingly dull. After school he went to university and then became a lawyer, which was painfully predictable.

Like most lawyers, Holt entered politics, joining the Menzies government as Minister For Looking Slightly Like Menzies. The first Menzies government fell apart in a violent orgy of general lameness, but the loyal Holt stayed around and waited for the Liberal Party to be invented. When it was, by Menzies himself no less, Holt joined up and after Menzies won the 1949 election, Holt served as Minister for Labour, which was confusing because 'Labour', as in the ministry, was spelt correctly, while 'Labor', as in the party, was spelt incorrectly.

By the end of the 1950s Holt, who had little knowledge of or interest in economics, naturally became Treasurer[187]. This was a strong indication that he would become prime minister when Menzies either retired or was caught in sunlight and turned to stone. And indeed, this was what came to pass. On Australia Day 1966, Harold Holt officially became Australian Prime Minister, and the Age of Holt began.

Holt, by all accounts, enjoyed being prime minister. The big car he got to ride in was fantastic, and his new house was just lovely. He also got to meet many interesting people, such as US president Lyndon B. Johnson, who was the basis of his catchphrase, 'All the day in my PJs.' This was in reference to the frequent slumber parties Holt attended at the White House, at which the two men discussed where to bomb next between pillow fights.

---

187 This remains a time-honoured tradition.

Yes, life was good for Prime Minister Holt, but life was about to take a sudden, unexpected, and thrilling turn. On 17 December 1967, Holt took a break from being harangued in the press and repeatedly owned in public by Gough Whitlam, and drove from Melbourne to Cheviot Beach, on Point Nepean near Portsea. With him was Marjorie Gillespie, his neighbour and rumoured lover: and by 'rumoured', I mean, come on, the prime minister is taking holidays with his *neighbour*? Don't be so naïve. Also with them was Marjorie's daughter, who inexplicably was named 'Vyner', Vyner's boyfriend Martin Simpson, and a man called Alan Stewart who was just, kind of, there. Although these people might seem unimportant, it's impossible to overstate just how irrelevant they are to this story.

At Cheviot Beach, Harold put on his swimming trunks, and announced, 'I know this beach like the back of my hand', illustrating the point by holding up his hand and showing everyone the tiny lifeguards' flags planted on the back of it. The surf was high and rough that day, and Holt was a 59-year-old man with a heart condition. Furthermore, he had a sore shoulder and was on powerful painkillers. With all these factors in play, it seems miraculous that he ever survived.

Yet on that fateful day, Harold Holt, Australian Prime Minister, did something quite remarkable. Swimming blissfully out into Port Phillip Bay, the PM left the stresses and crises of leadership behind and simply enjoyed the soothing sensation of cold seawater on his wizened Liberal flesh[188]. Diving beneath the waves, he discovered a whole new world of underwater adventure, passing exotic fish, strange crustaceans, and cunning octopuses hiding among the swaying seabed grasses. As he swam further and further from shore, Holt found himself feeling less and less like returning to his old

188 Yum.

life. All the meetings, all the speeches, all the moral compromises and internal squabbling: that was what he had to look forward to if he went back to land. But here under the sea, he was feeling an incredible sense of freedom. Was it just a crazy dream? Was it just the severe oxygen deprivation he was now suffering after several minutes underwater? No – he felt great. He'd never felt more alive. He'd never felt more certain of anything: his future was not in Canberra, it was in the cool, welcoming waters of the Pacific.

Obviously, Holt's plan to live under the sea was not the most practical idea he'd ever had. It was positively ludicrous: how could a man, raised on land since birth, possibly make a life under the sea, among the fish and the squids and the anemones? Where would he live? What would he do for a living? The whole idea was doomed to failure – or at least it would have been, if at that moment Prime Minister Holt had not made a remarkable discovery.

Gliding smoothly through a thicket of seaweed, Holt emerged into a wide, sandy clearing, and his jaw dropped as he beheld the most astonishing sight of his life. Before him stood a vast transparent dome, and within the dome was spread a glittering city, more magnificent than the most spectacular metropolis he'd ever seen on land[189]. Holt gargled in amazement, and began swimming again, his stroke faster than before, straining every sinew to reach the shining city on the ocean floor. At the gates he was met by two tall mermen in glittering coral armour. 'Greetings, land-walker,' they burbled melodically. 'Finally, our peoples greet each other. Come, learn our ways.'

Up on land, the search was on for the missing prime minister. Police, Navy divers, Air Force helicopters, Army personnel and local volunteers rushed to the beach in an attempt to find any scraps of prime ministerial material bobbing around the bay. Never

189 Perth.

before had a prime minister completely vanished; there was no real precedent for a large-scale operation to recover a prime minister from the icy embrace of Poseidon. Predictably, they found nothing, although they could never have suspected the reason why.

On 19 December 1967, the government announced that Harold Holt was believed to be dead. On 5 January 1968, the search was called off on the grounds that everyone was really tired and wet. A memorial service had already been held, on 22 December, which seems really disrespectful to the searchers, because it: a) assumed they were going to fail; and b) meant they didn't get to come to the service because they were out combing the kelp and so forth. Attending the memorial service were dignitaries including Prince Charles, British Prime Minister Harold Wilson, South Vietnamese President Nguyen Van Thieu – who frankly was probably happy to get away for a bit – and of course Harold's old BFF, Lyndon B. Johnson, who broke down in tears as he remembered those long nights when the popcorn was fresh and it seemed like love would last forever.

Did Harold Holt, as he walked the moist streets of the ocean-floor city, learning the ways of the Water People and taking eel-riding lessons, think of his old pal the President and feel a pang of homesickness? Did he fret for the welfare of his wife Zara, or for that of Marjorie, with whom he had enjoyed many joyful days making Zara's steadfast loyalty a cruel joke? Was there even a moment, as Holt gained an audience with the Council of Elders and taught them the ways of the Above, that the ex-PM wondered if he had done the right thing in leaving Australia behind for the Kingdom of the Deep? We can never know for sure, unless Holt someday returns to give an exclusive interview to Buzzfeed[190].

---

190 '27 Reasons Why These Pictures Of Harold Holt's Watery Realm Are Everything.'

As it was, life moved on in Australia. Holt was succeeded as prime minister by John McEwen, a rugged country bloke who had been nicknamed 'Black Jack' due to his habit of hitting people on the back of the head.

McEwen's prime ministership was simply a caretaker arrangement, and he was succeeded by John Gorton, a kindly orangutan who had been coaxed into parliament with promises of melons. Coincidentally, it was around this time that Harold Holt, eager to give something back to the aquatic paradise that had already given him so much, explained the basic precepts of representative democracy to the oceanic establishment. So impressed were the sea-people with Holt's exciting new ideas about democratic government and equality between all citizens that they immediately made him Emperor-For-Life, and he moved into the Palace of Neptune. Wielding the mighty dolphin-head sceptre, Harold Holt was now ruler of all the seven seas, a fate that had seemed almost improbable back when he was serving his articles at Fink, Best and Miller.

As Gorton hung on to win the 1969 election despite a huge swing against the incumbent government, Holt was modernising the seabed road and rail systems and introducing a system of progressive taxation to help fund major social programs aimed at lifting the poorest marine-dwellers out of poverty. 'The lowliest sandsweeper has as much right to happiness and dignity as the most gloriously-attired brineduke,' he famously announced, and despite pushback from members of the afishtocracy, his reforms were implemented and ushered in a new age of peace and prosperity around the ocean. His attempts to extend voting rights to all vertebrates, however, did not meet with success, due to entrenched anti-manatee prejudices.

Nowadays, few remember exactly what, if anything, the Holt prime ministership achieved for Australia. Holt is mainly remembered for the unconventional manner in which he left office: despite the country's status as an island, it never occurred to any other PM that it was an option to simply walk into the sea; although surely plenty would have found the prospect incredibly tempting. Most Australians feel an urge to walk into the sea just from hearing about federal politics, let alone being directly involved in them. Overall, Harold Holt's legacy on land can be said to be solidly non-existent. Yet his legacy under the sea is vast.

Even today, Holt sits on his pearl throne, master of all he surveys. The saltwater has granted him greatly extended life, and he is expected to reign for many years yet – upon his demise one of his thousands of Holtspawn will assume the crown, hopefully bearing in mind the wisdom and lessons of their father. All who live in the oceans of the world pay tribute to Holt The Liberator, Holt The Benefactor, Holt The Destroyer: his works are many and his glory is blinding, his temper is quick yet his mercy is endless. How fortunate for all mermen, mermaids, friendly whales and sharks that on that fateful day in 1967, Harold Holt decided to leave the bland and colourless world of humanity behind, and enter a more fabulous existence, forevermore.

As for we poor landlubbers, the closest we'll ever get to the magnificent marine life is when we go for a refreshing swim at the Harold Holt Swim Centre – true testament to his greatness.

FUN FOR YOU AT HOME: Walk into the sea. How far did you get? Keep trying until you get all the way.

VINCENT LINGIARI
The Immovable Object

THE GREAT AUSTRALIAN songwriter Paul Kelly has immortalised many real-life Australians in his catchy rock compositions – Don Bradman, Billy Baxter, Mr Gravy: The King of Prison – but of all his finely drawn musical sketches of his noblest compatriots, probably the most evocative and important is one he co-wrote with Kev Carmody: 'From Little Things, Big Things Grow', the tale of Vincent Lingiari. And if few songs have more perfectly told the tale of a true hero, by the same token few people have more deserved to be remembered in song. For Vincent Lingiari was a living legend whose story merits singing to future generations for as long as this country endures. Opposed by a society that had dedicated the best part of two centuries to the brutal dispossession and oppression of his people, Lingiari stood firm and declared he would not submit. He changed not only the course of his people's lives, but that of Australia itself. It's more than Billy Baxter ever did.

Vincent Lingiari was born in 1919, a member of the Gurindji people of the Victoria River region of the Northern Territory. Vincent's parents worked on the Wave Hill cattle station, 600km south of Darwin, and even further away from any actual city. It was a starkly remote place in the middle of some of the world's most unforgiving country, seemingly designed less to raise cattle than to punish them for their sins. At the time of Lingiari's birth, Wave Hill was owned by William Vestey, the employer of Vincent Lingiari's parents, and later the boss of Vincent himself, when the boy was put to work at the age of 12 at the Wave Hill stock camps. Today it might seem appalling that a 12-year-old could be forced to work mustering cattle, but these were different times, when child labour was a cherished part of everyday life. As was institutionalised racism and the belief that Aboriginal people were subhuman.

Forcing Aboriginal people to work for them was a longstanding tradition for the Vesteys and the Wave Hill station. Like many Aboriginal nations, the Gurindji had found their traditional way of life somewhat squeezed by white settlers. The white settlers, of course, were only following their own traditional way of life, i.e. theft and genocide, so it was a real clash of cultures.

The waterholes that Aboriginal tribes had depended on had been fenced off by pastoralists or polluted by their cattle, which also destroyed desert plants that were an important resource for the original inhabitants. Meanwhile white hunters shot the Aboriginal hunting dogs and the kangaroos that were a staple food for the locals – kangaroos were a threat to the white invaders because they competed with cattle for grass and water, and were also symbolic of natural grace and beauty, two things that the British Empire had vowed to wipe off the face of the earth. With their traditional food sources running short, the Aboriginal communities came up with the eminently practical idea of grabbing a bit of British beef for themselves. This seemed only fair since it was the cattle that had decimated their society, but the whites, operating on the tried and tested imperial principle of 'when in doubt, shoot everyone', did not take kindly to the people whose land they had stolen trying to stay alive.

And so the Gurindji found themselves forced to move to the cattle stations and work as stockmen and servants, for meagre rations.

For years, conditions on the Wave Hill station had been drawing opprobrium. An inquiry by the Northern Territory government found that Vestey Group had been 'quite ruthless in denying their Aboriginal labour proper access to human rights'. And that was in the 1930s. When the Northern Territory government of the thirties accuses you of racial oppression, you know you're really plumbing the depths. It's like being called out for sexism by Sam Newman. Or Kyle Sandilands asking you to mind your manners. In 1945 another inquiry found that Vesteys was paying its Aboriginal workers less than five shillings a day – the minimum legal wage for Aboriginal people – while non-Aboriginal male workers earnt £2/8[191]. At the time, it was actually illegal to pay Aboriginal workers more than a specified amount, so again, Vesteys was falling short of the standards set by some of the most racist people in the history of the world. Moreover, the little money the Gurindji did receive, from government benefits, was paid directly into company accounts which they did not control.

Besides the almost heroically unjust pay grades, Gurindji employees at Wave Hill were living in corrugated iron humpies with no lighting, plumbing, furniture or floors – literally no floors. The Wave Hill worker Billy Bunter Jampijinpa said of conditions on the station:

> *We were treated just like dogs. We were lucky to get paid the 50 quid a month we were due, and we lived in tin humpies you had to crawl in and out on your knees. There was no running water. The food was bad – just flour, tea, sugar and bits of beef like the head or feet of a bullock. The Vesteys mob were hard men. They didn't care about blackfellas.*

191 Two pounds, eight shillings, or in today's money, six hundred francs.

That Vesteys didn't care about blackfellas certainly seemed to be the case, although Vesteys would probably defend itself by pointing out that not caring about blackfellas was a constitutional requirement at the time – along with not caring about Asians, women, asbestosis, etc.

There must always come a limit to how much people will stand, and the Gurindji were approaching it. The tipping point came when Vincent Lingiari, who had begun work on Wave Hill at the age of 12 and had continued working, for a pathetic pittance, in inhuman conditions, for 35 years, was made leader of the community by his Gurindji brethren. Ascending to leadership in August 1966, Vincent drew his line in the sand, declaring that he would go no further and demanding a real floor to draw lines on. He called upon his people to refuse to accept the Vesteys' abuses, and with two hundred other Indigenous Wave Hill employees and their families, walked off the station. They set up camp at Wattie Creek, called Daguragu by the Gurindji.

Lingiari's actions caused uproar. Vesteys were bewildered. Lingiari demanded better pay and rations, and protection of the Aboriginal women; all things that would mean pretty major lifestyle changes for the white men of the area. At least, these were his demands at first: it soon became clear that Vincent had a vision that went far beyond simply begging for something approaching human conditions to live in. He was after something bigger and more fundamental: the return of Gurindji lands to their rightful owners. Gaining support from prominent Australians such as the novelist Frank Hardy and trade union leader Brian Manning, he pushed Vesteys to give back the stolen property they were squatting on. The broad consensus was that Vesteys would struggle to make a case that their occupation of Wave Hill predated Gurindji settlement, and would have to depend on other arguments: like for instance showing the receipts from when they'd bought it from the people who'd stolen it; or threatening a nationwide beef shortage. Or, obviously, going back to their standard argument: that white people were great and should have everything.

The Gurindji made maps showing which land they wanted returned: in 1967 they petitioned the Governor-General, the Right Honourable[192] Richard Gardiner Casey, for 1295 square kilometres near Wave Hill. Casey responded, 'I'm just the Governor-General, I really have no power whatsoever.' But even after they got in touch with someone who could do something, the request was denied. The government felt, fairly logically if less than charitably, that the principle of returning stolen land was one that could be quite dangerous in a country in which basically all the land had been stolen.

Lingiari, together with Billy Bunter Jamijinpa and others, travelled around the country to give speeches and hold fundraisers for the Gurindji's cause. It was the first time that a bid for Aboriginal land rights had gained popular support, and the Wave Hill strike was backed by unions, lawyers and politicians across Australia. Demonstrations were held – and arrests made at them – in support of the Gurindji. The Australian establishment, so secure in its belief that the golden days of sadistic discrimination would last forever, had become complacent, and were suddenly blindsided by the discovery that not only did Indigenous people believe themselves to be, you know, *people*, but that there were actual white people who agreed with them. It was crisis time.

There were attempts, naturally, to break the strike. At the outset Vesteys tried to attract the Gurindji back, offering increased wages. Vincent replied, 'Nah, we'll just stay here, I reckon.' Late in 1966, when the strike was still in its infancy, the NT government offered a

192 Relatively speaking.

125 per cent pay rise, but the strikers remained intransigent, refusing to accept anything less than the return of land and wages equal to those of white workers – something the government understandably refused on the grounds that if people of different races received equal wages, they might start considering themselves equal people, and that was a terribly slippery slope for a democratic racist government to roll down. The government also offered houses, which were refused, and when enticements failed, tried to cut off Gurindji food supplies and threatened to have them forcibly removed.

The strike continued. In Kelly's song, Lingiari is quoted as saying, in response to a suggestion that he accept the offers and give his people relief from the hardships of the walk-off, 'No thanks, we know how to wait'. They did: the Gurindji dug in at Wattie Creek as the years went by, defiant, immovable and completely consistent in their message: until we get our land, we are going nowhere. In response, the company and the government replied, you can't have your land, we're using it right now. In 1969, three years after Vincent first led his people off the station, the federal government received a proposal to give eight square kilometres – a positively minute area – back to the Gurindji. Cabinet declined to even consider it. Perhaps they thought they could outlast Vincent Lingiari. If so, they did not know Vincent Lingiari. And neither did they know themselves, or how bad at politics they were – three years later the Coalition was out of power and Gough Whitlam had swept in his patrician, intellectually snobbish way, into The Lodge.

The tide had already turned by that time. In 1967 the country voted overwhelmingly in the affirmative to the famous referendum granting the Federal government power to make laws for Aboriginal people. Clearly much of the population had begun to develop some rudimentary idea of Indigenous Australians as deserving of equality – they weren't quite all the way there yet, but it was moving that way.

The newly-minted Whitlam government, elected six years after the beginning of the strike, made land rights a priority. Suspending mining exploration licences in the NT, and stopping development leases that could infringe on Aboriginal rights, Whitlam's regime moved to grant the Gurindji a small piece of land at Wattie Creek. The wheels were in motion: soon the momentum would be irresistible, as the avalanche Lingiari had triggered came crashing down like a ton of mixed metaphors.

The Gurindji were not the only people putting on the pressure for action on land rights. In 1971, the Yolngu of Arnhem Land sued the mining company Nabalco, claiming that they had the right to deny the company access to their ancestral lands. Their case was not successful, Justice Blackburn finding that when Europeans came to Australia they declared the land *terra nullius* – not owned by anyone – and that under British law as it then stood, patently idiotic and bigoted principles must take precedence.

But the Yolngu's failed suit led to the establishment of the Woodward Royal Commission into Aboriginal Land Rights, which led to the Aboriginal Land Rights Act. This act would not be passed until 1976, when the Fraser government was in power, but the Whitlam government drafted legislation in 1975, and it would be unfair to give credit to Fraser since everyone knows Whitlam was the nice one. That year, Gough Whitlam travelled to Kalkaringi, near Wave Hill, for a formal ceremony granting the Gurindji the return of some of their land – his government had brokered a deal with the current Lord Vestey to lease 3236 square kilometres of Wave Hill to the Gurindji, even though the company's constitution clearly forbade either forgoing profits or being decent to others.

Speaking to Vincent Lingiari and his countryfolk, the prime minister said:

> *On this great day, I, Prime Minister of Australia, speak to you on behalf of all Australian people – all those who honour and love this land we live in. For them I want to say to you: I want this to acknowledge that we Australians have still much to do to redress the injustice and oppression that has for so long been the lot of Black Australians. Vincent Lingiari, I solemnly hand to you these deeds as proof, in Australian law, that these lands belong to the Gurindji people and I put into your hands part of the earth itself as a sign that this land will be the possession of you and your children forever.*

It was such a gracious speech by Whitlam that it would be incredibly churlish to mention his policy on East Timor or his fiscal recklessness at this point, so I won't. Instead let's focus on what a history-shaping moment this was, not just for the men present, but for every Australian from that point on. In one of the most iconic images ever captured on film, Whitlam poured a handful of sand into Lingiari's hand, to symbolise the handover of land.

That ceremony took place on 16 August 1975. It was a week short of nine years since the Gurindji had walked off Wave Hill. Nine years of telling their story, putting their case, and waiting, waiting, waiting for the change to come. It's almost unthinkable today, when modern life moves so fast and attention spans are so short that most people can barely go one minute without making a disparaging remark about how often children look at their phones, that there was a time when people could wait nine years for justice. The forces of big business and big government tried to bribe them off the land, and then threaten them off the land, but nothing was moving Vincent Lingiari and his steadfast army. He had been so patient, so defiant, and so strong in his convictions that the nation of Australia was forced to do the right thing, against all its carefully honed instincts. The actions of Vincent Lingiari and his countrymen were massively influential in bringing about legal recognition of Indigenous people's rights to their own land: a mighty inspiration as long as you don't consider how depressing the whole affair was, at its heart. But then, without great injustice, where would we get our heroes from? The football mainly, I guess[193].

Vincent Lingiari's legacy continues to resonate to this day. If Australia has never properly come to terms with its history, the Wave Hill walk-off at least forced us to start making an effort. Upon the prime minister pouring sand into his hand, Vincent said, 'Now we can all be mates', but after all he'd achieved we can forgive him this moment of tragic naïveté. After all, he'd inspired not just Indigenous Australians, but anyone who was ever discouraged about the futility of fighting the rich and powerful. Not that you're wrong to be discouraged – obviously fighting the rich and powerful is incredibly inadvisable – but every now and then, if you've got the stomach for a nine-year fight, things just might swing your way. As Kelly sang sixteen years after the hand-back:

That was the story of Vincent Lingiari
But this is the story of something much more
How power and privilege cannot move a people
Who know where they stand and stand in the law

Today the anniversary of the strike is known as Freedom Day, and thousands gather at Kalkaringi to re-enact Lingiari's walk-off and celebrate his victory. The walk-off route is now on the Australian National Heritage List, but then, so is the Great

193 Though this is also a source of great injustice, i.e. the 1989 NSWRL grand final.

Barrier Reef, so walk-off route fans shouldn't get complacent. Besides Kelly's famous one, other songs by Irish singer Damian Dempsey, and Australian Ted Egan – who wrote 'Gurindji Blues' with Lingiari himself during the strike – commemorate Vincent's achievement. His name is borne by the federal electorate of Lingiari in the Northern Territory.

Vincent Lingiari died in 1988, in his late sixties. The battles he inspired, for justice and respect, live on. Surely no man has done more to serve his people or expand his country's heart. His name is indelible in the story of Australia, a reminder of the time a poor stockman led a couple of hundred folks off their worksite, and stared down millionaires and ministers until they gave in. For Vincent Lingiari knew where he stood, and big things grew from it.

FUN FOR YOU AT HOME: Go on a camping trip to the remote 'Top End'. Stay out there for nine years. Not so much fun now, eh?

RUPERT MURDOCH
The Good News

WHAT CAN YOU SAY about a man who has so profoundly shaped the modern world? Seriously, what can you say? In a legal sense? I feel like I should tread pretty carefully here, because Rupert Murdoch is, in a manner of speaking, still alive at the time of writing. Perhaps he always will be – he certainly has no plans to die, and history suggests that what Rupert does not plan will not happen. For Murdoch is a man who perhaps more than anyone else, embodies the characteristic central to all great Australians: the ability to get what he wants.

Murdoch's happy knack for acquiring whatever he desires began way back on 11 March 1931, when, after having expressed a wish to have a father who owned newspapers, he found himself in possession of exactly that. Keith Murdoch was a journalist and former war correspondent who had made waves in World War One by helping to expose the fact that the Gallipoli campaign was less well-planned than *Blues Brothers 2000*. Keith named his only son Keith, but luckily his son started going by his middle name, Rupert, when he grew up, or this passage would probably be quite confusing.

Rupert was born in Melbourne, and went to Geelong Grammar School, because Melbourne at the time had no schools good enough to educate a boy who would one day be as rich as Rupert would be.

At Geelong Grammar Rupert showed his aptitude for the family business, editing the school journal *The Corian*[194] and student journal *If Revived*[195], and becoming excited by the possibilities that journalism offered for lowering the tone of public discourse. Murdoch also took Geelong Grammar's cricket team to the National Junior Finals, and from all reports, just left them there.

After school, young Rupert continued his education in the eldritch ways of the editor, working part-time at the *Melbourne Herald.* Discovering that his father still hadn't died yet, he passed the time by going to Oxford, England's foremost university for bright young Australian megalomaniacs. At Oxford he managed Oxford Student Publications, publisher of student newspaper *Cherwell*, which became the first student newspaper of the 1950s to adopt the Page 3 Girl.

At the age of 21, Rupert discovered that his father was dead and knew instinctively that this was the ideal moment to claim his inheritance[196]. Returning from Oxford he took control of News Ltd, the family business.

News Ltd was not, of course, the corporate behemoth it would become when Rupert assumed control. Its main asset was Adelaide paper *The News*, and no company had ever risen to global domination with a main asset in Adelaide. But young Murdoch saw in *The News* an opportunity to surpass the achievements of his father.

His first move was to make the *The News* a success, something that hadn't occurred to any of its previous proprietors. The profitability of his flagship newspaper sparked in him an audacious yet ingenious idea: if you could make lots of money from a newspaper, could you not make even *more* money from *more*

194 Meaning 'Man who loves Corey'.

195 Meaning the founders were deeply disturbed.

196 Timing is everything.

newspaper, could you not make even *more* money from *more* newspapers? People told him he was mad, and perhaps they were right, but Rupert Murdoch would never be the type to listen to naysayers.

Over the next few years, Murdoch stormed through the Australian press landscape like a well-dressed swarm of locusts: if instead of eating the crops, locusts bought them, increased the proportion of them devoted to sport and celebrity gossip, and slapped sensationalistic headlines all over them[197]. He began by buying Perth's *The Sunday Times*, and then proceeded to devour suburban and provincial papers across the nation, including Sydney's *Daily Mirror.*

Murdoch was not only intent on acquiring papers, but value-adding to them, increasing sales and circulation by cutting back on less popular aspects like reportage and analysis, and boosting investment in crowd-pleasing elements like nudity and hatred. To a world that had hitherto thought of the newspaper business as a bastion of decency and rectitude, it was a shock, but also a relief, as the entire world had only recently gotten over World War Two and was frankly sick of pretending to be nice.

Murdoch's devastatingly effective combination of rapacious corporatism and populist pandering had placed Australia in his grasp. But few people who have never actually ordered a bombing have been as hard to satiate as Rupert Murdoch: dominating one country was never going to be enough. In 1964, he learnt that the British-Canadian newspaper tycoon Lord Thomson of Fleet[198] was planning to buy the New Zealand daily paper the *Dominion.* Having never realised that people besides himself were allowed

197 Which would really shake up the farm sector.

198 Who was either named after Fleet Street, or Fleet Street was named after him, or possibly neither of those.

to buy newspapers, Rupert was outraged, and launched his own counter-bid. In a four-way tussle for the newspaper, Murdoch was triumphant, and the world trembled at the emergence of a new titan. The New Zealand bit of the world trembled, anyway. The rest would come soon enough.

Later in 1964, Murdoch founded *The Australian*, Australia's first national daily newspaper, which remains an influential voice in the Australian socio-political discourse to this day, and is worth every cent of the millions and millions of dollars that Rupert squirts up against the wall each year to keep it running. Because for Rupert Murdoch, the newspaper business has never been about money: it's been about using newspapers to tell politicians what to do so he can make more money.

Having tasted the sweet tang of international expansion with the *Dominion*, Murdoch began studying his atlas for suggestions of other countries whose pies he could shove his fingers into. In 1968 he bought the British *News of the World*, the venerable organ that really put the 'news' into 'this is a wildly inappropriate approach to reporting the news' from its foundation in 1843 to 2011, when it was shut down after allegations that its editorial staff had been behaving in an utterly predictable manner.

After the *News of the World*, Murdoch bought British broadsheet *The Sun*, which had been struggling due to a string of injuries caused by people trying to open it on trains. The new owner slashed costs by making *The Sun* a tabloid[199] and using the same printing press for both it and the *News of the World*. Murdoch's approach to the news was encapsulated by a story told by Larry Lamb, the editor appointed to the *The Sun* upon its acquisition. As Lamb tells it, Murdoch instructed, 'I want a tearaway paper with lots of tits in it'. A loyal and obedient man, Lamb refused to ask

199 Latin for 'little paper'. Probably.

Murdoch what the hell he was talking about, and simply went off and did as he was reasonably sure he had been asked. *The Sun* went from strength to strength with its bountiful tits and tearawayness, and a formula that would soon rule the world was born.

In 1973, Rupert invaded America, buying the *San Antonio Express–News*, then founding the *Star*, a supermarket tabloid especially designed to be read while swearing under your breath at the old lady in front of you paying by cheque. In 1976 he purchased the *New York Post*[200], and his foothold in the States was well and truly established. Back home he had acquired Sydney's *Daily Telegraph*[201] from Sir Frank Packer, the legendary mogul known as the Keith Murdoch of the Packer family. Packer later regretted selling the *Telegraph* to Murdoch, as his own dreams of hiring dozens of racist illiterates came to a jarring halt.

As the 80s dawned, Rupert Murdoch found himself rich, powerful, and in what one could term the prime of his life, once you realised that he will live until he's 150. The decade was the era of Thatcher and Reagan, and Murdoch found that the times suited him – he had always wanted to generate mass unemployment, and the winds of change gave him the chance. The introduction of electronic production processes saw big job cuts in his businesses in Australia, Britain and America: great news for Murdoch and lovers of efficiency, but bad news for the unions, notorious for their hatred of progress and tacky obsession with poor people. The print unions in the UK flew into a frenzy over the excellently named Wapping dispute, a dispute that took place in Wapping and not, sadly, a dispute caused by whatever sexual act 'wapping' might be[202].

---

200 Motto: 'For people who love *The New York Times* but hate quality'.

201 Not to be confused with the *Daily Telegraph*, or the *Daily Telegraph*, or of course the now-defunct *Daily Telegraph*. Got it?

202 Let your imagination run wild.

The Wapping affair began when Murdoch built a new publishing facility in Wapping, in East London, moving operations from Fleet Street. At the new plant, 670 printers could produce the same output as 6800 had at the old facilities, and the unions, as usual, got all snotty about 'jobs' and 'fairness' and 'potential starvation', and went on strike. Murdoch responded by sacking the 6000 striking employees, which was a pretty elegant solution. The printers responded by picketing the plant and trying to block shipments from it. Thatcher responded by being a real hardarse and sending the cops in. Things from there got somewhat tense.

The printers' strike went on for a whole year, an impressive length of time for something that achieved absolutely nothing. In the end the Wapping imbroglio brought about 1500 arrests, 574 injured policemen, and the unions scurrying off with their tails between their legs. Within two years all of the UK's major papers opened new plants away from Fleet Street, proving yet again that in a struggle between the wealthy and the workers, the workers are hardly ever violent enough to make a real difference.

Thatcher's cooperation with Murdoch in the Wapping dispute was emblematic of Rupert's close relationship with governments of all stripes – but mainly of the 'let's give Rupert a present' stripe. He spent the 80s cosying up to Thatcher – hopefully not literally – and when she was deposed by John Major, Murdoch's *The Sun* claimed credit for assisting Major to an upset win in the 1992 election. In the three subsequent elections, the *The Sun* backed Tony Blair's Labour[203], and Blair sailed merrily home. After the retirement of Blair, Murdoch switched his allegiance back to the Conservatives, with eerily familiar results.

Murdoch's activities down the decades were not restricted to newspapers, of course: which is fortunate, given that by the

203 Or to give it its proper title, 'Labour-ish'.

time this book is published, there may not be any left. In 1983 he bought a controlling interest in Satellite Television, which he renamed Sky Channel, in honour of, I guess, the sky. Murdoch stated that cable and satellite television was 'the most important single advance since Caxton invented the printing press', but he was way off-base: actually Gutenberg invented it. Although in its early years Sky lost money hand over fist, and also via direct debit, the business eventually pulled a reverse-*Australian*, moving from loss to profit. A merger between Sky TV and British Satellite Broadcasting, producing the new entity BSkyB, was the turning point: today, under the name Sky UK Limited, the company is the UK's largest pay-TV broadcaster, and also provides broadband internet, phone services, and Shane Warne.

While he was reshaping the British media world in his own image – or rather, in Samantha Fox's image[204] – Murdoch was not neglecting the land of his birth. Although in a way, he was, because in 1985 he became an American citizen and gave up his Australian citizenship. But if he disowned us in a personal sense, Rupert never gave up his sincere love of Australian money. In 1984, he had been made a Companion of the Order of Australia for services to publishing, which made the citizenship-renouncing thing seem kind of spiteful, and caused many people to scrutinise their dictionaries in search of the definition of 'services'. In 1987, he bought the Herald and Weekly Times, a company which today publishes Melbourne's *Herald Sun*, Adelaide's *The Advertiser*, and *The Weekly Times*, Australia's foremost fertiliser-scented farming newsletter. In 1995, Murdoch's News Corporation partnered with Telstra to launch the Foxtel pay-TV network, which in the ensuing two decades became Australia's number one source of overpriced lifestyle programming.

---

204 Ask your dad.

Foxtel, of course, was named after the Fox Broadcasting Company, founded by Murdoch in the US in 1986. Fox would prove to be extremely lucrative for Murdoch, and make its mark in American TV history with a three-pronged approach: cheap-yet-hilarious reality shows; adult-oriented animated comedies filled with loathing for everything that Rupert Murdoch stands for; and the Fox News Network. This last has been a particular success: a carefully honed mixture of naked aggression, chemically-imbalanced bigotry, and touching self-delusion, Fox News has become one of America's – and indeed the world's – most trusted sources of confirmation bias.

It's incredible to think that the gigantic Murdoch octopus currently wrapping its financially cunning tentacles around the globe began with a humble newspaper in Adelaide. News Corp has grown to encompass so many diverse businesses in so many sectors of the media and communications industries that you could make a book by simply listing all of Murdoch's acquisitions over the years. Not necessarily a very interesting book, but certainly an easy one to write. It's worth considering. Besides those already mentioned, Murdoch either owns or has owned interests in Dow Jones, the *Wall Street Journal*, MySpace[205], IGN Entertainment, *The Times* of London, *The Courier-Mail,* Festival Mushroom Records, Star TV of Hong Kong, Sky Italia, and something called 'the Moraga Estate' which is either a vineyard or a dead guy's storage locker. In a nutshell, anyone who says that Rupert Murdoch owns a whole lot of stuff is in no way exaggerating: in fact, it's probably that no Australian has ever owned more – not even Greg Norman.

But you don't get to be incredibly rich and powerful and a hollowed-out caricature of a human soul without making a few

---

205 Remember MySpace? It was like Facebook except Sandi Thom was on it. Remember Sandi Thom? Lucky you.

enemies, without stepping on a few toes, without bending a few rules, without destroying a few innocent lives. Controversy has dogged Rupert Murdoch throughout his life and career, and brought down on him stresses and pressures that might've crushed a lesser man or one who cared in the slightest about it.

The main source of controversy has come from Murdoch's close association with politicians. In the countries where his companies have a major presence, he has been seen to exert great influence on political decisions, either by instructing his editors to push a certain line, or just by going round to the prime minister's house and handing them their orders for the day. So it is that many government decisions, particularly of the conservative or pro-business kind, are seen by some as being the result of Murdoch's manoeuvres. This may be slightly unfair, however, as Murdoch himself is only partially responsible for such government actions: they're also caused by politicians being spineless toadying creeps. It's just difficult to separate out the policies that were caused by spineless toadying creepiness PLUS Murdoch interference, from the policies that were caused by spineless toadying creepiness by itself.

The biggest single controversy to surround Murdoch was perhaps the News International phone-hacking scandal, when employees of the *News of the World* and other Murdoch papers in Britain hacked the voicemails of celebrities, politicians, crime victims and relatives of deceased soldiers. Fortunately they did all this without Rupert Murdoch's knowledge, and the day he informed the world of this was one of enormous relief for the world: imagine if he'd known what his employees were up to! It would've been just awful. The hacking revelations, including the shocking story of the *News of the World* hiring private investigators to hack into the voicemail of murdered schoolgirl Milly Dowler, caused massive public outcry, and the high-profile resignations of Dow

Jones CEO Les Hinton and News International CEO Rebekah Brooks among others. Even the London Police Commissioner Paul Stephenson resigned, in order to demonstrate his complete innocence of all charges.

The widespread criminality and corruption revealed by the hacking scandal shocked the world, while at the same time feeling pretty in-character for everyone involved. These were certainly dark times for Murdoch, who had to deal with the news that he had inadvertently hired a big bunch of nasty crooks who had taken advantage of his optimistic, trusting nature. Testifying at the Leveson Inquiry into British media practices, Rupert proclaimed that 'this is the most humble day of my life', and that was a big admission when you think about all the invasive medical procedures he must have undergone in his time.

But if opinions of Rupert Murdoch vary widely wherever his gigantic shadow looms, some things are undeniable. Whether you think of him as a mighty captain of industry, peerless wealth creator and giant of the noble fourth estate; or as a shameless hustler, degrader of public debate and promulgator of large-scale corruption[206], you can't argue with his success. And if you do argue with his success, *The Australian* will run op-eds about you until you shut up, so might as well save time. No Australian has spread their influence so far and so thoroughly; no Australian has racked up cash in such obscene quantities; no Australian has made it so blatantly clear that they don't really want to be Australian[207]. For his wealth, for his business acumen, for his transformation of the staid world of media into a dazzling wonderland of glamour and breasts and class warfare – Rupert Murdoch deserves a place, if not in the pantheon of great Australians, at least in the pantheon of terrifying ones.

---

206 This one, probably.

207 Well, Germaine Greer, I guess.

FUN FOR YOU AT HOME: Start your own newspaper! Use your home computer and printer to write, edit and publish a newspaper reporting on the hot issues around your neighbourhood. Make sure to include sections for sport, sections for showbiz news, and sections for poorly-educated screaming. Sell your paper to your friends and family. Calculate how much money you have lost. Write a one-page essay on why print is dead.

MODERN TIMES

AND SO, TO TODAY. Modern Australia has come a long way from the country that was once best-known for nobody knowing it was there. Today, we take our place proudly on the world stage, participating confidently in global culture, diplomacy and trade, and hardly ever going into a great big hysterical sulk because someone from another country said they don't like us.

The Australia of the 21st century is a country so certain of its national identity that it is comfortable flat-out denying that it is what it said it was. It is a country that has attained such a level of sophistication and self-aware complexity that within its warm, welcoming bosom can harmoniously nestle art and science, sport and religion, lethal spiders and surprisingly vicious koalas, *Masterchef* and *My Kitchen Rules*. It is, in short, a well-rounded country, and while every Australian throughout history has made a unique contribution to it becoming such, the last few decades have produced their own special breed of Aussies who have helped usher us into our current state, god have mercy on them.

The ructions of World War Two, followed by the prosperous complacency of the post-war period and the increasingly problematic and turbulent 60s and 70s, gave way the 80s, an era of excess and innovation. The opening up of the economy and the rise of a new variety of charmingly criminal business leaders stamped Australia as a nation well in tune with the spirit of the times. Political leaders began to take a more outward-looking approach to governing, looking to new allies beyond the traditional friends of the western world – Australia had discovered that Asia existed, and was both fascinated and intimidated, and frequently obnoxious about it. Prejudices were by turns stoked and overcome as Australia, like all nations, was forced to grapple with an increasingly interconnected world.

Sometimes it seems that in the modern era, Australia has to reflect more than ever on its past. The wrongs of history continue to echo and be argued over, and the efforts of Australians to distract themselves from troubling thoughts have at times been truly Herculean. There has been unprecedented glory for Australians in the recent past, in sport, entertainment and the arts – but an increased visibility on the world stage means an increased scrutiny on us as a nation, and like a teenage boy without a lock on his bedroom door, Australia is frequently caught with its pants down.

Through it all, Australia has continued to be led by men and women of vision, talent and a sort of aggravating upthemselfness[208]. Whether conquering the world on the biggest stage of all, breaking new ground in political achievement, or winning hearts with simple Aussie enthusiasm, these folks have propelled us into a new era whether we like it or not[209]. These are their stories.

---

208 Patent pending.

209 We don't.

ALAN BOND
Hit Me with Your Best Yacht

EVERY AUSTRALIAN REMEMBERS the America's Cup victory of 1983. Even some who weren't born yet remember it – that's how powerfully the memory has penetrated the soft, yielding outer skin of our national consciousness. The wild nationwide celebrations, the feeling of being a part of history, the brief yet intoxicating mass delusion that any of us were in any way interested in sailing: it was a unique time for Australians. Then-Prime Minister Bob Hawke's famous announcement that it was now illegal for anyone to lose their job brought hope and good cheer to a despondent nation, ground down by years of Malcolm Fraser's dour, yachtless premiership.

Many elements have to come together to make a successful bid for an international sailing championship. At least, I assume they do: I can't say for sure because, like all normal people, I know almost nothing about sailing and do not anticipate a day when I will be so bereft of options that learning more about sailing starts to look like an attractive course of action.

The point is, that though my best guess is that sailing victory requires a synthesis of excellence from a dedicated team of sportspeople pushing themselves to the very limit of putting up sails and pulling on ropes and so forth, there is one man without whom no America's Cup may be won: the man with the money. You can't win a boat race without buying a boat, or at the very least renting it for a relatively lengthy period of time. And in the case of the 1983 America's Cup, the guy who came through with the cash to put a team on the water was Alan Bond, Australia's favourite billionaire playboy of the 1980s.

But Bond wasn't just a boat-purchaser: he was also a felon. But even that doesn't completely sum up this complex, driven, possibly sort-of-intelligent man. To fully understand Alan Bond, it's necessary to examine not only the man's own life story, but also the exciting, economically adventurous climate of Australia in the non-stop 80s. The story of Bond and the story of Australia dovetailed to bring about the greatest love affair between a nation and a criminal since Ned Kelly.

The Bond saga began in earnest on 22 April 1938, when baby Alan was born to Frank and Kathleen Bond. Unconventionally for an Australian, he was born in Hammersmith, London: the first of many flamboyantly non-conformist acts that would come to characterise his life. At the age of 12, Alan moved with his parents and sister to Fremantle.

Little Alan didn't take long to adapt to his new home; he was charged with stealing and being unlawfully on premises within two years of arriving in Australia. At the age of 18, he confessed to planning a robbery after being arrested again for being unlawfully on premises. Already, the young man was showing a definite aptitude for being unlawfully on premises, and his parents had high hopes that he could forge a successful career in the home invasion sector.

But for this ambitious tyro, illegally occupying other people's property was only the beginning. A brilliant lateral thinker, he was struck with a thunderbolt of inspiration: if being unlawfully on properties was easy for him, how much easier would it be to develop properties of his own? As Bond saw it, property development offered two major advantages: it would be a lucrative source of income; and if he owned the properties, nobody could arrest him for being on them.

Rather than finishing high school like a loser, Bond had begun a signwriting apprenticeship at the age of 15, reasoning that to control property, one must first control the signs out the front of the property. The really talented signwriters are often able to make a killing in the property market just by erecting extremely convincing signs out the front of various buildings reading 'MINE'. Bond never got that good, but his later business activities often rose to a similar level of sophistication. At night he studied accounting, gaining a thorough grounding in all the laws and regulations that he aspired to one day ignore.

In 1959, Bond formed the Bond Corporation, which we should've seen coming. According to his official website[210], Bond Corporation 'opened the way for a new style of entrepreneur', which is pretty big talk from a man who was, at the time, a 21-year-old signwriter. This snotty little brat's 'new style' was apparently 'acquiring companies and using his drive and innovation to build them into world class corporations'. For the next three decades myriad companies would be well and truly drive-and-determinationed by Alan Bond. He went and drive-and-determinationed their brains out. The business world hadn't seen such passionate, red-blooded drive and determination since Dick Turpin.

Bond first amassed his fortune in property development, demonstrating a unique ability to buy bits of land, build things on them, and then sell them. This modus operandi having never occurred to anyone before, Bond's innovation took the business

210 Nowadays, this website is not, to be honest, in great shape.

world by storm, and today, buying land and then building on it and then selling it is one of the most common activities engaged in by property developers, surpassed only by bribery and running for local council. Bond's genius was already manifesting itself, and his creativity continued to change the industry: on one occasion he had the sandhills surrounding one of his developments spraypainted green to make the photos in the brochure look more lush; is it any wonder he won the hearts of Australians, a people famous for their embrace of pathological liars? Of course, your average Australian is an honest fellow, who does not condone mendacity of any kind: but there is a soft spot in his heart for a self-made man who, though he may lie, does so for the right reasons or for money.

Bond had already proven himself as a better person than us by becoming rich, but in 1970 his legend truly began. Buying three America's Cup challenge yachts from Sir Frank Packer, in what would become a cherished tradition of Alan Bond giving the Packer family large amounts of money, Bond entered the wonderful world of sailing, a realm beloved throughout history by millions of rich idiots with no capacity for forethought.

Some background: the America's Cup, also known as 'the Auld Mug', 'the Venerable Vessel' and 'Ol' Juggy', was first awarded in 1851 by the Royal Yacht Squadron for a race around the Isle of Wight, won by the schooner *America*, after which the cup was then named. Shortly afterwards it was discovered that there was also a country called America, and everyone agreed it was only fair the cup should go there. The New York Yacht Club held it for the next 132 years in the sporting world's longest ever winning streak. The NYYC was aided in its continued defences by the rules of sailing, which nobody has ever known, making it difficult for anyone to determine whether they'd actually won the cup or not – every time someone thought they might have won it, the Americans told them they'd made a foot fault or were carrying non-regulation hand towels, and take the cup back home again. Bond planned to change this, declaring that he was willing to spend whatever it took to find out what the rules were and promising that the crews of his boats would always be informed in a timely fashion whether they had won a race or not.

Bond's first attempt at winning the America's Cup was unsuccessful, as were his second and third. Even worse, in the second challenge he was beaten by a yacht skippered by American billionaire Ted Turner, who wasn't even aware he was in a boat for most of the race. Bond determined to keep on fighting for his dream of bankrolling an international sporting triumph that did not directly involve him in any meaningful way. It's possible that he was encouraged in this by his receiving the Australian of the Year award in 1978, the criteria for the award at that time apparently giving considerable weight to material wealth and sporting failure. He shared the award with Galarrwuy Yunupingu, which is one of those examples of extreme juxtaposition that has always made history a laugh.

The turning of the tide in Bond's naval fortunes was down to Ben Lexcen, a plucky[211] young marine architect who had battled his entire life against the quite justifiable public perception that 'marine architect' isn't a real job. Unable to make a living from the underwater housing industry, Lexcen had worked on the boats for Bond's three unsuccessful challenges, an experience which had granted him the insight that to seriously challenge for the America's Cup, it would be necessary to abandon the traditional method of using a slower boat than your opponent's. I know it seems obvious after the fact, but back then this was quite the jaw-dropper.

---

211 Examination of Australian sporting history reveals that our champions have been, in over 95% of cases, plucky.

Lexcen's plan was to build a boat that would revolutionise the whole field of whatever it is that sailing boats are supposed to do. His idea was to equip the yacht with a 'winged keel', which in layman's terms can essentially be described as a keel with wings. What did this mean for the boat? Well, put simply, the winged keel served to increase the effective keel aspect ratio in order to reduce the level of lift induced drag resulting from a tip vortex[212].

Bond loved Lexcen's idea, or at least was uninterested enough in the details to pay for it without asking too many questions: thus transferring his business strategy to the field of sport. And so *Australia II* was born: a boat that, as its name suggested, was like Australia but better[213].

When Bond showed up at Newport Yacht Club, Rhode Island in 1983 with *Australia II* in his bumbag, it caused much controversy amongst the yachting establishment. The New York Yacht Club, which was defending its title, protested against *Australia II*, claiming that having a boat with wings was cheating, since boats are supposed to float not fly. However, much like a high school football team in a movie where a donkey becomes the star quarterback, Bond smoothly declared, 'Show me where in the rules it says that a yacht CAN'T fly!' The New Yorkers had no answer, and *Australia II* was allowed to compete, and to win – its winged keel proving irresistible against the sad, wingless keel of the Americans' sorry excuse for a boat.

When *Australia II* crossed the finish line, or whatever happens at the end of a yacht race, in the early hours of 27 September 1983, the entire nation erupted in joy, having collectively decided that what the hell, let's act like we're interested in sailing for a bit[214]. Many

---

212 Put less simply would take way too long.

213 If only it were so easy to create a sequel to the country itself.

214 The football season had just finished, and the cricket hadn't started yet.

Australians saw it as a landmark moment in the nation's history: the day when we simultaneously found out what sailing was, and proved we could beat the world at it. It was like a drunker, less violent Gallipoli. Prime Minister Bob Hawke, who had had his own 'America's Cup' moment earlier in the year when he had sailed the ship of Labor skilfully around the buoy of representative democracy, went down in history when, at a victory party, he famously declared, 'Any boss whose sack isn't working today can kiss my bum', or something along those lines.

The America's Cup cemented Alan Bond's status as a hero in the eyes of Australians. It was Lexcen who designed the winged keel, and it was a bunch of what I presume were sailors of some kind who sailed the boat, but it was Bond who signed the cheques, and this made him the most important – if not the most impressive, talented or praiseworthy – person in the whole operation. An inspiration to little boys with less than robust physiques everywhere, he was now firmly ensconced in the highest echelons of Australian society, and it seemed to many that once thus ensconced, he would never be un-ensconced. How wrong those many were.

Yachting had not been Bond's only occupation over these years: his business interests had swollen to enormous, unsightly proportions[215]. He diversified his portfolio, expanding into retail, mining, and for some reason airships; and in 1981 he bought the Swan Brewery for $164 million. Finding that making beer put him in a good mood, he went on to pay $1.2 billion for Castlemaine Tooheys, which put him in control of half the country's beer market, meaning he could get beer anytime he wanted, even for kids and stuff. He was the Willy Wonka of beer, and every bit as neglectful of occupational health and safety.

215 As had he.

The Castlemaine Tooheys purchase was the biggest corporate takeover in Australian history, and the price was four times the value of Bond Corporation at the time. I know that's hard to get your head around, but you and I are neither corporate tycoons nor career criminals, so we can't be expected to fully understand the world of high finance and expensive liquor.

Upon merging his own iconic Australianness with the iconic Australianness of Tooheys, Bond further enhanced his public image by telling the publicans who sold the company's beer that they no longer had an interest in their pubs – which came as a surprise to the publicans, who had honestly believed that they were very interested in them indeed – and that they would therefore be kicked to the kerb as soon as their leases expired. This act of brutal oppression of the lower classes, which caused a protracted legal battle, nervous breakdowns for several publicans, and at least one suicide, was a perfect example of the kind of whimsical corporate showmanship that endeared Bond so to the Australian public. If there's one thing Australians love, it's a battler. But in a pinch, they'll settle for a man kicking battlers to death as well.

Seriously, some might question how a greedy lying sociopath like Bond managed to achieve such widespread popularity, but it's important to remember that this was the 1980s, a time when the philosophy of 'greed is good' gained great currency among moviegoers who didn't understand the plot of *Wall Street*, and when people loved nothing more than a fabulously rich man who had not yet been arrested grinding the poor beneath his boot heel: from Bond, to Christopher Skase, to Mel Gibson, we just couldn't get enough of 'em.

The turning point in Bond's fortunes might be said to have been his bold move to acquire the Nine Network in 1987. As Bond later told it, the transaction went thusly: he told legendary billionaire, straight-talking business tough guy, and terrifying giant rubber hand puppet Kerry Packer that he wanted to buy Channel Nine.

'I don't want to sell Channel Nine,' Packer replied.

'Look,' retorted Bond. 'Maybe I haven't made myself clear: I really, *really* want to buy Channel Nine. Like, I'm gagging for it.'

'I don't care what you're gagging for,' the Great Kerry snarled. 'I like having Channel Nine. You can't have it. It's mine.'

'Would it change your mind,' asked Bond, leaning forward and waggling his eyebrows significantly, 'if I told you this: I want to buy it.'

'Look,' Packer said in exasperation, frankly wondering how this weird little man had even been allowed into his office, 'Channel Nine is my most treasured possession. I wouldn't sell it for less than a billion dollars.'

'Oh,' said Bond, 'okay then.'

Packer stared. 'What?' he said, slightly confused.

'I'll pay a billion dollars,' said Bond. 'Will you take a cheque?'

'Yeah, okay, let's, ah,' Packer snorted hysterically, 'let's do this.' And so the deal was done.

Packer would later say, 'You only get one Alan Bond in your lifetime, and I've had mine', an extremely insensitive remark to those of us who never even get one Alan Bond and have spent our whole lives slaving away in the gutter, cursing the total absence of Alan Bonds on the horizon. But he was right that the deal turned out well for him – two years after buying the Nine Network, Bond was forced to sell it back to Packer at a colossal loss in a classic example of what business experts call 'pretty funny'.

It was a sign that the Bond mystique was starting to crack. His financial savvy was becoming questionable – he was a profligate spender, squandering millions on gifts for his family and at one point buying a village in England, which doesn't even sound like something a person can do.

In the wake of the 1987 stock market crash, Bond purchased *Irises*, by Vincent Van Gogh, for $54 million, half of which was loaned to him by the auctioneer Sotheby's, which had slightly misunderstood the purpose of their business. It was becoming clear that Alan Bond's success was to a great extent dependent on the generosity of people with poor judgment.

In 1989, Bond took what is usually the final step in a businessman's downward spiral into total irrationality: he founded a university. Australia's first privately-funded university, Bond University was a place for young people who wanted to learn the secrets of business success and had literally nowhere else to go. When in 1992, Bond declared bankruptcy, many Bond University students probably regretted their enrolment, but to be honest if it took them that long education was never their natural home anyway.

That bankruptcy didn't come as a shock to anyone who'd been paying attention, although Bond's entire career to that point had been a testament to the fact that most people hadn't been paying any attention. Some said it was Bond's hubris that had caught up with him: others said it was all the money he had spent that he didn't actually have. Maybe there was truth on both sides.

Sadly for Alan Bond, his woes did not stop at bankruptcy. The same year he was also sentenced to prison for his role in the collapse of a merchant bank, but only served 90 days, being acquitted on retrial. However, four years later he discovered that criminal charges could also have their dark side, getting three years for fraud relating to the purchase of Edouard Manet's painting *La Promenade*. It was around this time that Bond made the startling discovery that he was suffering severe brain damage and could not remember anything he had ever done in his entire life. I'm sure we can all relate.

It was a tragic sight, as the once-mighty Australian of the Year and champion boat-buyer sat day after day in court, in both criminal and civil cases, fighting fraud charges and a variety of angry creditors, totally defenceless. Rendered feeble and vulnerable by the mysterious and sudden ailment, it tugged at the heartstrings to see Bond respond 'I don't recall' to question after question regarding things he had done, companies he had defrauded, and money he had stolen. Where did the truth lie? With Bond's memory gone, it was impossible to tell. Australians were united in their sympathy for their fallen hero, with thousands of messages of support reaching the stricken tycoon, who sadly couldn't read any of them because of the baffling brain fever that had overcome his once-keen senses much like the hero of classic story *Flowers for Algernon*, except that Bond had never befriended a mouse and the guy in the story hadn't committed larceny on a grand scale.

Even in his weakened state, Bond remained a high achiever, continuing to break records and make history by being convicted of the largest fraud in Australian corporate history: the cheeky removal of more than $1 billion from Bell Resources in 1988, possibly money that he needed to make the interest payments to Kerry Packer. After pleading guilty to failing to act honestly as a company director – a pretty unrealistic thing to make illegal when you think about it – he was sentenced to four years in jail, which was convenient because he was already in there. This became seven years after the Director of Public Prosecutions appealed but then became three, and Bond was out of prison by 2000.

His release began a happier chapter in the Bond saga, as his mysterious brain disease had just as mysteriously disappeared. He had pulled off the rare reverse *Flowers for Algernon*, like a disabled mouse brought back to life. Even better, Bond returned to the business world, gladdening the hearts of all those who had missed his dynamic presence at the top of the corporate ladder, and especially those of his creditors who had years earlier received 0.6 of a cent in the dollar on his debts to them and were no doubt relieved to see how well he was looking these days. In 2008, Alan Bond returned to Australia's rich list, with his worth estimated at $265 million, a fitting end to the inspirational underdog tale that had been his life, following the inspirational overdog tale that had been the slightly earlier bit.

In 2015, at the age of 77, Alan Bond passed away following complications from heart surgery, and was survived by his money.

Alan Bond left a legacy of excess, extravagance and extremely poor choices, but in the typical manner of the classic Aussie larrikin, he breezed through all difficulties with a smile, a wink and a declaration of amnesia. A memorable tale of a man's triumph over adversity and simultaneous infliction of adversity on many, many other people, the Alan Bond story epitomises that famous line in the national anthem:

> *With golden soil, and wealth for toil, and an enduring love of unrepentant criminals.*

FUN FOR YOU AT HOME: Become a property developer! Find a vacant plot of land in your neighbourhood and build a house on it from old cereal boxes and plastic cups. See how much you can sell it for, then plunge all your earnings into high-risk resource plays. Ask a parent to help you find a lawyer.

STEVE IRWIN
The Crocodile Monetiser

AUSTRALIAN HISTORY is full of moguls, tycoons and entrepreneurs of every stripe and speckle. John MacArthur built an empire of sheep for the country to ride on the backs of, and had a governor dragged from under his bed in the process. Rupert Murdoch proved that even an Australian can achieve genuine world domination as long as he stops being Australian as early as possible. But perhaps no Antipodean wealth creator has had such a thrilling and surprising rise to prominence as Steve Irwin, the first Australian to truly recognise the business potential of crocodiles.

Humans and crocodiles had, of course, had a long relationship way before Steve Irwin came along, but that relationship had been mainly of the culinary variety. Australians have long been enthusiastic crocodile feeders, and in the croc world our species' selflessness in laying down our lives for the nutrition of our reptilian brothers is legendary. As an apex predator, crocodiles pose an extreme danger to humans, especially ones who fail to understand the meaning of the term 'apex predator'. The saltwater crocodile is the most dangerous of the lot, building up its muscles through regular ocean swims and possessing a bite force that has been measured at over 16,000 Newtons[216]. This makes the saltie the most powerful biter in the animal kingdom, placing it ahead of other animals such as the hyena, the honey badger, the Bactrian camel or Geri 'Ginger Spice' Halliwell. Such a powerful bite is impressive enough, but when you add in the fact that the average crocodile also has teeth, it all adds up to one very credible fact: being bitten by a saltwater crocodile hurts like an absolute bastard.

The first thing people noticed about Steve Irwin is that even though he was completely aware that a crocodile bite was bad for you, he was still very willing to get inadvisably close to crocodiles, and even to touch them, which is not just inadvisable but positively reckless: being touched is one of the average crocodile's pet peeves. This meant one of two things: either Irwin enjoyed being bitten by crocodiles, or he thought that a crocodile bite was a small price to pay for the joy of touching one of the beasts in an irregularly intimate fashion.

It probably helped that as a child, little Steve spent his formative years at the Beerwah Reptile Park, a wildlife refuge that his father Bob Irwin had built after moving his family from Melbourne to Queensland to chase his dream of surrounding himself with all Earth's most terrifying creatures. In many ways, the reptiles at the park were Steve's family, although in many other ways, this was a very strange attitude to take and you couldn't exactly say it's normal. But if Steve's upbringing was abnormal, it was an abnormality that would prove to be profitable beyond his wildest dreams[217].

As a boy, Steve took part in feeding and animal care at the park, which is probably a violation of some kind of regulation, but

216 I think this is some kind of biscuit.

217 Not to imply I have any special knowledge of how wild Steve's dreams were.

it was a different time and people were fairly relaxed about both child labour and child devouring-by-wild-animals. On his sixth birthday, Steve was given a four-metre python, the pair quickly becoming the best of friends à la an unusually unsettling Disney buddy movie[218]. Many parents will tell you that you shouldn't give a six-year-old an enormous snake for their birthday, but the vast majority of those parents' children will never be multimillionaires, so who's the real fool?[219]

By the age of nine, Steve had not only had a solid three years' practice at being a snake's best friend, but was allowed to handle crocodiles, and even wrestle them, thanks to the years of education on reptiles that his father had provided him from an early age. Or to put it another way: despite the years of education on reptiles that his father had provided him from an early age.

Reaching adulthood, as many boys of his generation did at the time, Steve began working for the East Coast Crocodile Management Program, in the course of which he captured more than a hundred crocodiles, earning him the nickname 'The Caloundra Crocnapper' in the crocodile community. Old crocodiles would tell the youngsters chilling tales of Steve Irwin and his Ropes of Doom, and crocodile parents across Queensland warned their children to always come directly home and not loiter, for fear they would be snatched. Some thought that Steve Irwin was just a legend, and scoffed at the idea that a malevolent khaki demon was lying in wait to abduct them – they soon learnt.

In 1991, Steve took over the management of the reptile park, and the next year changed the name from Beerwah Reptile Park, which wasn't exactly catchy and created a lot of confusion over what exactly a 'Beerwah' was, to 'Australia Zoo', a name that perfectly

---

218 Working title 'Monty and the Python'.

219 It's still them.

encapsulated everything that Steve wanted the park to represent: a) that it was in Australia; and b) that it was a zoo.

As manager of Australia Zoo, Steve had become a fully-fledged reptile tycoon, a job that didn't even exist until he invented it, just another example of his peculiar innovativeness. But his career was yet to explode into the stratosphere of wealth and celebrity. When it did, it would be, as has been the case with countless great men throughout history, the result of marrying a naturalist from Eugene, Oregon. Terri Raines visited Australia Zoo in 1991 and she and Steve fell in love at first sight, bonding over their shared love of cold-blooded killing machines. Marrying in 1992, the happy couple spent their honeymoon trapping crocodiles, the dream of young lovers since the dawn of time. But that honeymoon turned out to be far more significant than the average ordinary romantic carnivore-snaring getaway: it would be the key to what became the Steve Irwin empire.

On honeymoon, the Irwins were filmed crocnapping by Steve's friend John Stainton, a film director with no particular qualms about tagging along on other people's honeymoons and filming them. The footage he captured was eventually turned into the pilot of a TV program that would change the world: *The Crocodile Hunter.*

Steve Irwin was obviously not the first Australian to think of making entertainment out of crocodiles. In the 1980s loveable larrikin Paul Hogan had become a global superstar thanks to his movie *Crocodile Dundee*. But Hogan had only capitalised on the cachet of the word 'crocodile': the movie itself had precious little reptile action, and turned out to be basically a comedy of manners about surprising toilets and the ongoing debate over cutlery classification. Irwin was taking the commercialisation of crocodilians further, by bringing live man and live croc together in a physical sense, over and over again, on camera.

In 1996, four years after the honeymoon that produced the footage, *The Crocodile Hunter* made its debut on Australian TV. Critics immediately pinpointed the distinctive element that would become the show's trademark: the title was a bald-faced lie. Steve Irwin did not, in fact, hunt crocodiles. He was more accurately described as a 'crocodile trapper'; and perhaps even more accurately, a 'crocodile harasser'. It would rapidly become clear that Steve had no intention of killing any crocodiles: in fact he didn't even enjoy killing crocodiles. The sense of betrayal was palpable.

To some extent, what Steve was actually *doing* with the crocodiles on his honeymoon was not important[220], as long as Terri consented. What was important was that, like Paul Hogan, he was a real larrikin, a word which was originally coined to describe violent street gangs, but had by the 1990s come to mean anyone who spoke like Alf from *Home and Away* and wore shorts in public. But unlike Hogan, whose larrikinism took a relaxed, laconic form, Steve was a more breathless, hyperactive brand of larrikin, like a crazed spider monkey smashing all your windows and trying to have sex with your face. He was a stunning breath of fresh air, especially coming from Queensland, a wide sultry land where the oppressive heat and laidback lifestyle causes most inhabitants to speak slowly and sparingly and racistly. Steve Irwin could pack more words into half an hour than most Queenslanders did in half a year, even if 70 to 80 per cent of those words were 'crikey' and 'wow'.

A year after *The Crocodile Hunter* was introduced to Australian audiences, it aired on American TV. Americans, never having had to talk to anyone like Steve Irwin at a barbecue, found him a fresh and fascinating novelty and not an intolerably obnoxious dickhead.

---

220 Indeed, many modern churches now say that whatever you do with a crocodile on your honeymoon is between you and God.

The original honeymoon pilot was expanded into a series, the first season of which saw Steve and Terri meet spiders, beavers, raccoons, snakes, turtles, alligators, and of course crocodiles, the heartiest of all the Irwin meal tickets. The series also acted as an invaluable source of publicity for Australia Zoo, bringing the zoo's scaly charms to international attention.

Liked well enough in small doses by other Australians, Steve was positively adored by viewers in other countries, particularly the USA. His boundless enthusiasm and suicidal courage, combined with his broad ocker accent and willingness to wear shorts regardless of circumstance, endeared him to a population desperate for an entertainer with genuine authenticity and a love of animals bordering on the unnatural.

The first season of the show was just four episodes long, but production quickly went into overdrive. In the end *The Crocodile Hunter* would run for five seasons and 55 episodes, plus four specials. Over these episodes Steve and Terri travelled all over the world, met a dazzling variety of wild beasts, and challenged the logic of the food chain to an extent never before seen. Highlights of the show's fabled run include:

- The time Steve's assistant Wes was severely injured by a crocodile named Graham, but Steve saves his life by jumping on Graham.
- The time we witnessed the subtly erotic sight of giant saltwater crocodiles eating pigs whole.
- The time Steve got up close with spitting cobras and was forced to seek medical assistance in a totally unforeseeable development.
- The time Steve flew in an F-16 even though this has nothing to do with animals whatever.

There were many more magic moments from the intrepid Crocodile Non-Hunter, who was busily building his brand into an unstoppable commercial juggernaut, like a kind of reptile-focused Olsen Twins. The TV show was broadcast into more than 130 countries, and its success allowed Steve to keep expanding his beloved Australia Zoo. From its humble beginnings as an arena for Bob Irwin to stage his child-snake fights, it had become a world-class wildlife exhibition, with exciting new features such as:

- The Crocoseum, a museum staffed and operated entirely by superintelligent crocodiles.
- The rainforest aviary, where visitors could learn what it was like to be pecked on the head by real jungle birds.
- Tiger Temple, where pilgrims could offer tribute and beseech the divine tigers not to bite their faces.
- The Disabled Toilets.

Steve even spoke of the possibility of opening an Australia Zoo in Las Vegas, making use of the natural synergy between large predators and gambling addiction. This project never came to fruition, but the idea raised intriguing questions. Would an 'Australia Zoo' make any sense outside Australia? On the other hand, would a foreign-based Australia Zoo expose the fact that it didn't make any sense *in* Australia, like when they open an Outback Steakhouse in Australia and nobody quite knows what's going on? I guess we'll never know.

The Irwins had become the richest crocodile wrestling couple in history, and possibly the richest carnivore-touchers of any kind[221]. But much of their growing fortune was ploughed back

221 With the exception of Bill and Melinda Gates, the well-known bear-fingerers.

into the zoo and their ceaseless efforts for animal conservation, a cause close to their hearts, not least because if animals aren't conserved, you can't film yourself wrestling them. Although their projects were aimed at a commercial audience, they stuck fast to the philosophy that the animals must always come first. Then again, Gina Rinehart can say that her philosophy is that the rocks must always come first too – you can say whatever you please comes first when the cash keeps rolling in. Not that I want to be cynical: Steve Irwin undeniably loved his animals. You could tell by the way he kept cuddling them.

It was easy to overlook how savvy a businessman Steve Irwin was, because you were too busy paying attention to the shouting and the shorts and the gigantic jaws about to close around his head. But his achievement in parlaying a modest wildlife park and a stunning disregard for his own safety into a global multimedia empire should never be underestimated. With his beloved Terri by his side, Steve had become an unlikely corporate behemoth, and it didn't stop at *The Crocodile Hunter* and Australia Zoo: Steve also established the Steve Irwin Conservation Foundation and International Crocodile Rescue, and fronted advertising campaigns for FedEx, the Ghan railway, and Toyota.

In fact, the early years of the new millennium were dominated by Steve Irwin, who found the world had suddenly developed an insatiable thirst for him, and was only too happy to pour himself down its dry dusty throat. In 2001, he entered the world of film, scoring a cameo in *Dr Dolittle 2*, a movie which many critics rate as one of the top three Dr Dolittle-themed films of all time. As Steve himself could, in a way, 'talk to the animals', or at the very least 'manhandle the animals and make them a bit jumpy', it was a role tailor-made for the hardy wildlife warrior, especially because he was playing himself.

The next step in Irwin's film career was, obviously, a starring role, which he achieved with *The Crocodile Hunter: Collision Course* in 2002. This opus, which has a 5.4 rating on IMDB – solid but unpretentious, much like Steve himself – told the real story of the Crocodile Hunter's story of success: assuming that that story was one about Steve mistaking CIA agents for poachers and trying to prevent them from capturing a crocodile which has swallowed a tracking drone. The soundtrack featured a cover of 'Crocodile Rock' by the Baha Men, as a special treat for fans of the pitiless abyss of existential terror.

Starring Steve Irwin as Steve, Terri Irwin as Terri, and Magda Szubanski in her signature role as Brozzie Drewitt, the film had mixed reviews, insofar as some critics hated it and others just didn't see it. Still, it grossed $33 million, having cost $12 million to make, so one could reasonably say that *Crocodile Hunter: Collision Course* was a hit, even if doing so is likely to induce a wave of indefinable sadness.

The same year as his leading-man debut, Steve, along with Terri and daughter Bindi, appeared in *Wiggly Safari*, a Wiggles video exploring the tantalising question of what would happen if a safari became wiggly. The answer: a whole bunch of enjoyable shenanigans! The video was set in Australia Zoo, which was a pretty happy coincidence because it saved the Irwins a lot of petrol money.

But these were sidelines – Steve's passion was for the art of wildlife documentary, an art he single-handedly revolutionised. Before Irwin the genre had been divided into two broad subcategories: the Attenborough school of calm detached observation and perfectly framed sequences of nature's most astounding phenomena; and the Disney's White Wilderness school of deliberately slaughtering large numbers of animals for the entertainment of children. Steve Irwin introduced an addictive third way of filming wildlife: Irwinism, which steered a middle course between detached observation and mass killing to find fertile ground in keeping animals alive while shouting hysterically at them Steve Irwin was an easy target for ridicule – that's why he's in this book – but in the game of life, the winner is not he with the most fashionable shorts, it's he with the biggest sack with a dollar sign on it. Steve Irwin famously had an enormous sack. And when you think about it, if a guy is going to build up a multimillion-dollar empire, mucking around with crocodiles and snakes and lions is a better way to do it than the way most multimillion-dollar empires are built, which almost always involves large-scale environmental vandalism and/or actual murder.

A man as full of life as Steve Irwin seemed invincible, not subject to the inevitabilities that plague ordinary mortals. But he was as human as any one of us, a fact that was brought home in tragic fashion on 4 September 2006, when an attempt to film a stingray off Port Douglas, Queensland, resulted in a fatal wound from the creature's tail. As unlikely as it seemed, the man who had devoted his life to provoking deadly animals had ended up being killed by one of them. The irony was devastating.

Like all truly great (rich) men, Steve Irwin's story did not end with his untimely death. His legacy lives on and becomes even stronger with the passing of time, much like Obi-Wan Kenobi or Tupac. He is commemorated in the names of Steve Irwin Way, the road running by Australia Zoo; the Steve Irwin Wildlife Reserve in north Queensland; and he is one of the very few people to have both a turtle and a snail named after him[222]: the Irwin's turtle and the *Crikey steveirwini*[223].

---

222 Others include Dannii Minogue and Charlemagne.

223 That's a real thing. What can you do, right?

Most of all, though, Steve Irwin lives on through his family: particularly his daughter Bindi, who has had a stunning and varied career herself, beginning with appearances on her father's TV shows, before starring in her own projects including *Bindi the Jungle Girl, Free Willy: Escape from Pirate's Cove, Return to Nim's Island, Bindi's Bootcamp*, and various other things that nobody has ever seen. After winning season 21 of *Dancing With The Stars*, Bindi continues to pursue a successful career in being hounded by paparazzi. With Bindi, and her younger brother Bob, carrying on the family tradition of safari suits, Steve's invaluable conservation work, and even more invaluable making money from animals work, is secure.

Steve Irwin was a true original – or at least if he wasn't, he was unoriginal to a degree and volume that hadn't been seen before. He taught the world so much about animals, but did he not also teach us about ourselves? No, he did not. Not really. But about animals, we learnt heaps. The man earnt a fortune from his love for wildlife, but he also gave back so much, and if there were animals who felt traumatised by their contact with him, they never said so, because they are animals, so we have no real need to think about that too much. Good on him.

FUN FOR YOU AT HOME: Wrestle a crocodile. If you can't find a crocodile, try wrestling whatever animal you can find: a dog, a cat, a lizard, an ant – try wrestling a few and taking note of the differences in degree of difficulty.

JULIA GILLARD
The Ginger Pimpernel

JULIA GILLARD WAS, without doubt, the greatest Prime Minister Australia has ever had. Over her career, the only possible criticism that could be made of her was that she was, in fact, the worst Prime Minister Australia has ever had. This dichotomy, the two sides of Julia Gillard, is a shining example of the way in which she divided opinion. But love her or hate her, you could never deny that Gillard was a high achiever. Well, that's not strictly true: you could deny it, and lots of people did, constantly. But most of them were never prime minister, so chalk that up to jealousy.

In a way Gillard was always marked for greatness. Born in Barry, the town in Wales where Stacey from *Gavin and Stacey* came from, young Julia likewise dreamt of one day being laughed at by millions, and in due course her dream would be realised. But first she had to convince her parents that the best way to become Australian Prime Minister was to move to Australia, which they did, settling in Adelaide in 1966, the well-known 'city of churches/death'.

Julia Gillard attended the University of Adelaide, a prestigious institution whose alumni include Shaun Micallef, Christopher Pyne, Colin Thiele, and Nobel laureates Howard Florey, William Bragg and Robin Warren. It's also produced over 100 Rhodes scholars, although I think by now we've learnt that almost anyone can be a Rhodes scholar[224]. Anyway Gillard had more important things to do than swanning off to Oxford to race canoes. Instead she swanned off to Melbourne, which she had heard was where the action was, though it was possible she had confused 'action' with 'graffiti'.

Gillard gained her Bachelor of Laws degree from Melbourne University in 1986, and in 1987 joined the law firm Slater and Gordon, who will fight for YOU if you have been injured in a car accident. In 1990, at the age of 29, she became one of the youngest ever partners at Slater and Gordon.

Like every lawyer ever, Gillard was easily bored, and in the days before *Masterchef*, the traditional path for lawyers wishing to quit their jobs was politics. In 1996, therefore, she quit her job and took a position as chief of staff to Victorian Opposition Leader John Brumby, himself a fiery up-and-comer who would one day go down in history as a man who almost certainly was Premier at some point I think.

Gillard proved herself a formidable operator as chief of staff. In one famous story, a male colleague, overcome by rage, threw an orange at her. Without so much as a flinch, Gillard caught the fruit and, with icy calm, told the angry man, 'You don't chuck it, you peel it.' She then proceeded to eat the projectile. This display of composure and sangfroid stunned many in the party machine: myriad aspiring powerbrokers had in the past tried and failed to grasp the true purpose of oranges, and for such a relative newcomer to do it so effortlessly marked Gillard for greatness.

After two years as the power behind the Brumby, Gillard was elected to the Federal House of Representatives in 1998, representing the electorate of Lalor. Her maiden speech to Parliament established a

224 Almost any white person anyway.

theme that would be constant throughout her career: talking about things. In it she outlined the ways in which Lalor's inhabitants were poor and dirty and frequently kicked and spat on by snotty rich knobs. The fiery rhetoric of the new MP struck a chord.

In her first year in office, Gillard achieved every child's dream: membership of the standing committee for Employment, Education and Workplace Relations. Yet despite this, Labor somehow contrived to lose the 2001 federal election, Prime Minister John Howard's exploitation of anxieties about asylum seekers and terrorism proving far too powerful for Opposition Leader Kim Beazley's total acquiescence to Howard's exploitation of anxieties about asylum seekers and terrorism. Seeking to rebuild the party, Simon Crean became Labor leader, sort of.

Gillard had by now moved into the Health portfolio, placing her in direct opposition to Health Minister Tony Abbott, and beginning a rivalry that would echo through the ages and give Abbott some extremely fevered dreams. These two political bomb-throwers went head-to-head with a ferocity the Australian voting public rarely sees, and even more rarely cares about.

Gillard was emblematic of the new, more aggressive Labor. Latham was discombobulating the government with his bold tactics and imaginative policies such as burning down every third private school and punching you in the face if you looked at him funny; the Howard regime looked in trouble. Gillard's dream of being in government was so close she could taste it, but it turned out to just be gas: Latham fell in a heap in the 2004 election after voters rejected his pledge to break both John Howard's arms in public. The Labor leader responded to his defeat with all the phlegmatic calm of a ferret trapped in a lifesaver's speedos, and the party turned once again to Beazley, who had lost two elections already but was at least neither insane nor Simon Crean.

Beazley did not last long in his second stint as opposition leader, due to the perception that he was a loser, bolstered by the way he kept losing. It wasn't long before Kevin Rudd, a small shiny technocrat who had risen in the ALP not through traditional factional means but via a mind control ray of his own invention, took on the mantle – and Gillard took the momentous step of assuming the role of Rudd's deputy opposition leader.

As Deputy Leader, Gillard provided a relatable, down-to-earth counterpoint to her leader's somewhat aloof megalomania, and Rudd-Gillard became a dream team that gave John Howard nightmares, assuming that John Howard was capable of sleeping at night. As the 2007 election loomed, the Rudd-Gillard message began to seriously penetrate the public consciousness, and voters slowly came to realise that, despite what their grandparents had told them when they were small, voting for Labor *was* legal.

On 24 November 2007, the Labor Opposition swept the 11-year-old Howard administration from office, crushing the tired, complacent Liberal-National Coalition and causing Howard himself to transform into the form of a crow and fly into exile in the Mountains of Shadow. This meant that Julia Gillard became the first female deputy prime minister in the nation's history, a massive achievement that proved, once and for all, that sexism didn't exist.

With 11 long years of authoritarian smugness to unravel, the Rudd government got straight to work on its hefty agenda. Rudd had taken an ambitious policy platform to the election, and the people loved him for the tireless way he worked day and night to transform his big plans into slightly smaller plans.

There were two great achievements of the Rudd government in its first term: the official apology to the Stolen Generations, and the survival of the Global Financial Crisis. This latter was genuinely impressive: as the world's financial systems went into meltdown, the scintillating brains trust of the Australian government hit upon the ingenious idea that when the economy is flatlining, it might help if people had more money to spend. This counter-intuitive brainwave, which contradicted conventional economic thinking that the best way to stimulate a slowing economy is to make everyone as poor as possible, worked a treat. A direct fiscal stimulus payment to taxpayers, combined with a major program of public works, kept the Australian economy relatively strong throughout the worst financial crisis the world had seen for decades. Although there were some quibbles over details of the government's plan, such as the size of the stimulus payments and the left-field decision to murder thousands of Australians in their own homes with burning insulation[225], nobody could deny that on a macroeconomic level, whatever that means, the government's policy had been an enormous success.

The financial crisis quashed, Prime Minister Rudd could now move ahead with his long-term agenda of sleep deprivation and verbal abuse. Revolutionising hidebound political theory with his fresh new approach to alienating Cabinet members and reforming the public service by screaming the 'C word' at them until they resigned in tears, Rudd left more of an imprint on public life in three years than most men manage in three years and a few weeks. And through it all Julia Gillard was at his side: encouraging, advising, cautioning, supporting, negotiating, and periodically checking to see whether the numbers had turned far enough to let her knock him off yet.

For Julia Gillard was many things: a class warrior, a feminist icon, a brilliant orator, an accomplished full-forward; but more than anything else, she was a woman of vision. She saw herself at

---

225 Some economists say murder is no way to bring about prosperity, but can you argue with results?

the vanguard of a new era of Australian politics, when no prime minister would be safe from sudden defenestration, no cabinet minister restrained from following the dictates of their heart, no voter permitted to have any idea what was going on. Gillard saw a future where federal politics was in a constant state of flux and the thrilling backroom machinations of party apparatchiks made the idea of smooth, efficient governance the hilarious dream of a madman.

By 2010, Kevin Rudd had been struggling for some time. His obsessive attention to detail and insistence on staying up late every night thinking up new insults to yell at his staff had caused him, some were saying, to crack under the pressure. With relentless attacks on his every move by the new Opposition Leader Tony Abbott – installed at the head of the Liberal Party in 2009 in what many pundits assumed had been the completion of some kind of dare – Rudd's popularity had begun to dip.

Gillard saw her chance and went in for the kill. As the old political saw has it, 'when a man is hated by every single person he works with, that is often a good time to try to take his job'. With Rudd surrounded by MPs who loathed him, and a public who didn't understand why he had promised to undertake serious action on climate change and then hadn't, and didn't understand why he had promised to introduce a major mining tax and then hadn't, and didn't understand him in general because he used long words, the deputy's time had come. It all happened so quickly: one minute Gillard was stroking the prime minister's hair while he drifted off to sleep mumbling about Chinese trade barriers; the next minute she was holding the prime minister's severed head aloft by that very same hair and announcing that a 'good government' had 'lost its way'. This assertion, suggesting that somehow the Rudd government, while out nation-building, had wandered into a thick fog and found itself stranded in the woods, would come to be a source of some conjecture in coming years. How, exactly, had it lost its way? How, exactly, was it a good government? And how, exactly, would Gillard be any better than Rudd, besides the reduced likelihood of her swearing at air hostesses?

The most pressing question, however, was: just how long would Gillard *be* prime minister? An election was looming, and the Gillard experiment risked being cut very short indeed if she could not fend off the challenge from her old sparring partner Abbott, who was running on a platform of budget repair, fiscal responsibility, and gazing intensely at people with barely-concealed hunger.

The 2010 election proved to be one of the tightest in history. In the end, neither Abbott nor Gillard could gain a majority in the House of Representatives – the decision as to who would rule the country came down to three independent MPs: Tony Windsor, Rob Oakeshott and Bob Katter.

All three men were former National Party members, which might have seemed to make them more sympathetic to Abbott's Coalition. But these were no ordinary MPs: Oakeshott was an idealistic youngster from regional New South Wales with a philosophy of economic conservatism, social progressivism, and generalised bafflement. Windsor was a grizzled veteran of both state and federal politics who disliked Tony Abbott as a result of getting to know him. And then there was Bob Katter, a wild salamander who hatched on the fringes of a nuclear test site and gained the ability to run for election and operate a firearm. Katter was first to decide, declaring that he would be supporting Abbott, because though Gillard may have many memorable qualities, Abbott would be the more likely to win a knife fight against a baboon. It came down to Windsor and Oakeshott – if they did not plump for the nation's first female prime minister, it would be back to sausage town for another three years.

Finally, Windsor and Oakeshott called a press conference at which Windsor announced that he would be supporting Gillard, the only major party leader who didn't make him vomit blood. Oakeshott then stood to announce his decision, and several months later, said it would also be Gillard.

And so, Julia Gillard, the first woman to become Australian Prime Minister, also became the first woman to sort-of win an election to a certain extent. The glass ceiling remained broken, temporarily. But to keep it broken would require all of Gillard's political savvy. Or if possible, all of someone else's.

And thus the Gillard Era began. Early in her prime ministership, Gillard had said in an interview that she didn't 'support the idea of a big Australia', and she was determined to work assiduously throughout her reign to make Australia as small as possible. Her greatest accomplishment in this regard was the passage of legislation to excise the Australian mainland from its own migration zone. This meant that Australia instantly became much smaller, as it now no longer contained itself. In practical terms, it also meant that any asylum seeker who reached Australia could be legally sent to an offshore detention centre, where they would be abused and assaulted and given debilitating lifelong mental illness in order to showcase the Australian government's compassion.

Unfortunately, though Gillard was successful in her bid to make Australia's migration zone disappear, she failed to implement her grand refugee plan, the so-called Malaysia Solution. Under this plan, 800 asylum seekers would be sent from Australia to Malaysia, in return for which Malaysia would send 4000 refugees to Australia, which would then receive Malaysia's third and fourth-round picks in the AFL draft, while Malaysia got 40 per cent off its next purchase of any main meal not including drinks.

Having devised this scheme, which would solve Australia's

refugee problem in ways that our feeble mortal brains cannot even comprehend, Gillard was devastated when the Malaysia Solution was shot down by the High Court. Yet again a brave and innovative politician had been stymied by interfering lawyers, and the High Court, which had a history of deliberately and blatantly knowing what the law was, had poked its nose into someone else's business and come out with blood all over its nostrils.

The Gillard years were about more than just asylum seekers though: there was a wide range of policy areas in which she took an interest. Education had always been dear to Gillard's heart, ever since she learnt to read and had the idea that other children should too. This resulted in the Gonski Report, a landmark report named after the Education Minister's favourite brand of yoghurt, which recommended radical reforms to the national education system, such as spending money in places where it would be of most use and other such revolutionary concepts. Gonski was widely hailed as a major breakthrough by education experts, and it is predicted that if state and federal governments can work together in a spirit of goodwill, the report's recommendations may eventually be implemented as early as 2120.

Gillard's prime ministership also featured exciting developments in the areas of same-sex marriage, which she opposed, and poker machine regulations, which she promised to take action on and then didn't. It was an exciting time for anyone who enjoyed looking forward to things for a limited period of time.

But it was on another unfulfilled promise that Gillard's leadership was eventually to founder. The seeds of her greatest misstep were sown during the 2010 election campaign, when the new prime minister publicly vowed that there 'will be no carbon tax under a government I lead'. Nobody paid too much attention at the time, because they were mostly already asleep, but it was a nice reassurance to everyone who was terrified of the violence and bloodshed that a carbon tax could unleash.

All might have been well had Gillard, having once said that she would never introduce a carbon tax, remembered that she had said that. Unfortunately, in early 2011, she got together with the Greens – who were probably high at the time – and cooked up the Clean Energy Bill, which involved putting a price on carbon.

Even now, this did not have to spell the end for Gillard – after all, a price on carbon is not, technically, a 'carbon tax', and as a skilled communicator, the prime minister would no doubt be able to resolutely defend against allegations that she was introducing a carbon tax, by explaining the difference and refusing to waver.

It was just as Australia awaited that resolute defence that Gillard went on the radio to tell the country that the carbon pricing mechanism was 'effectively like a tax'. Many people saw this as a tactical blunder by the prime minister, inasmuch as it is difficult to argue that your plan is not a tax when you've already said that it is.

The carbon tax galvanised the country's right wing and inflamed many ordinary Australians who had already been suspicious of the claim that a woman could be prime minister, and were now more certain than ever that Gillard was bent on stealing their bodily fluids to feed her insatiable ovaries. Rallies were held to fight back against the Gillardian Reign of Terror. Truckers assembled to form the 'Convoy of No Confidence', in which they gathered in Canberra to protest and swap stories about the various head injuries they'd suffered as children. At one rally, Tony Abbott addressed an angry mob outside Parliament House, standing in front of protest signs reading 'Ditch the Witch' and 'Bob Brown's Bitch', which some observers thought might be references to Gillard, although others pointed out that they might have been directed at some other witch and/or bitch. Meanwhile the right-wing commentariat was in a frenzy: popular shock jock and part-time rugby-career-ruiner Alan Jones expressed a desire to take the prime minister out to sea in a chaff bag and drown her, prompting other commentators to call on Jones to publicly explain what a chaff bag is.

Emotions, in a nutshell were running high, which is always likely to be the case when the stakes are as high as an ideological contest between the drive to implement a mildly restrictive emissions policy aimed at achieving a minor reduction in greenhouse gases, and the desire to avoid near-imperceptible impacts on the economy. The battle raged on all sides, but Gillard had the numbers where it counted: in parliament, where the Greens, off their heads on absinthe, had the balance of power. The carbon tax passed in November 2011, prompting emotional scenes in the chamber as government and Greens members celebrated a historic legislative occasion, while the Opposition celebrated the government having written their next election campaign for them.

Gillard began to look fondly back on the halcyon days of 2010, when for almost six or seven minutes she was actually quite popular, as her approval ratings plummeted and the attacks on her by the Opposition and its cheerleaders in the media became more and more savage. Opinion was divided on the true cause of these attacks: some detected a powerful streak of misogyny in much of the criticism directed at Gillard, while others pointed out that she had formulated policies that alienated many people and displayed poor political judgment in her attempts to promote those policies. On the other hand, the first group noted, it seemed unlikely that a man presenting the same policies would have suffered the same treatment in the media. But then again, their opponents observed, if Gillard didn't want to be subjected to sexist abuse, maybe she shouldn't have made the undeniably provocative decision to be female, against all expert advice and official precedent. Here the two sides reached some consensus: nobody had held a gun to Gillard's head and forced her to be a woman, so she did have to accept the consequences of that decision. Many believed she had only been born female to get attention in the first place.

But Julia Gillard, of Barry, Adelaide and Lalor, was no quitter: she was born to fight, and the more the Opposition and media put the boot in, the more she kicked back like a donkey with a troubled childhood. The most famous example came on 9 October 2012, when Gillard delivered the now-legendary 'misogyny speech'. To clear up any confusion, the 'misogyny speech' was, in fact, a speech *against* misogyny, which made it quite a departure for an Australian prime minister, all of whom had previously been pro-misogyny and proclaimed the fact in public near-constantly.

Having endured another barrage of belligerent berating from Abbott, Gillard stood at the dispatch box, took a deep breath, and delivered the speech of her life. Referring to Abbott's assertion that misogynists were not fit for high office, the prime minister snapped:

> *I hope the Leader of the Opposition has got a piece of paper and is writing out his resignation. Because if he wants to know what misogyny looks like in modern Australia, he doesn't need a motion in the House of Representatives, he needs a mirror. That's what he needs.*

Having delivered this devastating rebuke, which was either calling Abbott a misogynist or saying that there was a misogynist standing behind him, Gillard went on to denounce the Opposition Leader's 'repulsive double standards' regarding sexism, quoting several occasions on which Abbott had said things which could be interpreted as sexist – although to be fair, you could only really interpret them that way if you heard them.

The speech struck a chord with many, not just in Australia, but across the world. In particular, Gillard's opening thrust, 'I will not be lectured about sexism and misogyny by this man' echoed throughout every media outlet for weeks, and remains the most memorable quote of her long career. The searing heat of the smackdown, mingled with the subtle intrigue of the unspoken question – which man *would* she like to be lectured about sexism and misogyny by? – roused powerful emotions in the heart of every woman who had ever felt insulted, diminished or generally hacked off with some dumb, arrogant, hairy man in lycra. On that day, Gillard was not just Gillard: she was all of us, although not me because I am a man[226].

The speech made Julia Gillard a global celebrity, with congratulations flooding in from dignitaries ranging from French President François Hollande to Danish Prime Minister Helle Thorning-Schmidt[227]. US President Barack Obama also praised the speech, as did Hillary Clinton, and some believed that if Clinton had made a speech like Gillard's, she might have won the 2016 election, although the people who believed that were not very smart. However, there were also negative consequences from the speech, such as people making YouTube videos where they set it to a ukulele backing, just proving that the evil of the human race truly knows no limit. Also, the fact that the speech was delivered on the same day that Gillard's government legislated to cut welfare for single mothers tainted its feminist credentials for some, but this is petty – is not true inspiration worth a few thousand single mothers dropping below the poverty line?

Unfortunately for Gillard, becoming a feminist icon could not save her from dwindling poll numbers and the ongoing

---

226 Technically.

227 Probably a real person.

white-anting of Kevin Rudd. Gillard's predecessor had turned out to not be one of those politicians who took being stabbed in the back with gentle good humour, and had worked tirelessly since the day he was deposed to destabilise his betrayer's leadership and lay waste to her dreams. It was working: the Labor Party was now split between those who wanted Rudd back in order to save their own jobs, and those who were willing to publicly call him a psychopath – a reasonably wide divide.

By June 2013, Labor's polls were starting to resemble the script of a horror movie where the heroine thinks she's escaped but it turns out the one friend she trusted was the killer all along and she gets impaled on her own competition javelin. The ALP was heading for a crash of Hindenburgian proportions, and there was only one way to stop it: be a lot better at their jobs. But since that wasn't an option, they'd have to get Rudd back.

On 26 June 2013, a leadership ballot was held and Gillard was toppled, 57-45. Kevin Rudd, 2007's Saviour of the Nation and Labor Hero, had returned in one of the least triumphant ascents in the history of people ascending things. But if what you want is to be prime minister, getting the job as the result of 57 people who hate your guts reluctantly deciding that you're their best chance of maybe not becoming unemployed is better than nothing.

Gillard's political career ended. Both she and Rudd had pledged to quit politics if defeated, and she stuck to her promise. Sadly, she had not pledged to abstain from writing books or appearing in TV documentary series, and she went on to do both of these things in what was a particularly harrowing time for the nation. A couple of months after her defeat, Labor lost the federal election, although the margin under Rudd was considerably narrower than had been expected under Gillard. The system was therefore seen to work.

The end was sad for Gillard, but it is impossible to ignore her achievements. As the first woman prime minister of Australia, she proved that a woman prime minister was a thing that could exist without even a little bit of blood raining from the sky. She inspired countless other women and girls to believe in themselves and chase their dreams and reach for the stars so that they too could one day face a ceaseless torrent of bigoted abuse from thousands of people they'd never met. She also taught the nation a valuable lesson: when you are steadfast in your principles, when you stand up for what you believe in[228], you will be humiliatingly hounded from your job. The Gillard legacy is secure: nobody can take her place in history away from her. Not only did she blaze a trail for women, but she ushered in a new era of Australian politics. After Gillard knocked off Rudd, and Rudd knocked off Gillard, Abbott beat Rudd in an election, and then Turnbull knocked off Abbott. Who will knock off Turnbull? Who knows? That's what makes this time so exciting, and we have Julia Gillard and her farsighted treachery to thank for that. Julia made politics fun – how many prime ministers can say that?

FUN FOR YOU AT HOME: Find a friend or relative and lecture them about misogyny. See if they will be lectured about misogyny by you. Now you know how Tony Abbott feels.

228 E.g. 'being Prime Minister'.

CATHY FREEMAN
One Perfect Lap

IN ALL THE STORIED HISTORY of Australian sport, through all the majestic careers of athletic gods and goddesses, in all the titanic clashes and spine-tingling historic moments that the nation's love affair with the physically gifted had brought us, surely there had never been a night like this. The day: 25 September 2000. The setting: Olympic Stadium in Sydney. In the midst of a vast, black night, an oasis of blinding light, a tiny patch brighter than the sun in the heart of the city. Zoom down to that dazzling spot, and in the centre we find an arena, a wide green lawn surrounded by a moat of red-brown, lined with white. Around the strip, a hundred thousand people shout and whoop and fill the night with camera flashes and spill beer and accidentally elbow each other in the head trying to get back to their seats carrying trays of hot dogs and chips. They have come from every corner of the city, every corner of the country, and just about every corner of the world. Flags of a hundred nations fly, or possibly even more – I didn't count.

Every one of the people in the stadium has their own story. Rich and poor, old and young, university-educated and functionally illiterate mingle, united by their common humanity yet divided by myriad fault lines of race, sex and class. In other circumstances the stands would likely erupt in an orgy of savage violence as the natural human instinct to inflict injury on those different from yourself kicked in. But these are not other circumstances – tonight, the mood is one of celebration and joy. But not ordinary joy: this joy is suffused with tension, with stress, with the nerve-shredding agony of anticipation. Tonight is a happy night, but every one of this merry crowd knows how quickly delight can turn to misery. Every smiling face in the stadium has fear behind it, because every smiling face in the stadium is focused with laser-resembling intensity on one spot, and on one woman occupying that spot.

Down on the ground, she stands. A tiny figure in the eye of a gigantic hurricane. The track beneath her feet, the colour of the Queensland earth she'd first run on, probably, assuming she had an extremely cinematic childhood. There's definitely some places in Queensland where the earth is that colour. She might have run on it. Really makes you think[229].

There she stands. Rivals to the right of her. Rivals to the left of her. In front of her, only the long, lonely curve of the racetrack, the single lane that for now, is her whole universe – or should be, if she can only block out the deafening noise of this monolithic stadium and focus on what her whole life has been leading up to: this one moment.

She is dressed sort of like a spaceman; a gentle, intelligent alien who has come to Earth to teach humanity how to love each other and end all war and prejudice forever, but returns to its home planet defeated and disillusioned by the irreparably corrupt nature of earth-kind. A skin-tight head-to-toe onesie that seems to cry out for an accompanying ray gun. But this otherworldly visitor is not here to teach us about the ways of a sexless intergalactic utopia: she

229 That's what sets this book apart from more conventional history books: I never spoil the facts by checking them.

is here to teach us another profound lesson. She is here to teach us about the healing power of running.

Time seems to slow. The roar of the crowd recedes into the background, as if being heard down a long, narrow tunnel. Peripheral vision blurs in the manner of TV's Daredevil when his super-hearing is detecting nefarious activity. There is nothing for her but her lane, and the finish line, and the sleek lines of her futuristic onesie. She kneels ... she crouches ... she waits for the starter's gun. A sudden, earsplitting *crack* ... and she launches herself into the biggest forty-nine point one one seconds of her life.

The crowd rises from its seats as one. A nation holds its breath. The race has started, but in reality it started 27 years earlier[230], in the little town of Mackay, Queensland, the sugar capital of Australia. It was here that Catherine Astrid Salome Freeman was born – some might say, born to run, but that seems a little on the nose, so let's just say she was born, as this is an indisputable fact.

Freeman began athletics when she was just two years old, an age at which most children are still pathetic stumbling losers[231]. One could say that athletic excellence was in Freeman's blood. Her grandfather was Frank 'King' Fisher, the champion Queensland rugby league player known as the 'Wally Lewis of Aboriginal rugby league players'. Fisher, a star of the Queensland country in the 1930s, was described by the British captain Jim Brough as the best country player the touring Great Britain team had encountered, and offered Fisher a contract with the English club Salford. That contract was never taken up, however, due to an endearing little quirk of the Queensland government known as the *Aboriginals Protection and Restriction of Sale of Opium Act 1897.* This charming little rule, put in place so the government could control dangerous

230 Well, not in reality. In the opposite of reality, in reality.

231 Mine were, anyway.

substances like opium and black people, meant it was up to the state of Queensland whether Fisher was allowed to go to England to fulfil his dreams, and the state of Queensland decided it was for the best if he didn't. Thank God for that generous government, always there to protect Aboriginals!

Luckily, by the time Cathy Freeman's career began things were very different in Australia: back in Frank Fisher's day, a sports star could be held back for the colour of their skin, whereas in Freeman's time, an Aboriginal person who was good at sport had a half-decent chance of being mostly tolerated if they kept their mouth shut. It had really been a huge leap forward. Well done, Australia.

Clearly Freeman's genes were of the robust sort, and that night in Sydney, as she exploded from the blocks in her spacesuit, it might have seemed like glory was always her destiny. But nobody becomes a champion without hard work outside of *My Kitchen Rules*, and it was a long road from Slade Point in Mackay to the Olympic Stadium[232].

Her first coach was her stepfather, Bruce Barber, who guided her as a junior to multiple victories around the state and the country, in the 100 and 200 metres, the long jump, and the high jump. Jumping would gradually fall by the wayside, though, as she became more serious about her career and decided that taking lots of short steps really fast was more her style than taking one big step relatively slowly.

Freeman's first taste of international success came at the 1990 Commonwealth Games, the famous four-yearly festival of Australia beating up tiny poverty-stricken nations from around the world. The 16-year-old Queenslander won gold as part of the Australian 4x100 relay team, becoming the first Aboriginal person

232 Talking figuratively again: in fact there IS no road from Slade Point to the Olympic Stadium; you have to turn quite a few corners.

to take home a Commonwealth gold and making a lot of white Australians feel pretty proud of themselves for cheering her on. The encouragement and support given to Freeman, in fact, stands as one of the greatest achievements of white Australia, and her entire career is a testament to just how great we really are.

Cathy's first taste of the Olympics was at Barcelona in 1992, when she was 18 and legally permitted to drink, smoke and have sex. But if she was doing all of these things, she kept them well away from the track, reaching the second round of the 400m and the semi-finals of the 200m. I agree that doesn't sound impressive at all, but it means she was among the best 20 or so runners in the world: how many activities are you one of the 20 best on the world at? I thought so[233].

Freeman was showing she could mix it with the big girls of international running, and even with the small girls, who were usually quicker because of their lower body mass. At the 1994 Commonwealth Games, she bestrode the world – apart from most of the Americas, Europe, Asia and Africa – like a colossus, winning gold in both the 400 and 200. But it was also at those games that Freeman first felt the sharp lash of controversy, and sadly the brouhaha involved the issue of race, something that Australia had traditionally been so good at handling.

The whole thing revolved, as stupid pointless maddening problems so often do, around the matter of flags. Now, to you and me, a flag may just be a piece of cloth, but to a lot of pretty weird people, flags are incredibly important, to the point where they will actually expend time and energy on trying to police what flags people hold, and when, and where, and which fashion. We can't understand these people, but we owe it to them to respect

233 I myself am the 18th or 19th best writer in the world right now, and I can tell you it's a big deal.

their idiotic point of view, even when they are musty stiff-necked cauliflower-nosed numbnuts with a ham hock where their brain should be. Which is where Arthur Tunstall OBE, comes in.

Tunstall was a rugged sports administrator of the old school – you know, that school that told Cathy's granddad he wasn't allowed to leave the country. His background was in boxing, where for 60 years he worked tirelessly to advance the cause of young men inflicting brain damage on each other. Acting as referee, judge, team manager at numerous championships, and senior administrator, his contribution to Australian boxing was enormous, if that's the kind of thing you find admirable.

His contribution to Australian track and field, on the other hand, was slightly smaller, and consisted for the most part for an unfortunate incident in Canada during the 1994 Games. As *chef de mission*[234] of the Australian team, he was seen to splutter indignantly into his cocoa when he saw young Cathy Freeman, a slip of what Tunstall, in his blunt way, could only describe as a *girl*, walk a victory lap of the stadium after her 200m win carrying … brace yourself for the full horror … not one, but TWO flags.

Yes, Freeman celebrated her triumph by draping herself in both the Australian and the Aboriginal flags. The world responded swiftly and decisively with a loud 'who gives a fuck?' But there were still some willing to uphold standards in the modern world, and Tunstall was the standards standard-bearer. His wrath was fierce and terrible and extremely wrinkly, and he threatened to send Cathy Freeman home for being so shamelessly disrespectful of her country as to admit that she was a member of its Indigenous population. Such unpatriotism made Tunstall's blood boil, and joining his corpuscles in the kettle was the haemoglobin of many of Australia's reddest commentators and opinion columnists. Could such a flagrant public

234 French for 'missing chef'.

display of Aboriginality go unpunished? The debate raged for days, and Freeman's career was in danger of being derailed by her own hubristic multiple-cloth-carrying.

Fortunately, tempers cooled and Freeman stayed in Canada, Tunstall's attention having been diverted by an even more pressing issue: the presence at the Commonwealth Games of athletes with a disability, whom he described as 'an embarrassment' in his usual calm and reasonable way.

(Several years later, the affair was finally put to rest when Freeman and Tunstall appeared together in a tea commercial, proving that despite our differences, there is one thing that will always unite us: being given large sums of money by beverage companies.)

The Commonwealth Games had established Cathy Freeman as both a shining star of sport, and a powerful spokesperson for her people. This presented a dilemma for the Australian people, who tend to love shining stars of sport, but hate powerful spokespersons for their people, unless their people are the same people as our people, which they rarely are, because if they were they wouldn't need powerful spokespeople. It's confusing, being Australian. But Freeman cut through the confusion with her grace and humility, her winning smile, and her ability to run faster than most of us could dream of, even if we went outside for a bit.

At Atlanta in 1996, Freeman finished second behind Marie-José Pérec of France, and since there was an Olympic Games on at the time, she got a silver medal for it. She also ran an Australian record time in the process, which normally wouldn't be a big deal because Australian records in athletics are mostly rubbish, but in this case it was actually quite speedy. Moreover, the one-two finish between the upstart Australian and the patrician French champion set mouths watering for the inevitably colossal clash between the two at the next Olympics, when Pérec would be defending her crown against a Freeman with four more years in her legs.

In 1997, Freeman took out the 400m at the World Championships. In 1998, she sat out the season due to an injured foot, one of the most important parts of the body for most runners. There was a fear that her foot would prove to be an Achilles heel, but fortunately nothing so cruelly poetic happened – the foot was just a temporary setback and she was back on the track in 1999, running as fast as ever.

In 1999, in fact, Freeman was undefeated in the 400 – her powers were only increasing. This was also the year she married Sandy Bodecker, a Nike executive who had become infatuated with how good Cathy made her shoes look. Although marriage is often the point at which the average person loses all their zest and purpose in life and becomes an idle embittered husk, this didn't seem to be the case for Freeman, who just kept on winning through the year and into 2000.

This was the year she'd been waiting for, and luckily spacetime had not ground to a cataclysmic halt before it came. The dream was to win her favoured event in front of a home crowd, at the 2000 Sydney Olympics, which even before they happened were well known to be the greatest Olympics ever. Sydney had won the right to host the Games in 1993, thanks to a slick, professionally-assembled bid, the adorable prattling of unnerving child Tanya Blencowe, and New South Wales Premier John Fahey's spring-loaded knees. As the best city in the best country in the world, Sydney had a huge responsibility to stage a successful Olympics, and they let nobody down, putting on a show that every Games since has failed miserably to match, and every Games beforehand has felt bad about in retrospect.

Cathy Freeman lit the flame for those Sydney Games, just as she'd lit the flame of hope in the hearts of Australian people or something of that nature. But having lit that hopeful flame, the nation now expected the shy Mackay youngster to refrain from extinguishing it in the cruellest manner. Basically, she now had to win, and if she did not she would go down in history as the woman who broke a nation's heart. Every professional Australian sportsperson makes the same deal with the public: they will win and allow us to vicariously experience the glory they achieved and bask in their reflected glow, or else we will loathe them and everything they stand for forever. It's not an easy deal, but it has the advantage of being extremely fair.

Freeman knew, crouching on the blocks on that clear balmy September night, that it was time to hold up her end of the deal. A Commonwealth Games gold was all very well, an Olympic silver was lovely, and the World Championship victories were quite nice, but it's Olympic gold that athletes prize above all else, and it was Olympic gold we demanded from our own golden girl: who if unsuccessful would forfeit her right to be called that as well.

One obstacle she had already cleared: Pérec had gone home, abandoning the race of the century due to what she called 'harassment' from members of the public, but what most decent Aussies called 'gutlessness', and what some slightly less decent Aussies called 'being French'. Pérec's absence meant the greatest threat to Freeman's fulfilment of her destiny was history. And what chance did the other runners in the race have, up against a woman who they knew was so fast her closest rival left the country rather than try to beat her?

Still, running is a tricky business. So many things can go wrong, even for an extremely fast person. You can trip. You can slip. You can have a stroke mid-run. You can get cramp. You can get hayfever. You can get shot by a sniper. A magpie can attack you. A sinkhole can open up in your lane. The risks are innumerable.

The courage it takes to even step onto a track is often underrated, but Cathy Freeman had stepped onto this one, and as the gun went off and she burst forth from her block, the whole country resting on her bony shoulders, that courage came to the fore.

For she did not slip. She did not trip. She suffered no cardiovascular events, geological upheaval, or unfortunate wildlife encounters. All she felt was the wind on her face, all she saw was the looming finish line, all she did was run. And run. And run.

Imagine what it must be like to have a hundred thousand people madly cheering for you. It's almost enough to make you want to go for a run yourself. As Freeman flew around the bend, one could imagine the collective screams and shouts of encouragement forming a mighty gust of wind to drive her onward, although realistically, probably most of the momentum was being generated by her legs.

Whatever the case, the fact is that less than a minute after that gun had rent the night air, Freeman had crossed the finish line, and she'd done it, as the industry jargon says, in first place. The crowd went literally insane. The giant breath that Australia had been holding was let out in a mighty national puff of relief. It was all going to be all right. We didn't have to hate her.

Cathy Astrid Salome Freeman, the humble country girl with too many middle names, stood in the middle of the mad commotion, and breathed deep the air of victory. She sat down on the track, pulled back her space hood, removed her shoes, and for a moment, simply allowed the world to wash over her. She had carried a nation's hopes and dreams on her back, and never once let herself buckle under the weight. She had taken the dream of a little girl from conception to fruition. She had, to put it simply and briefly, run bloody fast. This time nobody cared that her victory lap featured both Australian and Aboriginal flags, because this time everybody decided to be normal human beings with reasonable priorities – that's the magic of the Olympics.

Cathy Freeman didn't make it to another Olympic Games. She retired in 2003, having lost the insatiable will to win that pushes otherwise intelligent people to strain muscle and sinew beyond breaking point and sometimes also get shin splints, just for the chance to have three quarters of a minute in the spotlight every four years.

Freeman has not been idle since retirement, working assiduously for charity and in the community, particularly to assist Aboriginal children. The good she's done over many years resounds throughout the country, yet to most people, the name Cathy Freeman brings to mind just one moment in time, a brief moment that was over almost as soon as it had begun. But that one moment shone more brightly than most people's entire lives – when you have a moment like that, what else do you need?

FUN FOR YOU AT HOME: Gather a dozen or so friends, and take turns timing each other running 400 metres. Can you run it in less than 49.11 seconds? Of course not. That's why Cathy Freeman is better than you. Don't forget it.

MALCOLM TURNBULL
All You Need is Cash

MALCOLM TURNBULL'S LIFE is a modern-day fairytale: proof that dreams really do come true. The endless succession of dizzying highs that make up the Turnbull story illustrate a profound truth: that in our modern egalitarian society, being a white male with an expensive education is no barrier to inheriting significant wealth from your parents.

Malcolm Bligh Turnbull was born in Sydney on 24 October 1954, the same day that Hungary's Sándor Kocsis scored his sixth international hat-trick against Czechoslovakia: a powerful omen, as young Malcolm would go on to kick many goals himself in his adult life. It was also the day that a US Air Force transport plane strayed off course and crashed in the Alps, although it's hard to think of any metaphorical way to relate that to Turnbull's career.

Turnbull's parental circumstances are of particular interest to the history buff. Descended from John Turnbull, a Scottish tailor who arrived in New South Wales in 1802, Malcolm's father Bruce shared his middle name of Bligh, symbolising that the Turnbull family, like the former sea captain and governor William Bligh, were devoted to duty and tended to get on people's nerves. The really fascinating bit is Mal's mum: Coral Lansbury was not only an accomplished writer and academic in her own right, but was also the second cousin of

Angela Lansbury. Which means Malcolm Turnbull is related to Jessica Fletcher from *Murder She Wrote*! Isn't that fantastic? If I were him, I would be constantly bringing this up at social gatherings. I would have *Murder She Wrote*-themed dinner parties[235]. I would seriously consider establishing a detective agency. As we will see, Malcolm Turnbull achieved many great things throughout his life, but nothing he has ever done is as impressive as being Angela Lansbury's cousin, in my opinion[236].

Anyway, moving on: young Malcolm attended Sydney Grammar School, well-known as one of the best places in Sydney for boys to learn grammar. He showed great promise here: so good was he at grammar that he won the Lawrence Campbell Oratory Competition, a prestigious public speaking contest wherein a prize is awarded to the student who delivers the speech that comes closest to guessing who Lawrence Campbell was. Teenage Turnbull was already displaying the ability to speak eloquently and persuasively in public provided there was no requirement to actually create anything or bring about any kind of practical change that would one day serve him well.

Following his bewitching of the Sydney Grammar community with his mellifluous, Saruman-like voice, boyish Malcolm moved on to Sydney University, where he gained a Bachelor of Arts and then a Bachelor of Laws, which is like a Bachelor of Arts but meaningful. While studying at Sydney Uni, he also worked as a journalist for Nation Review, Radio 2SM and Channel 9, which shows how lax journalism standards were back then: these days a uni student could never get regular work in the mainstream media unless they had proven themselves to be an above-average level of racist.

Having become two different kinds of Bachelor at once, Turnbull decided he'd had enough of this student life, and it was

235 Yeah. I do this anyway to be honest.

236 I wish Angela Lansbury were Australian: I'd love to write about her.

time for him to embark on a slightly different student life. He won a Rhodes scholarship and attended Brasenose College, Oxford. At Brasenose he gained a Bachelor of Civil Law degree, making him one of the late 20th century's most bachelored men. He also continued his journalistic work, or put another way, he continued to neglect his studies, working for the *Sunday Times*, a newspaper famous for its willingness to employ any random foreigner that turned up on its doorstep.

An Oxford don once said that Turnbull was 'always going to enter life's rooms without knocking', and it's true that even at an early age he was an extremely rude person. But you need more than rudeness to succeed in life[237], and young Malcolm had that something extra: call it courage, call it intellect, call it money – it's the indefinable X factor that leads to glory, and glory was what Malcolm Turnbull was chasing.

Glory was not slow to come his way after university: returning to Australia from Oxford, Turnbull began working as a barrister, having accidentally discovered one night at a birthday party that he looked great in a wig. Leaving the bar[238] in 1983, he stood for Liberal Party preselection in the seat of Mosman, but lost out to Phillip Smiles, the famous politician who everybody remembers so well. Following this humiliating setback, Malcolm Turnbull vowed to never again dabble in politics, a promise that as far as anyone can tell, he has kept to this day.

Turnbull's next career move, in his ongoing quest to collect as many different jobs as possible like an especially poorly written character on *Neighbours*, was to become general counsel and secretary for Kerry Packer's Australian Consolidated Press Holdings, publisher of *Women's Weekly*, *Woman's Day*, and various

237 Not much more, mind.

238 The legal bar, I assume, although records are sketchy on this point.

other magazines whose publishing schedules do not align with their titles[239]. In this position, it was Turnbull's job to make sure that no legal obstacles prevented the publication of photographs of smiling women in tailored blouses sitting in expensive kitchens.

His biggest challenge at ACP, though, came during the Costigan Commission[240], which had implicated an Australian businessman, codenamed 'the Goanna' because of his reputed thick hide and ability to run on hot sand, in tax evasion and organised crime up to and including murder. Packer, never a man to defend on the back foot, outed himself as 'the Goanna', and denied all the allegations. On his boss's behalf, Turnbull went on the attack and denounced the Commission, accusing it of misusing its powers.

The 'Goanna' allegations went nowhere in the face of Turnbull's ferocious legalism, and were formally dismissed by the Attorney-General in 1987, despite lingering doubts over a $225,000 loan Packer received from a bankrupt Queensland businessman – although that characterisation is slightly unfair, as in the 1980s if you didn't deal with bankrupt businessmen you'd hardly ever get anything done. Asked why he took the loan in cash, Packer told the Commission that 'I like cash. I have a squirrel-like mentality'. The revelation that squirrels like cash sent shockwaves through the zoological community, and Packer's behaviour made a few people look askance also. His reply caused the Commission to codename him 'the Squirrel', which had been altered to 'the Goanna' by the National Times when they reported on the Commission's report. So basically Packer, who resembled a squirrel, was turned into a

239 E.g. *Women's Monthly*, which came out every two years, and *Teen Girl Fortnight*, which was published every six hours.

240 Full title: The Royal Commission on the Activities of the Federated Ship Painters and Dockers Union. Was it really worth your time reading all that?

goanna in order to prevent all those who knew how squirrelly he was from knowing that the goanna was him, since if people knew the goanna was a squirrel they'd know the squirrel was Packer, but then Packer admitted he was the goanna, which meant everyone knew he was a squirrel anyway. All clear? Good.

Turnbull had done fine work in defending his master and slapping down the Costigan Commission, and that silver tongue was making an impact on a national scale. Feeling bored one day, and possibly watching a TV show where someone started a law firm, he thought that might be a bit of a laugh, and so he did, in partnership with Bruce McWilliam, another high-profile public figure who is indelibly stamped in all of our memories. Turnbull McWilliam's most prominent case was the 'Spycatcher' trial, wherein former MI5[241] agent Peter Wright fought the British government's attempts to prevent publication of his book *Spycatcher* in Australia. In the book Wright detailed his spycatching activities, boasting shamelessly about all the spies he had caught and how great he was at catching spies and how the Peter Gunn theme played wherever he went. The UK government, naturally alarmed at the thought of people finding out how much spycatching was going on right under their noses, insisted it was too dangerous a book to allow the Australian public to read, not realising that the Australian public honestly didn't care.

The British government, which had once ruled half the world, was no match for the Turnbull Tongue, and after a closing submission in which the dashing young lawyer stated, 'every person who has ultimately changed the course of history has started off being unpopular' – an assertion which, though blatantly untrue, really struck a chord with the judge – the United Kingdom slunk off home with its tail between its legs, while Turnbull stood atop the legal mountain, a shaft of heavenly sunlight illuminating

241 Remade starring Tom Cruise years later.

his magnificence. The phrase 'more God than Man' is thrown around pretty cavalierly nowadays, but there's no doubt it applied to Turnbull at this point: governments wilted in the face of his withering rhetorical agility, and whole nations bowed before his mercurial wit and marsupial-like good looks.

Like everyone who has ever been a lawyer, though, Turnbull was bored, and so he decided to stop doing law and do business instead, having occasionally watched Kerry Packer doing business and thought it looked like fun. So it was that in 1987 he formed the investment bank Whitlam Turnbull and Co, in partnership with prime ministerial offspring Nicholas Whitlam and former New South Wales Premier and dry-eyed Balmain boy Neville Wran, who was given the position of 'Co' so as to let him know just how highly Turnbull and Whitlam thought of state politicians. In 1990 Whitlam left the firm, which became known as Turnbull and Partners Ltd: there was just no way that Neville Wran was going to get any recognition from Malcolm. Turnbull and Partners continued until 1997, when Turnbull left to join Goldman Sachs, having for some time been fretting that people didn't see him as plutocratic enough.

The 1990s were a time of furious activity for Turnbull, whose nature was such that he was easily bored, and even more easily greedy. Besides his work as an investment banker, which saw him tirelessly taking other people's money and thinking up ways to persuade them that he was doing something useful with it, and his subsequent job at Goldman Sachs, in which he did basically the same thing but with larger amounts, he served as a director of FTR Holdings and Star Technology Systems, a company best known for trying to mine gold in Russia but then not actually doing it[242]. He

242 Later on, Turnbull's tendency towards trying to do things but then not doing them was remarked upon by some.

was also chairman of Axiom Forest Resources, finally fulfilling his lifelong dream to cut down trees professionally.

Perhaps Turnbull's greatest achievement in the 1990s was inventing the internet[243]. He did this by purchasing a stake in the company Ozemail, which according to contemporary reports, is a play on the words 'Aussie Mail'. Or 'Aus Email'. One or the other – the point they were trying to make was that they provided some form of mail and were Australian. Ozemail was an internet service provider, but was finding it difficult to make headway in the marketplace because Turnbull had not yet invented the internet, meaning that pitching to prospective customers became a problem: whenever the conversation got to the point when the punter asked, 'what service does your company actually provide', Ozemail could do nothing but shrug and blush. With the addition of Turnbull's Midas touch, and his farsighted idea for a global system of interconnected computer networks linking devices around the world, Ozemail's business plan really came into its own.

Like everything else Turnbull had turned his hand to (with the possible exception of Russian goldmining), OzEmail was a huge success, to the extent that five years after he bought in, his initial $500,000 stake was worth $57 million. Satisfied that his work changing the face of human communications forever and providing affordable access to inept erotica was done, Turnbull smiled peacefully and sold out. Immediately, the dot com bubble burst, the tech industry finding itself directionless and lost without its father and creator. But such is the nature of unstoppable genius: it is inherently restless, refusing to stay still, constantly moving, like a shark crossed with a lemur on speed[244].

The next move for the high-flying Renaissance polymath was

243 Abbott, Tony, *Collected Sayings*, p. 129.

244 The lemur isn't on speed, its offspring is; the baby it had with the shark.

to turn Australia into a republic. To this endeavour he brought all the energy and brilliance he had always brought to his business affairs, with the exception that he failed miserably. As chairman of the Australian Republican Movement, Turnbull led the charge to cut the strings that still bound the nation to the Queen's apron[245], and in 1999 the Australian people voted on the proposal, deciding that they were still big fans of apron strings. Turnbull, shattered at the discovery that not getting his way was even physically possible, declared that Prime Minister John Howard, a staunch monarchist and ferrety little liar, had 'broken the nation's heart'. In reality Howard had only broken around half the nation's heart, and even that half was mostly not so much broken as mildly irritated: the rest of the nation's heart was pointing and laughing at Turnbull, a savage blow to his pride, which had by this time grown to frighteningly massive proportions.

But Malcolm Turnbull was not the kind to let disappointment distract him from his goals. All his life he had lived by the simple axiom, 'When life gives you lemons, amass phenomenally large quantities of cash', and he was not about to change course now. His experience with the republic referendum had taught him a harsh but valuable lesson about himself: he was not cut out for constitutional reform. He was born for one purpose, and one purpose only: to uphold the great Australian tradition of grotesque income inequality. And if he was poor in republicanism, in financial terms he was rich indeed.

The 21st century brought fresh triumphs for Malcolm Bligh Turnbull, as he appeared before the HIH Insurance Royal Commission in regard to his role in HIH's purchase of FAI Insurance – while at Goldman Sachs Turnbull had advised FAI during the sale, which had contributed to HIH's collapse. The

245 Why she wears that thing all the time I've no idea.

Commission found no evidence of wrongdoing on Turnbull's part, a mighty vindication of Turnbull's commitment to never leaving any evidence of wrongdoing.

There seemed to be many years of profitable non-wrongdoing ahead of Malcolm Turnbull, the golden child of 20th-century Australian business, but fate has a habit of intervening in strange and narratively effective ways. In 2004, with the world at his feet and the future his oyster, Turnbull mysteriously disappeared from the corporate landscape. Suddenly his name was no longer a permanent fixture in the business pages, and the stock exchange no longer felt the smooth velvety touch of his sure hand upon its indices[246].

Many theories have been offered to explain Turnbull's unexpected disappearance. Chinese defection; terminal illness; religious conversion; all are plausible, but none have been proven. Today, more than a decade after Australian business was rendered Turnbull-less, we are none the wiser as to what happened to this bright burning comet of a man. Many Turnbull disciples, or 'Malcontents' as they style themselves, still hold out hope that their messiah will one day return to lead them, or at least himself, to glory.

The rest of us can only speculate on just what happened to Malcolm Turnbull, the man who would be – figuratively – King, but who would also – literally – prevent there being any Kings in the future. What happened to Turnbull may be impossible to know, but what we do know for sure is that he was a true colossus of this country. In his life he conquered the worlds of journalism, of law and of business, dominating every field he entered with his titanic intellect, his razor wit and his adorable koala face. Such a

246 'Malcolm roughly grabbed the index, thrusting his all-scrip offer deep inside its margins.'

multi-talented individual, as good at making money as he is at keeping it, comes along only once in a generation, and Australia is less exciting for his absence.

If any readers have any information about the whereabouts of the corporate giant formerly known as Malcolm Turnbull, pass it on to the author at pobjie.ben@gmail.com.

FUN FOR YOU AT HOME: Become a stock market player! Diversify your investments so you don't have excessive exposure to any one sector, and build your portfolio until you are in a position to launch a hostile takeover of a tech company. Stake your entire fortune and sense of self on one high-risk play and keep a diary of your mood fluctuations. Find some decent, honest work as you attempt to pick up the pieces.

EPILOGUE

OBVIOUSLY ONE BOOK cannot hold the story of every great Australian. Legendary Aussies like Joan Sydney, Francis de Groot and Joe Bugner sadly had to be left out of this volume for reasons of length, but that is no slight against them and the many others who have made our country what it is today. The history of Australia is literally littered – or at least figuratively littered – with people who can without fear of contradiction be described as 'inhabiting the Australian continent for at least some of the time'. I encourage all readers to make an effort to learn the stories of these remarkable individuals, and to accept that the example they set is one that is utterly impossible to live up to. If nothing else, knowing what great things our forebears accomplished should inspire us all to abandon any futile attempts to achieve greatness ourselves.

What is the future of Australianness? The concept of what an Australian is has changed so much over the years, from the early days when the answer to the question, 'What is an Australian?' was, 'You made that word up', to the modern day, when the answer is, 'Leave me alone'. Our forefathers and foremothers had to carve their concept of national identity painstakingly, by hand, out of hard rock, whereas in today's digital world anyone can develop their own sense of unique Australian character online – or at least they could, if the internet was faster. It could be that the meaning of Australianness is going to become more fragmented, even atomised, as we lose sight of the sacrifices and wars and violent crimes that made our ancestors what they were: dead.

But in reality it has been ever thus: Australian identity is not a fixed point in the heavens, but a speeding comet that blazes brightly and flits restlessly around the night sky, refusing to remain stationary until at last you realise it is not a comet but a burning pigeon. Like the wanderlust of the typical Australian, our national spirit has never been able to sit still. There was a time when to be Australian was to be English, only sunburnt. There was a time when to be Australian was to be a dangerous criminal, but far enough away georgaphically from normal people for them to feel relatively relaxed about you. There was even a time when to be Australian was to be a giant short-faced kangaroo, and it's amazing that today barely anyone even remembers what life was like back then.

As national identity has changed in our own lifetime, it changed in our great-grandparents' lifetime, and even in their great-grandparents'. Before Gallipoli nobody knew Australians could fight in trenches. Before Errol Flynn nobody knew Australians could be sexy in front of cameras. Before Julia Gillard nobody knew Australians could be women. Australia is a process of revelation, of unveiling to the world the surprising facts about ourselves that nobody knew. In a way, Australia is less a country than a colourfully illustrated reference book, delighting all with obscure pieces of trivia and the amazing measurements of spiders. For the pub quiz afficionado, Australia is a goldmine. For people who live here, it is if anything even more significant.

What great Australians will define us in the post-modern era? When the 50th edition of this book is published, in the late 21st century, the lineup will probably be unimaginably different. Instead of legendary sportspeople, artists and activists, we will most likely be lauding agile pop-up mobile-app entrepreneurs and YouTube pranksters. As well as, obviously, the myriad military strongmen who seize control of various parts of the country during the water wars: they're the greatest heroes of all, and their inclusion in revised versions of this text will be suitable tribute to their courage and wisdom, and not merely a statutory requirement under the laws of District Fourteen B as enacted in the Great Cleansing.

I guess what I'm saying is: we should let the celebration of great Australians be not only a reflection on our past, but a salutary lesson for our future. We need to learn from Weary Dunlop and Caroline Chisholm and Vincent Lingiari and all their historical kin, so that we can become the Australians we aspire to be, and more importantly, create the Australia we aspire to live in. But even while we do so, let's remember the words of a great Australian whose identity remains a mystery to this day: there's never been a more exciting time to be Australian … than right now.

ACKNOWLEDGEMENTS

As much as I would love to claim 100 per cent sole credit for the production of this book, the fact is I, like any author, had loads of help and support from many lovely and talented people, so it's only fair I give them a shout-out. Big thanks go to the team at Affirm Press: I'll single out Martin Hughes, who has been a tower of strength and will have my eternal gratitude for thinking I'm funny. Also big ups to Grace Breen for helping me feel like a proper author. And an extra-special, outstanding cry of appreciation to Cosima McGrath, the best editor I could hope for, without whom this book would not be as good as it is. Writing books is a much more enjoyable experience with these guys by your side.

I would like to thank my wife Bec, for being the absolute best in an all-round, universal way. And profound appreciation to Jonah, Kaia and Layla Pobjie, who every day make me laugh and render me awestruck at their general fabulousness. Thank you to my parents, Les and Helen Pobjie, who made me what I am – whatever that might be. Thank you to my sisters, Rebecca, Emily and Alice, the three geniuses who inspire me to be better always.

For artistic inspiration, moral support, solidarity and friendship, thanks go out to Peter Fitzsimons, Noni Hazlehurst, Mike Carlton, Wil Anderson, Wendy Harmer, David Hunt, Greg Fleet, Roz Hammond and Shaun Micallef. I live in hope that I can someday repay you in kind for all you've given me. A special diamond-encrusted, all-caps THANK YOU to Cam Smith, my best friend, comrade-in-arms, and human security blanket. You are my hero.

I want to acknowledge those giants who helped make this book possible, though they would never have known it: to Dave Barry, Douglas Adams, Terry Pratchett, Woody Allen, WC Sellar and RJ Yeatman, Richard Armour – thank you kindly. And to John Clarke – we will miss you forever.

But finally and most of all, thank you to all the great, good, magnificent and slightly dodgy Australians who made this book possible simply by living their lives. I'll always be grateful that you existed for me to recklessly mock in print. Good onya, every one.